WOMEN
CONNECTING WITH
WOMEN

Linx

WOMEN
CONNECTING WITH
WOMEN

Equipping Women for
Friend-to-Friend Support
and Mentoring

VERNA BIRKEY

WINEPRESS WP PUBLISHING

Women Connecting with Women
© 1998 by Verna Birkey
Second Printing

Published by:
WinePress Publishing
PO Box 1406
Mukilteo, WA 98275

Unless otherwise noted, scripture quotations are taken from the Holy Bible, New International Version, Copyright © 1973, 1978, 1984 by the International Bible Society. Used by permission of Zondervan Publishing House. The "NIV" and "New International Version" trademarks are registered in the United States Patent and Trademark Office by International Bible Society.

Verses marked TLB are taken from The Living Bible, Copyright © 1971 owned by assignment by Illinois Regional Bank N.A. (as trustee). Used by permission of Tyndale House Publishers, Inc., Wheaton, Illinois 60189. All rights reserved.

Verses marked AMP are taken from The Amplified Bible, Old Testament, Copyright © 1965 and 1987 by The Zondervan Corporation, and from The Amplified New Testament, Copyright © 1954, 1958, 1987 by The Lockman Foundation. Used by permission.

Verses marked NKJV are taken from the New King James Version, Copyright © 1979, 1980, 1982 by Thomas Nelson, Inc., Publishers. Used by permission.

Verses marked KJV are taken from the King James Version of the Bible.

Scripture references marked Phillips are from J. B. Phillips: The New Testament in Modern English, copyright © 1958, 1960, 1972 Macmillan Publishing Co., Inc.

Verses marked NASB are taken from the New American Standard Bible, © 1960, 1963, 1968, 1971, 1972, 1973, 1975, 1977 by The Lockman Foundation. Used by permission.

Printed in the United States of America.

ISBN 1-57921-087-2
Library of Congress Catalog Card Number: 97-62495

Contents

Part IV—Nourishing Others Through People-Helping

A Personal Word

For almost thirty years the call of God for me has included suitcases, airports, motels, and all-day teaching sessions in churches of all varieties and names. It has been an awesome privilege to listen to the joys, the challenges, and oftentimes the pain and hurt of countless women. It was these many encounters, coupled with my God-given spiritual gifts, that birthed my passion to equip women to become loving, caring friends, mentors, encouragers, and supporters to other women the Lord places in their sphere of influence.

When Hannah said she had turned to a group for the spouses of alcoholics for support instead of to the church, my heart cried. Why was she drawn to them? "They accept me and allow me to express my anger. They don't condemn or accuse or judge or preach at me when I struggle. I feel safe there. At church they *say* they love you, but too often their remedy is a quick verse that should solve your problem."

Several years ago when I shared my burden with a pastor's wife in Indiana she commented, "Christians are the only ones who shoot their wounded, but we've got to change that!" That's my passion, which I feel must be shared. We must all help change that!

Actually, mentors shooting their wounded is not new. It is vividly illustrated in the oldest book of the Bible, Job. After long days of listening to their accusations and "preaching," Job labeled his three friends "Miserable Comforters." I have done the same—probably you have too.

In brief, *Linx: Women Connecting with Women* is designed to help us avoid being miserable comforters like Job's friends and instead become "God with skin on" to others. My goal is to help us know how to become "comfortable comforters," so that the life of Jesus "may also be revealed in our body" (2 Corinthians 4:10–11).

Linx has become the handy designation for our weekly classes, as I have taught this material at my own church. In a succinct way it reminds us of our ultimate goal, which is to link up with other women as wise, understanding mentors and friends: women who know how to nourish themselves and others; women who are together learning truth that sets us free.

What's in This Book?

The major concepts in the pages of this book can be briefly summarized. *Linx* seeks to train (equip) women:

- To recognize that it is right to nourish (take care of) ourselves
- To identify and correct our own twisted thinking
- To learn how to draw appropriate boundaries
- To become aware of our self-talk
- To be good listeners and know what to listen for
- To ask helpful questions
- To give godly responses to others

In the Titus 2 model, Paul told Titus to *train* mentors. Training (equipping) must happen *before* women can effectively connect; so that's where we start. *Linx* is probably 90 percent training and 10 percent connecting. The training becomes the foundation for deeper, more helpful connections.

How to Use This Book

For individual study and personal growth. Read straight through to get the total message.

- Read a chapter each week, highlighting ideas relevant to you.
- Answer the questions in the *Study Guide*.(See page 333 for how to order.)
- Work through the *Practicing and Journaling,* applying the truths to your own life.
- Read with Bible in hand, looking up the scriptures, marking them in your Bible.

For group study and to help others. You can easily involve others with the help of the *Linx Study Guide.* This guide gives questions for discussion and interaction, whether with one other person or a group. Leader's helps are included.

- Reading and working through each chapter along with the *Study Guide*, with one or two other people who meet in your home is a simple and easy way to reach out to others.
- Use it in small groups, at Sunday school, or in weekday classes.
- Make *Linx* the basis for a churchwide women's study. Women can read the chapter at home, answer the questions in the *Study Guide*, then come together, first in small groups for discussion and then all together for a "wrap-up" by a leader/teacher.

I Am Deeply Indebted

To Jeanette Turnquist, my longtime friend and teammate in ministry. I couldn't have done it without you, Nettie. To you, my gratitude for your perseverance and your tireless, patient rewriting and editing.

To some special mentorees who have so freely shared your questions, struggles, feelings, insights, and victories. I've learned so much from you. And to all who have been *my* mentors, in person or through their writings.

To the women of the Enriched Living Workshops and Linx classes for your continued encouragement and urging to put these truths that you have found life-changing into book form so that you can review them and pass them on to others.

Most of all, to my Lord, Jesus Christ, Who called me and thrust me into this work of helping women and Who gives me the joy of helping them to help others.

A Word About the Stories

The stories throughout are true, but names and places have been changed.

Part **I**

The Truth
Will Set You Free

1

Needed: Safe People, Safe Places

My ninety-three-year-old dad lived in a retirement home in Illinois. Every Sunday at three I called him, and we chatted about whatever was on his mind. Sometimes he liked to reminisce. During one of those Sunday calls, his recollections took me back to the time when he was about seven years old and was assigned to babysit for his uncle's children.

While babysitting, he was also expected to do all kinds of other work on his uncle's farm. He always obeyed, but for all his hard work he received no pay—only an abundance of criticism for the way he did or didn't do things. As time went on the work increased, with still no pay and no praise.

Even walking to this uncle's farm was a frightful experience for my dad. The route required that he pass a pasture where a bull was kept. Whenever the bull saw him, it would come bellowing and charging as close to the fence as possible. My dad would be scared to death. He would try to skirt the pasture so the bull could not see him, but it always would see him and come at him, kicking the dust and acting as though it would charge with fury right through the fence. My dad said, "That was always frightening, but my uncle's attitude was even worse. He was very harsh and critical!"

Then he added thoughtfully, "Dad should not have allowed the man to take advantage of me. But then, my uncle was so critical and strong that my dad couldn't stand up to him. Dad wasn't that kind of man."

Though he kindly excused his own father, my dad's soul was hungry for something he didn't get from his family; and still, eighty-six years later, the remembrance of this lack caused him great soul-pain.

Instead of so vividly recalling the pain, how good it would have been if, as he sat in his chair reviewing his life, he could have said, "My family really respected me as a person. They:

- understood my problem and defended me from my uncle's injustices,
- supported me on my fearful walk past the bull, and
- praised and affirmed me

My dad then gave an account of a different situation in his life. "I often stopped in at the home of a neighbor who lived nearby. It was always such a joy to go to see them. They made me feel like a real person. Hilda would have a good, big dinner for me. And, as I grew older, I helped Martin shuck corn.

"I always knew that when I finished *that* job I would be paid. I worked hard, but I enjoyed going to their house and helping them. My uncle wanted me to shuck corn for him, too, but I did every-thing I could to get out of it. I knew he wouldn't treat me right, he wouldn't pay, and I would get nothing but criticism for my work."

Do you see the contrast? "They made me feel like a real per-son." Acceptance, affirmation, belonging.

Our Deep Soul Hunger for Connection

Children need a safe place: a family environment that gives more than steak and potatoes and the latest jeans and shoes. That's what my dad was hungry for. That's what we all long for—children and adults alike. We each have a deep soul hunger for justice, re-spect, affirmation, understanding, connection.

Isn't that our expectation when we go to *this* Bible study or become a part of *that* group? We want to connect. We want to sense that someone understands us, accepts us, hears us, knows us, believes in us. When we don't find that special link with another believer in *that group,* we look for it in another group. Some of us weary ourselves in looking yet never really finding a satisfying connection with others in the body of Christ.

My passion in this book is to equip each member of the body to become the someone who understands, accepts, hears, knows, and believes in another so that we can have satisfying connections. Our two key words are *connecting* and *equipping.*

Key Word: Connecting

First let's examine why connection is so vital.

Our General Need for Affirmation

A primary reason women need to connect with other women is because we all have need for affirmation and encouragement in general—in our homes, at church, and at the workplace. So many women feel that failing at one point in their lives pronounces them "a failure" in all points. Rachel said, "Verna, you are the only one who has ever encouraged me in my mothering. I always feel like such a failure." She's an excellent mother and has good open relationships with her daughters. She encourages, affirms, and lovingly guides them, but she focuses on the few areas where she hasn't fully achieved and feels like a failure. She needs someone to come alongside to encourage and affirm her.

The Scriptures are clear on our assignment. They often admonish us to encourage one another, to support one another. Just three examples from 1 Thessalonians:

> And we urge you, brothers, warn those who are idle, encourage the timid, help the weak, be patient with everyone. (5:14)

> Therefore encourage one another and build each other up, just as in fact you are doing. (5:11)

Now about brotherly love we do not need to write to you, for you yourselves have been taught by God to love each other. And in fact, you do love all the brothers throughout Macedonia. Yet we urge you, brothers, to do so more and more. (4:9–10)

Paul is saying that it's not that we don't know we are to love each other. It's not that we aren't doing it. We *are* doing it; but let's do it more and more.

Hannah's story is an example of that need to be built up. She had been excited when her husband made a profession of faith. But now things were different. After three years he had turned back to alcohol, and she had turned her anger toward the Lord. Why did God allow this? She called me to set up a time to talk. When we met she talked almost nonstop for more than two hours. I listened, but offered very little advice.

Full of anger toward her husband and toward God, she exploded, "For seven years I've been a patient and submissive wife. Why did God allow this?" She shook her fist in God's face and decided to go her own way. Now, several months later, she realized that turning from God was not the answer. She wanted to come back to Him, but she would not go to people in the church for help. Instead, she went to a secular support group for the spouses of alcoholics.

WHY NOT THE CHURCH?

After she had talked for quite a while, and I had simply listened without speaking many words at all, I asked, "Why do you prefer going to that group?"

She responded, "They accept me for who I am and how I feel. They listen without interruption or accusation. They don't condemn me or say I shouldn't feel that way. They allow me to express my anger. They allow me to have struggles. They don't sit in judgment or accuse me or preach at me. I feel safe there.

"The people there do not *say* they love you, they just really *show* that they love you. They listen to you, and being listened to makes you feel loved. At church, people say they love you, but they don't listen to you. Instead, they just want to give you a verse that is supposed to solve your problem."

In a few days this note came: "Thank you for the gift of love you gave me in spending time with me. You accepted me, loved me, and didn't judge me. Your acceptance of me has helped me to accept myself and others and to turn back to the Lord, believing in His acceptance of me and love for me, too."

All of the things that Hannah said her secular support group does is what we believers want to do—and more—because we have the gospel, the truth, and power of God. And we have the Spirit of God to shed abroad the love of God in our hearts (see Romans 5:5).

Our Confused and Twisted Thinking

Another reason women need real connection today is because of the legalistic upbringing of many members of our Christian community. Exposure to legalism results in some women being burdened by confused and twisted thinking.

Any woman suffering this way needs someone serving as God's instrument to help free her from errors in thinking, false guilt, and shame. She needs someone to help her sift through what is true and what is untrue, wise and unwise; someone who will help her understand her boundaries, rights, privileges, and responsibilities.

The way she can most effectively meet her need is by spending time with someone in a one-on-one safe connection—a safe place where she is free to talk about her thoughts, questions, and frustrations. A place where she is listened to without judgment. A place where no one will immediately try to fix her by quickly giving "wise words of advice" that are supposed to bring instant healing or change in thought patterns.

Some would ask, Isn't being raised in a Christian home and a church environment all that's needed for thinking truthfully? Not necessarily. If that were the case, why have so many books been written by well-respected Christian authors with such titles as:

- *Grace Awakening*—a book by Chuck Swindoll that deals with grace versus legalism
- *Lord, Heal My Hurts*—Is Kay Arthur writing only to those who have not grown up in Christian homes?
- *The Dangers in Growing Up in a Christian Home*, by a committed Christian counselor, Dr. Donald E. Sloat
- *When God's People Let You Down,* by a very experienced teaching and counseling pastor, Jeff VanVonderen

Are these authors talking only to people who have no Christian background? No, realistically there is a lot of hurt and twisted thinking that occurs within some Christian homes and some Bible-believing churches. We may already be grace-giving people or be part of a grace-giving church, but as Paul said to the Thessalonians, we want "to increase more and more" in giving grace and in continuing to grow as a true *grace community*.

KEY WORD: EQUIPPING

Our second key word is *equipping*, or training. Think of this book as a Titus 2:3–5 training manual, useful and applicable to all women of all ages and stages—mothers, wives, friends, mentors, and mentorees. Equipping ourselves with better people-relating skills will make our connections much deeper and more grace giving. Therefore, the bulk of this book is geared toward equipping. However, we have found that in our Linx study groups deep connections begin to form.

Why is training necessary? One day a woman from Spokane called me. When she first came to an Enriched Living Workshop that I was teaching, she said her marriage had been reduced to a pile of ashes. She related that her husband often screamed at her saying, "You don't show respect to me!" But he couldn't give her any specific examples, and she didn't know what to do to show respect to him. She felt frustrated and inadequate.

At the workshop she learned some specific ways for showing respect. Through them, she said, the Lord saved her marriage. She was so excited about what the Lord had done that she wanted to help others by sharing with them just exactly *how* she now gave honor and respect to her husband.

But she was confused. Her Bible teacher, a person she respected, told her, "Oh, you don't need to tell them *how.* All anyone needs is to have grace in the heart. Grace in the heart will cause the person to know how to respect their husband."

So she asked, "Which is right, Verna? Do you give them some how-tos or is my Bible teacher right: 'You only need grace in the heart'?"

True, the heart does need to be changed, but there is still a proper place for some possible how-tos and suggestions as to possible ways to show respect—not formulas or sets of rules that will, when obeyed, be certain to bring forth the desired result in every situation. These are very appropriate and helpful for anyone—just as they were helpful to that woman.

Equipping Is Part of God's Plan

In Titus 2:3–5 Paul told Titus that he must "teach the older women to be reverent in the way they live, not to be slanderers or addicted to much wine, but to teach what is good. Then they can train the younger women to love their husbands and children, to be self-controlled and pure, to be busy at home, to be kind, and to be subject to their husbands, so that no one will malign the word of God."

He asked Titus to tell them the sort of character that should spring from sound teaching. He wanted them to develop the character and right living that identifies true Christians. He was relating truth to life. We take from his words that he expected the older women to be examples of this character and to give specific help out of their years of experience. They were to give good counsel and be teachers of what is right and noble. In this way they would wisely train the younger women how to live godly lives, so that they would be a good advertisement for the Christian faith. (See Titus 2:3–5 AMP and Phillips.)

That is what women are to be in the business of doing. Our emphasis should be on ways we can put the principles of the Word to work in our little or big world of influence. Sometimes it's more comfortable to keep on studying to gain more knowledge, instead of concentrating on actually applying and practicing what we have learned. Each of us needs to answer the question, "How do I help fulfill God's plan for women as He lays it out in Titus 2?"

Equip the Reluctant

Some women feel very inadequate and are reluctant to take part in mentoring others according to Titus 2; but, they often are some of the most competent, gracious, and qualified people for such a ministry. These women need guidance and encouragement to get involved.

My friend Janelle is an excellent hospice nurse, very knowledgeable in her field and consistently learning more to become even more effective. In addition to that, she is a very caring person. She prefers hospice nursing to hospital nursing because she can get closer to the patients, spend time with them, and help them on a one-on-one basis. She has the opportunity to talk to the close family members, and she loves to help each of them according to her area of expertise.

But when I read our Linx class brochure to her to ask her evaluation of our wording, she said, "That is a much-needed ministry, but I could never do anything like that. I could never be a mentor."

I about dropped my eye teeth! She not only *is* an excellent mentor in her professional field, she would be one of the most effective mentors in the Titus 2 model. Even though she would be one of the best qualified, she feels inadequate.

Even *thinking* of the Titus 2 model is scary for some of the best-qualified women—scary because of preconceived ideas about what mentoring really is. Many think it means *counseling,* and they say, "That's not for me. I could never do that." Mentoring is not always counseling. Mentoring is simply coming alongside another woman to give encouragement and support. A true mentor has a servant's heart that asks, "Is there any way I can help you achieve your full potential?"

Equip the Confident

On the other hand, some of us—both older and younger women—can appear overconfident, insensitive to real needs, and too ready to give our "wise counsel." We can actually be more like Job's "comforters." They had good words of truth, but they spoke them to the wrong person at the wrong time. Instead of encouraging and helping, they unintentionally caused more hurt—*ungrace* instead of grace. That's not what women need.

SHOOTING OUR WOUNDED

The chairman of our Columbus, Indiana, workshop and I rode to the airport together one day, and the subject of how Christians hurt Christians came up. She remarked, "It's like someone once said, 'Christians are the only ones who shoot their wounded.'" But she went on to say, "We've got to change that. We've *got* to change it!"

Do Christians really shoot their wounded? Why, after thirteen years of practice, did the committed Christian physician turn to more study to become a Christian psychiatrist, which he has been for the past seventeen years? And why did he find it important to write the book *Why Do Christians Shoot Their Wounded?* Because he has seen a lot of wounded people being shot down by Christians instead of being shown the understanding, love, and compassion of Jesus.

One day I went to visit a woman I had hoped could be a mentor to me, a woman I had not known before our meeting on this memorable day. Actually, she was the trusted and revered mentor of a friend of mine. At that time I was feeling betrayed and deceived by a good friend whom I felt was disloyal. I thought good friends, really good friends, trusted each other and shared their lives; instead, this friend seemed to be moving away from me. I explained this to my new mentor, but she did not ask me any questions or take time to get in touch with the hurt in my soul. She wasn't interested in how I *felt*.

After starting to cry in her presence, I said, "Here I go again—crying for no apparent reason. I can't seem to keep the tears back. Do you think I should be over this by now?"

Her answer: "Well, I think you should be over it *pretty soon.*" She didn't have a clue about the grief and pain in my soul, nor did it seem to me that she cared. She was insensitive to me and my wound, and she shot me down.

Now my cry, my pain, was not because I was resisting the will of God, nor was it anger toward my friend or toward God. But the loss of this friend had resulted in major losses in many areas of my life.

I had to ask myself, How can this "mentor" help me heal if she doesn't understand the hurt in my soul? And how can she understand unless she listens to me? But why should I share with her more of my pain unless I'm assured that she is a safe person with a heart of empathy, understanding, and compassion? When I went to her that day, my unspoken question was, "Can I trust you with my hurts?" I was giving her an opportunity to prove or disprove her grace to me. We need mentors who are safe persons and grace givers, not those who shoot us when we are already wounded.

The Work of Encouragement

God knew what He was doing when He put Titus 2:3–5 in the Scripture as a model and assignment to Christian women. This work of encouragement can relate to many areas of a woman's life, such as training in domestic skills, discipling a new believer, giving suggestions for disciplining children, etc.

I received a call from a conference director in New York who had invited me to speak at a retreat. As we visited he asked what I was doing these days, so I told him about Linx. Immediately he said, "My wife was asked to be a mentor, but she said, 'No one has mentored me. How can I be a mentor?'" Then he went on to say that when their children were young she had longed for someone to give her some helpful support and direction. Women everywhere express this need and desire.

Our major emphasis in this book will be to learn to truly listen to others, to be sensitive to their hurts—their particular woundedness—and to discover how we can come alongside as a mentor. We want to cooperate with the Lord as He heals their hurts. He will do the work in the heart, but He may use us to encourage, affirm, and even clear up some confusions.

As we have seen, Titus 2:3–5 gives the model and the assignment for older women to train younger women. You might ask, Where are the boundaries for "older" and "younger"? In a sense all of us fit both categories. Any woman with a little more experience or maturity in a specific area of life is "older," and there's probably a "younger" who would benefit from that maturity or experience.

Remember Janelle, the hospice nurse? Though more than a decade my junior, she was my mentor several times. When not only both of my parents, but also a friend of mine passed away, I was the younger in experience, and I gained much help from her.

A CHALLENGE TO GET INVOLVED

Two statements from Henry Blackaby's excellent book, *Experiencing God*, will help us get hold of God's heart and ways. Let us examine them and see how we can become involved with Him in His Kingdom work. The first statement is that God is always at work around us. The second is, God invites us to become involved with Him in His work.[1]

God is always at work around us: This concept is the very one that attracted me to my church when I heard the pastor say, "We want to march off the map with Jesus." I don't have a clue what else he said that day, but I do remember those words were very significant to me. They said to me, "We believe God is working around us, He wants us to join Him, and we're looking for effective ways to do just that."

God is not only working around us, but *He wants us to join Him in what He is doing*—it's His program, not ours. We aren't necessarily going to do things as we have always done them. Rather, we want to be ready to listen and hear the Lord afresh, watch what He is doing, be ready to join Him in His work, and let Him do through us the new work only He can do. This is an awesome privilege and invitation. What is *His work?* We could express it in so many ways, but my church's mission statement says it well in a paraphrase of Isaiah 61:1–4:

> The Spirit of the Sovereign Lord is on me, because the Lord has anointed me to preach good news to the poor. He has sent me to *bind up* the brokenhearted, to proclaim *freedom* for the captives and *release* from darkness for the prisoners, . . . to *comfort* all who mourn, and . . . those who grieve . . . [that they might experience] . . . beauty instead of ashes, the oil of gladness instead of mourning, and a garment of praise instead of a spirit of despair. So that they might be *rebuilt*, *restored*, and *renewed* in Him, a planting of the Lord for the display of his splendor. [Italics mine]

When the pastor read this, I could hardly sit still! My mind raced back to a day more than thirty years ago now, when I was Dean of Girls at a Christian boarding high school. That day I was out on the campground adjoining our school, alone, meditating in the Word. The Lord brought these verses from Isaiah to my attention, and He seemed to be saying, "This is My ministry job description for you, Verna."

Since that day, Isaiah 61 has been my burden, my passion, my emphasis. In time, the Lord called me to pioneer in bringing this kind of help specifically to women. I saw that God's plan for women helping women as Paul outlines in Titus 2:3–5 is, in a sense, the same as the ministry description in Isaiah—that is, to minister to women in the area of their need, whether they are especially hurting or just in need of encouragement, direction, or instruction on the how-tos of responsible living in their relationships.

Join God in What He Is Doing

God is always at work around us and He invites us to become involved with Him in His work. That is all very good in theory, but it presents a big challenge to us. Too often we have in mind what we want to do for God rather than discovering what He wants to do through us. We are to join Him in *His* Work, not ask Him to bless our agenda. We are to be His coworkers as He leads, appoints, and does the work that only He can do.

Blackaby clearly acknowledges this when he states that to join God in what He is doing requires faith and action and results in having to make major adjustments in our thinking.

It surely did for me! I came to realize that God was working around me and that He was inviting me to become involved with Him in His work. Then came the need for acting in faith and making some real adjustments in my thinking about myself and especially about God. I felt very much like Moses, hearing God call to him from within the burning bush, "Moses! Moses!"

And Moses said, "Here I am." Here is the interchange between God and Moses, from Exodus 3:7–8, 10:

> The LORD said, "I have indeed seen the misery of my people in Egypt. I have heard them crying out because of their slave drivers, and I am concerned about their suffering. So I have come down to rescue them from the hand of the Egyptians. . . . So now, go. I am sending you to Pharaoh to bring my people . . . out of Egypt."

But Moses had some good arguments for not joining God in this work:

1. " '*Who am I,* that I should go to Pharaoh and bring the Israelites out of Egypt?' And God said, 'I will be with you.' " (3:11–12)
2. " '*Suppose* I go to the Israelites and say to them, "The God of your fathers has sent me to you," and they ask me, "What is his name?" Then what shall I tell them?' " (3:13)
3. " '*What if* they do not believe me or listen to me and say, "The LORD did not appear to you"?' " (4:1)
4. " 'O LORD, I have *never been eloquent*, neither in the past nor since you have spoken to your servant. I am *slow of speech and tongue*.' " (4:10)

The LORD said to him, "Who gave man his mouth? . . . Is it not I, the LORD? Now go; I will help you speak and will teach you what to say." (Exodus 4:11–12)

Moses still wasn't convinced:

"O LORD, please send someone else to do it." (Exodus 4:13)

This sounds like a humble response, but is it actually?

Major Changes in Thinking

Moses had to make some major adjustments in his thinking about himself and about God. One major adjustment in his thinking about himself is seen in his reply, "Who am I that I should go," implying, God, You aren't thinking straight—I can't do that! I'm far too insignificant and far too inadequate and ungifted for speaking.

Instead of taking this point of view, Moses needed to look at God's plan, realize that God was inviting him to join Him, and believe that God would take the responsibility to make Moses adequate. "I will be with you, help you, and teach you what to say." Moses had to choose to believe God and change his thinking about himself—his ability, his adequacy.

Moses also had to make some adjustments in his thoughts about God—His wisdom in calling him to this impossible task and His almighty power that would be totally adequate for the work He was calling Moses to do. God was not assigning Moses a task and then sending him off by himself to accomplish the work. No, God Himself was already at work and was now asking Moses to join Him so that God could accomplish a phase of His work through Moses.

Even though Moses still wasn't convinced, he went, and God accomplished His work through him.

As I said, I identified with these thoughts of Moses many times when God was calling me to join Him in the work of teaching women in the Enriched Living Workshops. I knew the Lord guides through His Word, through prayer and circumstances, through the inner witness of the Holy Spirit, and through the counsel of others; so I used all of these. They each seemed to witness the call of God for me to join Him in this "work"—whatever it was to be. It was a pioneer work, to be sure. It had no structure or pattern to follow. As I counseled with godly men and women, I got only strong affirmation and encouragement to launch out.

After spending a day with the Lord in the Word and prayer, I was definitely convinced, but I still felt very inadequate and wanted to go hide instead of becoming involved. I entertained one last argument that I felt might cause the Lord to change His mind: "But Lord, do you think I, as a single woman, can minister to both married and single women?" He won that argument too. I was going to have to move out in *faith* and make some major *adjustments* in my thinking about myself and about God. I chose to believe God had called me, was going before me, and would make me adequate for my part as I cooperated with Him.

By faith I started out on the five-day journey from the East Coast to the West Coast in a loaded-down VW bug. By faith I settled near Seattle and started teaching women, but the battle of faith would continue. More questions and more temptations to doubt came in the form of the same questions Moses had asked.

WHAT IF . . . JUST SUPPOSE

I recall sitting in my office (my one-bedroom apartment) at my desk (the kitchen table), making preparations for my first workshop, when suddenly the thoughts came, "*What if* no one comes? *Just suppose* it's all a big failure? *What if* you have to go back East defeated?" The same kind of misgivings began to haunt me as they did Moses. Almost immediately my faithful Lord reminded me of these words from John 15:16: "You did not choose me, but I chose you and appointed you to go and bear fruit—fruit that will last. Then the Father will give you whatever you ask in my name." Since that time God has been abundantly faithful and has done a work that only He could do.

Perhaps you can identify with Moses or with me in some of our feelings and excuses. Are you thinking, "God could never be calling me to join Him in His work of supporting, encouraging, and helping other women. I just don't have what it takes!" Titus 2:3–5 is God's purpose and pattern for all women.

As we acknowledge God's invitation to become involved with Him, we will inevitably have to make major adjustments in our thinking about ourselves, about God, and about others and step out in faith to see God do amazing things through us—things that only He can do. Our part is to remember 1 Thessalonians 5:24: "The one who calls you is faithful and he will do it." God fulfilled this promise for Moses, and for me!

FREE INDEED!

The Scripture says, "So if the Son sets you free, you will be free indeed . . . ." and "Then you will know the truth, and the truth will set you free" (John 8:32, 36). It is through grace and truth that Jesus sets us free.

In the following chapters we will discover, in practical ways, just *how* grace and truth can bring us into the freedom we need to experience growth in Christ, deepen our relationship with others, and reach out to others in love.

Are you willing to trust the Lord enough to join Him in the work that He wants to do through you? Are you willing to listen to Him and to make some major adjustments in your life, especially in your thinking about your own adequacy, about God and His ability to equip you for the calling, and about others and their real needs and hurts? If so, there are exciting adventures ahead for you.

THOUGHTS TO REMEMBER

God is inviting me to become involved with Him in His work of understanding, accepting, encouraging, and supporting the women in my sphere of influence. He has promised to make me adequate for what He asks me to do. I want to be a part of His Titus 2:3–5 purpose and plan.

And let us consider how we may spur one another on toward love and good deeds. Let us not give up meeting together, as some are in the habit of doing, but let us encourage one another—and all the more as you see the Day approaching. (Hebrews 10:24–25)

PRACTICING AND JOURNALING

Write out a prayer of commitment to become involved with God in His work—whatever that implies for you. Ask Him to direct you to someone this week who needs your word of affirmation or encouragement. Write what you said, along with the person's response.

2

Free to
Nourish Others

One of the joys of attending an intensive three-day seminar in Seattle a number of years ago was that I made many new friends from my own church. Several reached out to me in a special way, and I sensed that each wanted to become my friend.

During the last coffee break, for no explainable reason, I started crying. Not just a few sniffles, but real *boo-hooing*. One of my new friends patiently waited and invited me to share what was wrong. I was quiet, trying to understand it and put it all together. Finally, the light dawned. I wiped my eyes and mustered the strength to say, "I feel overwhelmed because you and the others have shown such love, and it tastes so good! I guess I don't want termination of this good thing! I'm afraid that after this seminar is over and we get back to church, we'll all have our masks on again, and it will be back to the way it was—*layer-to-layer fellowship*."

After I got home, my tears continued into the evening. Through the night my mind was busy trying to understand these emotional signals. Mentally, I marched through my life, beginning with my grade-school days, I was the only girl among eleven boys in a one-room school. There were no girls to be friends with. Then, because of family moves, I went to three different high schools. I had no church friends at that age—we lived too far from our church for me to have active friendships with anyone.

In my college and adult life I have had many good friends and coworkers; but, it always seems that after a short time, I become separated from them geographically. My work, which required constant travel for almost twenty-five years, has kept me from developing roots and deep friendships at church.

Tasting the Joy of Belonging

Now, tasting the joy of belonging to people right here in my own church brought the contrast of my whole buried, lonely past to the surface. In the process of seeking to understand my past relationships, I came to the startling awareness that I had been a very lonely person in my growing-up years. The emotional turmoil below the surface had triggered this volcanic response that was totally out of proportion to the present event.

Nevertheless, this whole experience helped me to see and understand a bit more the often unrecognized longing for meaningful relationships that is deep within all of us. We can call it a hunger, a thirst, a longing for satisfying connections—but our souls crave nourishment. God has planned for that deep hunger to be satisfied in a variety of ways, one of which is through connections with people.

(I must add this postscript: The Lord has over-compensated in this area in recent years, for He has showered me with wonderful friends and meaningful, deep relationships.)

NOURISHING OTHERS IS GOD'S IDEA

To nourish others is God's idea. He uses a variety of words to get that concept across to us. One is to love; another is to nourish and cherish. The principle is found in Ephesians 5:28–29 (NKJV):

> So husbands ought to love their own wives as their own bodies; he who loves his own wife loves himself. For no one ever hated his own flesh, but nourishes and cherishes it, just as the Lord does the church.

Though spoken to husbands, this mandate applies to all of us in the body of Christ. Just as the Lord nourishes and cherishes us, we are to do the same for others.

Another word is found in Isaiah 61:1: "Bind up the broken-hearted . . ." Nourish wounded ones. Another in 1 Thessalonians 5:11 (NASB): "Encourage one another and build each other up . . ."

God has put us on this earth not just for ourselves, but for others. We are to nourish others—spouse, children, friends, neighbors, and the family of God.

How Did Jesus Nourish Others?

A most significant thing about Jesus was the way He nourished others. He not only boldly stood for the truth, He showed grace. Jesus' manner and method were full of grace and truth.

The Scripture declares that He "came from the Father, full of grace and truth . . . grace and truth came through Jesus Christ" (John 1:14, 17). Grace and truth are the means Jesus used to provide satisfying soul nourishment for others. Let's take a look at what grace and truth looked like in His life as He related to the Pharisees and to a needy woman.

> The teachers of the law and the Pharisees brought in a woman caught in adultery. They made her stand before the group and said to Jesus, "Teacher, this woman was caught in the act of adultery. In the Law Moses commanded us to stone such women. Now what do you say?" They were using this question as a trap, in order to have a basis for accusing him.
>
> But Jesus bent down and started to write on the ground with his finger. When they kept on questioning him, he straightened up and said to them, "If any one of you is without sin, let him be the first to throw a stone at her." Again he stooped down and wrote on the ground.
>
> At this, those who heard began to go away one at a time, the older ones first, until only Jesus was left, with the woman still standing there. Jesus straightened up and asked her, "Woman, where are they? Has no one condemned you?"
>
> "No one, sir," she said.

"Then neither do I condemn you," Jesus declared. "Go now and leave your life of sin." (John 8:3–11)

JESUS SHOWED RESPECT FOR THE PERSON

Jesus understood this woman's deep needs, and as He stood against the hurtful behavior of the Pharisees, who had accused and shamed her, He showed respect for her as a person. He did not ignore the *truth* of her sin, but oh, the grace with which He dealt with her wounded and sinful heart!

Frequently we see Jesus standing against hurtful behavior that shames the other person and makes him or her feel inadequate, like a failure. His goal is not to shame, but to lead to conviction, repentance, and freedom from the sin. Jesus' way is grace and truth! Love comes first, then correction.

JESUS CONFRONTED AND CORRECTED

Jesus also nourished the Pharisees by giving correction with grace and truth. He quietly but firmly made His point to these accusers. They had nothing more to say. Confronting and correcting may not seem nourishing on the surface, but when done in the right way and with the right intent, this can nourish in a very significant way.

How Did Paul Nourish Others?

Paul willingly endured extreme hardships while traveling to visit the churches he had established. He also continually nourished them through letters of affirmation, instruction, and correction. Sometimes his words tasted good to his congregations, and sometimes they didn't. Start reading any one of his letters, and you'll get this flavor immediately.

Even as all nourishment might not taste good, so all that tastes good might not be nourishing. Paul directed the Corinthians to expel the immoral brother in their midst. To the man involved, this wrong conduct evidently tasted good, but it was not God's way.

How Did God Nourish Elijah?

God performed many miracles through and for Elijah (1 Kings 17–19). He commanded the ravens to bring Elijah food; He raised the widow's dead son; He followed that with a tremendous display of power on Mount Carmel, in the presence of the defeated priests of Baal.

But Jezebel, Ahab's wicked wife, was determined to kill Elijah. Afraid and running for his life, this man of God who had so courageously stood for God during many difficult times, now went into the desert, sat under a tree, and prayed that he might die. "I have had enough, Lord. Take my life," and he fell asleep. He was *depressed!*

Elijah in depression? Was depression reasonable and excusable for a man through whom God had shown His power by one miracle after another? If you had been there, what would you have said to him? Some of us would probably have a lot to say to him! We'd love to help him, since we're caretakers and want to fix people.

GOD SENT AN ANGEL

Well, God did send him some help. He dispatched an angel. Just imagine for a moment how the angel might have felt. Perhaps he was feeling terribly inadequate to help such a godly man who just wanted to die. Imagine the angel saying, "But Lord, I don't know what to say to a man like this. His case is beyond me! I've not had any experience with a depressed Elijah before."

Or perhaps the angel was more self-confident and thought, "Well, one thing he needs is some shaming for being a prophet of God who doesn't practice what he preaches. He should believe in God's power instead of running scared from a woman. So I'm going to confront him about his little faith. His depression is uncalled for. He should be ashamed and know how disappointed God is with him after all He's done for him."

No, it wasn't that way. What did the Lord tell the angel to do? Gently and lovingly the Lord said, "Take him some food."

"Food? Is that all? Lord, are you sure he doesn't need some wise counsel or a Bible verse or a reprimand for such little faith? Perhaps some shame for being so faithless and unbelieving?"

"No, no, right now he needs nourishment for his body and for his soul. Just touch him, let him know you understand him, and give him something to eat."

"And that's going to help him? Okay. I'll go, but I do feel kind of foolish, just doing that. Are You sure he doesn't need a spiritual rebuke, or at least *Three Steps to Overcoming Depression?* Well, I guess I'd better do just what You say—touch him, let him know I believe and understand him, and give him something to eat."

Now, you know I've added a bit of imagined dialogue, but I think you've already interpreted my parable. People need nourishment. God wants you to be like one of His angels that He can dispatch to nourish others—through a touch, by empathetic understanding, and by helping them see their need for nourishment themselves—so they will have renewed strength for God's journey for them.

Of course, at times it is appropriate to give good counsel or an appropriate scripture. But sometimes we tend to be too quick to give advice without empathetic understanding.

Nourishment Direct from God

Many times God does use other people to show us His nourishing grace. Sometimes that grace comes to us directly from Him. Psalm 142:2 says, "I pour out my complaint before him." Ann wrote how she poured out her heart to the Father:

> I spent quite some time sharing my anger with the Lord on my way to the store today: (1) anger because of past abuse, (2) anger because I didn't ask to have so many struggles, (3) anger that I seem so powerless to always live as I ought, and (4) anger at my slow progress. Verna, God was so gentle with me, so compassionate. He let me cry hard and then sent such comfort to my heart. I felt loved and cuddled and cozy in His arms, against His heart. I have been at rest since, knowing that He will take care of everything concerning me.

God uses people to help satisfy our soul hunger, but He also nourishes us with His Word and His presence.

Pattern for Nourishment: Grace and Truth

We are to follow Jesus' example as we see how He fleshed out grace and truth. We can see what grace and truth look like in the way He related to the woman taken in adultery and to the Pharisees. Jesus was full of grace and truth!

What does grace look like in Christ's representatives? My dad had been looking for grace from his uncle, but he didn't get it. His uncle was not a dispenser of grace. In fact, he dispensed just the opposite: *disgrace, dishonor,* humiliation, and shame. What a negative reflection of the character of Christ!

In her newsletter, *Hope for the Heart,* June Hunt wrote that she was helping her mother hang a pair of beautiful, expensive pictures on the wall. The nails would not go into the cement wall, so she bought wall hooks with adhesive backing.

Her mother asked, "Are you sure they'll hold?"

June answered, "Oh yes! Each picture weighs only eight pounds, but each hook will hold up to twenty."

June tells the rest of the story.

"I successfully hung the pictures. Mother oohed and aahed, but she did express a note of concern. I quickly reassured her of the adhesive grip.

"The next day when we walked into the living room, my heart sank as I saw one picture had fallen and was broken—beyond repair. Never shall I forget Mother's first words to me: 'Oh, June, things are just things. Now if you had been broken, that would be something to be concerned about.'"

Things are just things! What a relief to June. Her mother gave her grace instead of guilt. How easy it would have been for her to have said, "I told you so!" Instead, she looked beyond the fault, saw the real need, and gave grace.

A mother told how she showed grace to her daughter.

"As I was getting Jani ready for bed, I put on Christian radio. The preacher was talking about shame, forgiveness, and grace.

When the message was over I turned the radio off and was going to take Jani upstairs to bed, but she leaned against the wall and said, 'Mom, I'm *so* glad I told you about my sin! I kept that inside of my heart for two years, and it was so hard.'

"I picked her up, squeezed her, and said, 'And just think of all the pain you experienced because of it, when there was so much grace for you from Mommy and ever so much more from God!' She nodded and said she'd learned her lesson. I hugged her tightly!"

GRACE WILL LISTEN

A wife shared, "Last night my husband was on the phone making some business plans, so I went up to bed to read. He came up about an hour later and began talking about some of his struggles at work with staff. I listened and listened, but I had inner struggles. Earlier I had needed him to listen to me, but he hadn't.

"When he appeared to be finished I said, 'May I say something to you?' He nodded, so I said, 'I wish you'd give me some moments just to share myself with you, not for you to fix me, but just to listen.' I reminded him that at suppertime when I was sharing some facts about our financial matters, he had become impatient and reacted to something I had said. That ended the whole thing.

"He apologized for that but insisted that to communicate with his personality type I need to cut the 'feelings stuff' and get to the bottom line of what I want to share! Then he got back to talking about his troubles at the office—for another thirty minutes! It was difficult, but I listened as best I could and even made a suggestion, which he received."

Grace and truth.

WOMEN ARE TO NOURISH OTHER WOMEN

One special emphasis for us women as we think of nourishing others is the pattern given to us in Titus 2. Women need to be encouraged, supported, and listened to. Older women should pray for, be available to, and reach out to younger women. Younger women should take some prayerful initiative to seek out an older woman who might nourish them in this way. Both should pray to this end. This is the Titus 2 "business." Scripture gives us two powerful examples.

Biblical Example: Ruth and Naomi

During a time of famine both Ruth and her mother-in-law, Naomi, lost their husbands. Instead of going back to her people, Ruth chose to stay with Naomi to support her and to be supported by her. Together they went through some hard times. Together they learned to trust under the wings of the God of Israel. Together they saw God graciously provide for them. Naomi was a mentor to Ruth. Read the story of Ruth with that in mind.

Biblical Example: Mary and Elizabeth

Jesus' mother, Mary, was nourished by an older woman, Elizabeth. Mary spent three months in Elizabeth's home, sharing and learning from her. Mary was only a teenager, pregnant and engaged to be married. She needed a mentor to help her think about and prepare for the birth of the child and His training. Can you imagine how encouraging that time with Elizabeth must have been for her?

Younger Women Want to Connect

Many younger women desire to have a significant connection with an experienced woman who will be there for them. One day I received this letter:

Dear Ms. Birkey,

My name is Nancy Jacobson. I am thirty-five, married, and have two children, six and four. I attended your workshop in Montana last fall, and it was so helpful.

A job change brought us to Washington. In Montana, I was blessed by having a mentor. Since moving to Washington, I have been praying for a "Spiritual Mother." God has brought you to mind over and over again. I've thought, "No way—I'm sure she'd be too busy to meet with me two hours a month."

There's nothing I want more than to serve Christ to my greatest capacity—whatever the cost—and to make our home what Jesus wants it to be. But sometimes I'm so wishy-washy and confused. I have so many questions and few people I can entrust them to. Neither my husband nor I was raised in a Christian home.

Ms. Birkey, if I were to drive up to Kent once a month (a four-hour round trip), would you possibly consider being that Spiritual Mother?

Lois was persistent. At a time when I was stretched to the limit with commitments, she wrote:

Could I just write to you and share my thoughts and feelings? I find it a great help just to write it out. You don't need to respond. It's enough for me to know you're interested and would read my letters.

She didn't want to be an added burden to me, but her persistence led to a very precious friendship many years later.

After I offered support to a young woman in her forties, she wrote:

Thank you so much for taking time to help me with the difficulties in my life. I've prayed for many years for help and a way out of this entrapment of alcoholism. I know you are a part of the answer to those prayers. There are many challenges ahead of me; but, I know the Lord is with me, and the strength I receive through people like you will make the road not so lonely.

I've heard it said by some older women, "We want to be available, but the younger women don't seem to want us." Some don't, and there could be numerous reasons. Perhaps a young woman tried to reach out and was disappointed. Perhaps, instead of being met with compassion and empathy, she felt more judged and preached at than listened to and understood. Perhaps she just didn't realize the blessing this kind of connection could be to her.

You may recall my sense of rejection, grief, and pain over a traumatic event I shared with "Mrs. Mentor." As we were talking, I started crying again. When I asked, "Do you think I should be over this by now?" and she answered, "Well, I think you should be over it pretty soon!" I sensed no real understanding or allowance for my grief over my many losses. Instead, I felt judged for my slow progress, and I didn't go back to share my heart with her.

Older Women Need to Prepare

As I said in chapter 1, sometimes older women are afraid of being available to others because they feel inadequate; they don't know what to say. On the other hand, some older women are only too eager to give advice or a scriptural admonition, or they try to fix the person. To both I would say that most of the time you don't need to say much—just listen.

When Joy came for counseling, her first words were: "I don't want you to fix me. If I thought you'd try to fix me, I wouldn't be here. I know it's up to God and me to fix me. If I thought you'd try to show me how wise and able to give good advice you are, I wouldn't come to talk to you. But I knew you would give me some wise insight and let God and me fix me, so I felt safe to come."

After many, many hours of listening and giving some "wise words of advice" to the girls at the college, one girl said, "Thank you for listening to me." What about my wise words of advice? Not a word.

After a year of spending two hours a month together, Nancy said to me: "One of the greatest ways you have helped me is that you have listened. Many times when you have problems, they seem to be stuffed deep down inside and can't come out until you can begin to express yourself. So, if you can just talk out your thoughts in a safe environment, then you can sort through things. Often it becomes clear what needs attention and what you can do about it.

"Without someone to talk to, you feel so alone, get discouraged, and want to give up. It helps so much to talk to someone who will listen to me. I had to learn it was really okay for me to 'dump' on someone. Previously, I felt that I had to be the spiritual leader all the time."

Another friend in a time of unusual frustration expressed it this way: "What I really want is to just be with you and cry and cry, to have you listen to my heart, and help me think through everything and be able to sort it all out. Your tender understanding is so calming."

More than expecting us to fix them, they want us to listen. James 1:19 says: "Everyone should be quick to listen, slow to speak and slow to become angry." When people can freely express their thoughts and feelings—be it anger, guilt, confusion, or fear—they often come to their own conclusions about their need. But they need a safe person, one who won't shame, judge, or try to fix them prematurely. Instead, they need one who will listen to, believe in, accept, seek to understand, and when necessary, gently correct them.

This kind of mentoring support is especially needed today with so much abuse and so little connection with family and friends because of our busy and mobile society. Younger women: pray, reach out, pursue. Older women: pray, be available, and look for opportunities to be a mentor.

GUIDELINES FOR NOURISHING OTHERS

A friend frequently makes this statement, "I need 'God with skin on,' and that's what you are to me." If you know Jesus Christ as your Savior and Lord, then He lives within you, and you have the privilege of being "God with skin on" to others—God manifest in your flesh—showing His compassion, His unconditional love and acceptance, His forgiveness, His grace to others.

Please note I do not mean we should become *God* to others. There's real danger in that. We must not allow people to look to us or to anyone else as the voice of God. Too many Christian leaders have fallen at that point of power and control. Every human being is fallible. No one person has the whole truth, and neither do we.

So we need to acknowledge the privilege others have to disagree with us.

In his insightful book *Churches That Abuse,* Ronald Enroth states that leaders who are abusive develop that style over a period of time.

> [As they] became aware of the influence . . . and the power they could wield, . . . their ministries began to change. Consciously or unconsciously, they took advantage of vulnerable people, and convinced them that God had given them, the shepherds, the right to exercise full authority over the flock. . . . Unquestioning obedience and blind loyalty to a person are hallmarks of spiritual abuse. . . . [These] leaders are accountable to no one.[1]

He goes on to say that "the desire to control others and to exercise power over people, . . . has always been a part of human experience," whether as parent, spouse, teacher, or worker.

One pastor related, "that he was one of hundreds of pastors who had spent fifteen years picking up the pieces of broken lives that resulted from . . . extreme teachings and destructive applications on discipleship, authority, and shepherding."[2] If you want to read some strong words against false shepherding, read Ezekiel 34.

Can you disagree with the Bible teacher you most admire? Do you have the freedom to think for yourself, or do you expect this teacher to do your thinking for you?

In suggesting that you become "God with skin on," I am *not* talking about "lording it over those entrusted to you," as Peter so clearly warns against in 1 Peter 5:3. We must not seek to become *God* to the person, but we *can* be God's agent; that is, we can walk with others through their struggles, showing compassion, giving strength and support as Jesus would if He were here in His flesh. All the while we graciously help them keep their eyes on Jesus, the Author and Finisher of our faith.

We can nourish others in four very significant ways. Again, Jesus is our pattern.

Be an Advocate—a Defender; 1 John 2:1

Jesus is our heavenly Advocate who speaks to the Father in our defense when we sin. He was also a human advocate. An advocate is a person who pleads another's cause.

One woman said, "I need a 'human advocate.' I know I have Jesus as my Advocate before the Father, but I need a human advocate to help me figure out if I'm thinking straight."

We serve as advocate for another when we defend her against her own wrong thinking. We can lead her toward balance when her thinking is all black and white. As advocates we can help women think through the issues facing them so they can determine where their personal responsibility begins and ends.

People who have come from legalistic homes, abusive backgrounds, broken relationships, or who are in very difficult or confusing situations in the present need an advocate to defend them against:

- Their own accusing thoughts
- Misapplied truth and lies that are misguiding or harassing them
- An accusing conscience with legalistic overtones
- Others who would take advantage of them by using shame or guilt to control their actions

As advocates, we can help them determine where their personal responsibilities lie and where the other person's responsibilities begin and end.

Jesus As a Human Advocate

Jesus was a human advocate for the woman against her accusers. The story is in Mark 14:3–9. Recall when she poured the expensive perfume on Jesus' head and was accused of having unspiritual values and of being terribly inept at financial responsibility. Jesus became her human advocate—her defense. Here are His words from verses 6 and 7: "Leave her alone," said Jesus. "Why are you bothering her? She has done a beautiful thing to me. The poor you will always have with you, and you can help them any time you want. But you will not always have me."

Jesus nourished this woman by being her advocate, her Defender.

GRACIOUS, TRUTHFUL ADVOCATES

As advocates we can step in to help others who are wrongly assuming blame or shame, either from their own wrong thinking or from those who try to shame, manipulate, or control them.

And, like Jesus, we need to be advocates full of grace and truth. Some people have all grace, but no truth. Others have all truth, but no grace. We are to convey both grace and truth.

Robert was sharing with his prayer group the shock of receiving an eviction notice in the mail that day. He needed their support. You could see he was heavy with anxiety, pain, and anger. As he was sharing his deep frustration, someone in the group quickly spoke up, "Well, you know, all things work together for good. . . ." The statement was true, but was it given with grace? No. It was the wrong timing and the wrong manner! How do you think Robert felt? Unloved, not understood, preached at, not cared about. Truth, but no grace! No nourishing love. That person was more of an accuser than an advocate.

A young girl found an advocate in her mother. Dad was home again at last, after a long business trip, and the family decided to go out for a walk. Now twelve-year-old Susie felt she could share with her dad the joy and thrill of a recent event. She was in the midst of jubilantly sharing her delight, when she suddenly realized Dad had disappeared! He had seen a child sitting in a swing and went over to swing her a bit. Disappointed and hurt, Susie looked up at her mother and said, "Mom, Dad isn't interested in me."

Mother graciously acknowledged the hurt and that Susie had a valid point. She said kindly, "You must tell your dad about how you feel."

Mother was Susie's advocate, supporting her with grace and truth and encouraging her to address the situation. Susie did say something to her dad when he came back, and he showed more interest in her as they continued their walk.

Be a Paraclete—One Who Comes Alongside

In His last words to His disciples, Jesus promised four times that after He was gone the Father would send them another paraclete, the Holy Spirit (see John 14:16, 26; 15:26; 16:7). *Paraclete* is a wonderful Greek word with many nuances of meaning: comforter, helper, counselor, encourager, intercessor, one who stands by you.

Simply stated, a paraclete is one who comes alongside another to listen, to help carry a burden, to pray for, and to support the other in any way they can. When we discover how to serve as a paraclete, we learn clear ways to nourish others. We'll look at three of these ways.

COME ALONGSIDE AS AN ENCOURAGER

Speak grace-giving words. Scripture says we are to comfort, encourage, and build up one another (see 1 Thessalonians 4:18; 5:11). Paracletes don't have to look very far to find opportunities to encourage.

Parents, for example, need to be encouraged in the parenting job they are doing. Parents everywhere feel inadequate for the task. Many believe that they are failures. Parenting is a very challenging job. Dr. James Dobson expressed that idea in a book he called *Parenting Isn't for Cowards*. He confesses that even he didn't always know the best thing to do as a parent.

Bible teachers need encouragement too. Leaders plod on week after week not sure whether or not anything is getting through. Warren needed to hear affirming words on how he was doing as an adult-class discussion leader. When a person in his group commended him, he drank it in like a dry sponge. He was doing a good job, but he needed to be told, affirmed, and encouraged.

After Bettye attended the first workshops that I held in the Dallas area, she began to send a card of encouragement to me at every workshop. She did this faithfully from 1972 to 1987. Often the card would be humorous, and it would always have a hand-written note that said something like, "I just want you to know that I'll be praying for you while you're teaching the workshop in Lancaster [or wherever]," and it was signed, "Barny." I called her *daughter of encouragement.* (See Acts 4:36.)

COME ALONGSIDE AS A SUPPORT PERSON

Come alongside to understand, to listen, to intercede, to be there in time of need. The Bible says, "Two are better than one. . . . If one falls down, his friend can help him up. But pity the man who falls and has no one to help him up!" (Ecclesiastes 4:9–10).

One evening Rita called just as I was settling in to work seriously on this material after a day of interruptions. "May I come over and talk to you tonight? I really need to tonight."

This meeting was definitely not according to my planned agenda for the evening, but I was sure Rita needed my support, so I invited her to come. I was able to support her by listening to her with understanding. She was desperately afraid of going for some special counseling the next day because she would have to discuss her irrational fears. She needed to talk it out in a safe place first and be encouraged to go ahead and do the thing that she feared. People need support. Each of us needs "one-another*ing*," as the Bible mentions more than one hundred times.

A graphic picture of this concept of coming alongside came to a friend of mine at the time of the strong earthquake in California several years ago. She said, "On the news I saw a picture of two people hugging each other until the shaking stopped. They couldn't do another thing for each other. Their property and their possessions were being destroyed right before their eyes, but that didn't matter to them at the moment. All that mattered was that they had each other for support. They just held on to each other until the shaking stopped. Immediately, I thought, 'That's what I need so often, someone to hold me until the shaking stops.' Just hold me! You may not be able to do a thing for me—just hold me until the shaking stops." That's support!

Come Alongside As a Helper

The Bible says, "Carry each other's burdens" (Galatians 6:2). Help carry the load, both by guiding others to see real issues *and* by doing practical things for them—deliver a meal, do ironing or cleaning, teach some homemaking skills, etc.

When Rob was unexpectedly rushed to the hospital, people came alongside to help him and his wife, Barbara. There were days of tests that included anxious moments and much waiting to see what would happen next. Then came the angioplasty. Barbara said that during the day, many people from church came to express their concern, assure her of their prayers, or just to be with her during her waiting times.

Paracletes are available to others. They come alongside to help shoulder the burden.

Be a Refuge—a Safe Place

One of the most precious truths about God is that He is our Refuge. In a specific time of trouble most of us have clung to Psalm 46:1, "God is our refuge and strength, an ever-present help in trouble," or Deuteronomy 33:27, "The eternal God is your refuge, and underneath are the everlasting arms."

A refuge is a place of safety. The Bethany home where Mary, Martha, and Lazarus lived was a safe place, a refuge for Jesus. In a radio message, Charles Swindoll said: "For some reason Jesus chose their home as His place of refuge. It was a safe harbor, with people who didn't ask leading questions, who accepted Him as He was, who were not overtly critical, who didn't have a hidden agenda or didn't find a need to pump Him for answers. It was just a place to rest." Jesus was nourished in this safe place.

Ultimately, God is our *only* unfailing refuge. The Bible says, "Trust in him at all times, O people, pour out your hearts to him, for God is our refuge" (Psalm 62:8). Pour out your heart to God, for He is a safe place, just as he was for Ann (p. 34). You can express to Him all your anger, frustration, confusion, and questions— and it is safe. He doesn't change in His love and mercy. He feels compassion for you. He extends forgiveness. He's not judgmental.

He is patient and understanding and will be faithful to you to the end. He is your Refuge.

But He also wants us to be a refuge to others within our sphere of influence.

I want to be "God with skin on" as a refuge for others—a safe place where they can come and pour out their hearts. I want to be patient and understanding as they express their anger, bitterness, doubt, confusion, and even rebellion. I want to compassionately feel with them and not be judgmental toward them.

I told you about Hannah who said that when she had turned away from the Lord and then wanted to come back, she would not go to the people in the church for help. Instead, she went to a support group for the spouses of alcoholics because, "They accept me for who I am and how I feel. . . . They don't condemn me or say I shouldn't feel that way. . . . They don't sit in judgment or accuse me or preach at me. I feel safe there. . . . You did that for me. You accepted me, loved me, and didn't judge me."

I had the privilege of being a safe place for her. I want to be a safe place where others can pour out their fears and their anger, whether it is toward their husband, toward others, toward me, or even toward God. His ears and heart can take it—so can mine.

At the airport in Billings, Montana, a mother disgustedly picked up her child by the back of his clothes and carried him across the room. The little fellow was hanging there yelling, kicking, and crying. The father came, picked him up gently, sat down with him, and calmly pressed him close to his heart. As the father enfolded him in his strong, tender arms, the little fellow immediately relaxed and stopped crying. He felt safe, loved, healed. Soon he was off and away at the window happily watching the planes come in. All was well after he found a place of refuge, safe from Mom's temper and abuse.

Some wives have endured their husband's addictive sexual behavior for years. After perhaps years of repeatedly forgiving him, keeping his secret, and trying again to build the relationship, these women need a safe person in whom they can confide.

Sometimes the perpetrator is so smooth, so clever, so deceptive that he can deceive even the church elders. The elders may
not see the depth and extent of his sin; and often the abuser, instead of the victim, gets understanding and support from the
church. The leaders, and even friends, of the victim may admonish her, "If you will only forgive and submit, then all will work out
well." She is neither understood nor supported, just accused. Eventually she will have to find a new church—a new support system—because victims desperately need to find refuge in a church
body.

If we know a woman with this need, let's be ready to walk with
her through the sorrow and abuse she has experienced from her
husband and perhaps even from the church. You or I may be the
only place of refuge she has. As we become her human refuge, we
may also have the privilege of leading her to more fully trust God,
the One Who is her strong and secure refuge.

One of these dear, bruised women wrote recently, "As I was
again reading the story of the good Samaritan, I felt like I was the
person who was robbed, beaten, and left by the side of the road;
and the church has passed by on the other side."

Incidentally, my dad's uncle, whom Dad described as "harsh
and critical," was an elder and Bible teacher in the church for many
years. Yet he didn't know how to be a refuge for a little boy who
needed a place of safety.

Be a Confronter

Loving confrontation is a fourth way to nourish others, but
because of the significance of this concept, we'll take it up more
thoroughly in chapter 10.

BALANCING THIS TRUTH

Let me say a word about the balance to this truth of nourishing
others. Galatians 6:2 tells us that we are to bear one another's burdens, but Galatians 6:5 says that each of us must also bear his own

load. The other person is not to feed upon me like a leech, but I can *choose* to nourish her according to her need and my ability to meet that need. I must also discern those areas where she needs to carry her own load, a load I cannot be responsible for.

In 1 Thessalonians 5:14, the Word gives us instructions for dealing with four kinds of people.

1. Warn those who are idle (confront)
2. Encourage the timid (encourage)
3. Help the weak (be a refuge)
4. Be patient with everyone (support)

It doesn't take a lot of wisdom to do these things, just a listening ear; an understanding heart; a loving concern; and a willingness to be an advocate, a paraclete, or a refuge.

As an advocate, we provide a defense against the lies and accusations of the person's own conscience or those coming from someone else. As a paraclete, we come alongside with encouragement and strong support, helping to help carry their burdens. As a refuge, we are a safe place where they can come and pour out their hearts and be met, not with condemnation and judgment, but with grace—acceptance, understanding, and guidance.

In all these ways, we can help others experience the freedom that Jesus Christ died to give us. What a privilege we have to be "God with skin on," nourishing one another, fleshing out grace and truth.

The Scripture says, "So if the Son sets you free, you will be free indeed!" (John 8:36). It is through grace and truth that Jesus sets us free.

Perhaps you are thinking, "Me? Nourish others? I'm so dry myself, I have nothing to give!" We're going to speak to that in the following chapters. First we'll see how important it is to be nourished ourselves, and then we'll discover practical ways by which grace and truth can free us from the power of sin patterns in our daily living.

Thoughts to Remember

Because Jesus lives within us, we can be "God with skin on" to others, showing His compassion, His unconditional love, His acceptance and forgiveness.

"And we urge you, brothers, warn those who are idle, encourage the timid, help the weak, be patient with everyone" (1 Thessalonians 5:14).

Practicing and Journaling

Plan to do something this week to nourish another—a spouse, a child, or a friend. Be an advocate, a paraclete (supporter, encourager, helper), or a refuge. Write out one thing you did and how the person responded.

3

Free to Be Nourished!

As Dean of Girls in a Christian boarding high school, I lived in the dorm with about eighty high-school girls. For seven years I was available to them twenty-four hours a day, and I got very weary. At times I became impatient in spirit, and I dreaded having the girls knock on my door. Then sometimes I found myself hoping they would leave soon.

As I talked to the Lord about my weariness and my impatient spirit, it was as though He said, "Verna, why are you here?"

"To show these girls what You are really like."

"Have you been doing that?"

"No, I've been impatient with them sometimes; and You aren't impatient."

"Why have you been impatient?"

"I'm bone weary, Lord."

"Why are you so weary?"

"I stay up late at night listening to them share their conflicts, then I have to get up early the next morning."

"What can you do about that?"

"Get a rest in the afternoon perhaps."

"Right! That would be important."

I Needed Nourishment

How could I show the loving concern, patience, and compassion of Jesus Christ when my own impatient spirit showed through instead? To most effectively carry on the primary work God had for me there, I needed some physical and emotional nourishment. I came to realize that I was virtually ignoring my own need to replenish, and this was diminishing my ability to continue to nourish the girls.

I had to take responsibility to get some rest. The first step was a simple PLEASE DO NOT DISTURB sign that went on my door for a short time each day. That was a very difficult thing for me to do. I didn't like it, and the girls were disappointed when they discovered I was not available; but, I had to do it.

GOD MADE US WITH A NEED FOR NOURISHMENT

Psalm 107:5 says, "They were hungry and thirsty, and their lives ebbed away." Hunger and thirst in the physical realm do eventually lead to our bodies ebbing away. The same is true for the hunger in our souls. We long for emotional nourishment.

God has made us with a need for nourishment in three areas: physical, emotional, and spiritual. We will talk about all three areas; however, most of our emphasis will be on soul nourishment.

Meaning of Nourishment

What does it mean to have our souls, our inner beings, nourished? Webster says that to nourish is "to feed, or sustain with substances necessary to life and growth." Nourishment, then, is something that feeds my soul hunger so that life will be full, healthy, and growing, instead of fainting and ebbing away.

Sometimes we are so busy nourishing others—family, friends, church members, neighbors—that we don't realize how much we ourselves need some life-energizing "soul food."

This poet wrote humorously about someone who needed a little nourishment himself:

Mary had a little lamb.
It would have been a sheep,
But it joined the Baptist church
And died for lack of sleep.

We cannot nourish others very well if we are malnourished ourselves. We need to put our own spiritual, emotional, and physical health very high on our list of priorities. If we are worn out, short of patience, and depleted in spiritual vitality, we won't have anything to give and will fail in our ministry to others. Or we may appear very successful outwardly but fail at the central point: to manifest Jesus.

God Designed Us for Nourishment

God has made us with two vacuums in our soul, two empty spots for love. One vacuum is meant to be filled with God's love (1 John 4:9–11, 21) and the other with the love of other people. There are many commands in Scripture to love others. Both vacuums, both love cups, need to be filled with nourishing love. (See Matthew 22:37–39 and 1 John 3:23.)

Since nurturing love is a God-created need that everyone has and every human being wants and needs that kind of emotional nourishment, God has also made provision for these two vacuums to be filled.

Lois knew about these two empty spots when she wrote:

> I am experiencing a deep trial in my life at this time. My husband is very ill with cancer. Would you know of a woman who has experienced a similar trial and could reach out to another? I am in the Word daily and have a closeness to my Lord. I am also discipling four young women and am excited about the growth I see in their lives.
>
> I guess what I'm asking is for someone to hold my hand and tell me I'm going to make it. Do you think it's okay to desire that? I thought you might have contact with women who could help.

How Are We Nourished?

What nourishes us? What fills our emotional love tank? We could use many different words to describe ways to give or receive soul nourishment, such as *giving affirmation, encouragement, recognition.* For our purpose here we will boil them all down to two basic emotional needs: unconditional acceptance and continual approval.

UNCONDITIONAL ACCEPTANCE

Each of us needs assurance of unconditional acceptance. This fosters a sense of belonging, worth, and security.

Rich Buhler writes:

> There is a hunger that says, Please love me the way I am and don't take my faults and failures into account. Please ignore whether my teeth are straight or crooked or whether I get good or bad grades in school . . . whether I'm fat or skinny . . . neat or sloppy. Please [assure me] that you can . . . set aside my failures or even my successes . . . my possessions or my beauty and love me just because I'm me. That way I will know that if any of those factors change, you will still love me.[1]

That is the quality of love that each of us longs for—a love that has nothing to do with our performance, a love that cannot be earned and therefore cannot be lost or taken away. This is real security!

This kind of unconditional acceptance is communicated more through attitude than through words. It's so easy for children, or even adults, to get the impression that we are loved because we please another or because of the honor we bring to another through our good behavior or our great achievements.

A church leader might say to his child, "What do you think the people in our church are going to say if you act that way?" The implication: I love you when your behavior gives me honor.

A very athletic friend has a tremendous drive to achieve in sports. Now her teenage daughter is excelling in interschool track competition. Her mother is proud of her daughter's achievements, but she realizes the danger of putting too much pressure on her to achieve. She said, "I am trying hard not to live out my unrealized dreams athletically in her, because I know this would only communicate conditional acceptance to her."

CONTINUAL APPROVAL

Unconditional acceptance must be affirmed through continual words of approval. This gives a sense of significance, a feeling of competence, a sense of worth.

A sense of approval can be lost when it is based more on performance than on the person that I am. Therefore, I must be continually affirmed. I need constant approval from those who are the most important to me in order to know how they think I'm doing. Am I doing okay?

Nine-year-old Andrea asked her mother, "Mother, do you like to wear broaches and pins and stuff?"

Her mom replied, "No, I really don't. I haven't gotten into that kind of thing."

A few days later Andrea handed her mother a gift and said, "You aren't going to like this, but happy Mother's Day anyway." Andrea had made a special gift for her mother from two pieces of a puzzle. She was crushed, and Mother felt terrible.

Mother explained that, although she wasn't crazy over broaches, she loved this one because Andrea had made it especially for her. She loves anything Andrea gives her because she loves Andrea so much. They spent the next ten minutes crying together, with Andrea enfolded in her mother's arms as Andrea's sense of acceptance and approval was rejuvenated.

Unconditional acceptance and continual approval are the means of nourishing others.

THE FAMILY: GOD'S PRIMARY PLACE OF NOURISHMENT

God's plan is for everyone to have a nurturing environment. That's why He designed the family. When the family is functioning as God planned, the members are well nourished physically, emotionally, spiritually.

God's plan is for the husband and wife to be freely giving to each other's needs, nurturing one another with self-sacrificing love.

The child coming into this environment will have his needs graciously and lovingly met.

God wants all of us to receive nurturing love from one another. This fills our emotional tanks and supplies nutrients for life and growth. The family is the first and most important "filling station." Children can even nourish parents; wives can nourish husbands; husbands nourish wives; parents nourish children.

Sin Disrupted God's Perfect Plan

God's plan was perfect. If it had functioned as He planned, everyone would be abundantly nourished in every way. But sin marred the whole plan. With separation from God came a spirit of independence. This has been true from the Garden of Eden right down to you and me today. Sin introduced a new principle that has been plaguing us all since Adam and Eve.

When the family is not functioning in the way God planned, it is unhealthy. *Dysfunctional* is the current word for an unhealthy family, but the problem has been around for a long time. An unhealthy family environment does not provide adequate nourishment for its members. The root of all dysfunction is simply *sin*.

Every family since Adam and Eve's time has suffered from this independent, selfish spirit. Therefore, since *all* families do not function as God originally intended, everyone has some struggles in life, even Christians. And the degree of struggle depends a great deal on the degree of malnourishment that has resulted from the breakdown in the home.

You can probably think of many biblical illustrations of dysfunctional families. Isaac and Rebecca each had their favorite son; Rebecca preferred Jacob, and Isaac favored Esau. Joseph came from an unhealthy family system where there was favoritism, jealousy, and hatred. King David was an adulterer and a murderer.

TAKE RESPONSIBILITY TO BE NURTURED

Since all of us have experienced some degree of malnourishment as children, how and where do we find the measure of soul nourishment we need to be healthy, mature individuals? (In chapter 4 we will consider what can be done to actually *repair* the damage and the hurt in our lives.) Now, as adults, we are responsible to see that we are properly nourished—we might like to blame circumstances or people for our lack of nourishment. But bottom line: we are now responsible.

Certainly because my dad's uncle was not properly nourished himself, he found it very difficult to nourish my dad. Remember, it is much more difficult to give nourishment when you have not been nourished. But that uncle did not take responsibility to choose to change and break the unhealthy pattern; instead, he perpetuated that sinful behavior.

We cannot sit back and expect others to lavish us with love, encouragement, and approval. We are not to be a Dead Sea—always taking in, but never giving out. We are to be a flowing river, nourishing others as we have been nourished.

How can we get our own emotional tank filled in order to be free to nourish others?

Learn to Take Care of Yourself

Suppose a relief agency sends you to a famine-stricken area. You go to distribute food to the starving people who are all around you begging for food. As you try as fast as you can to distribute food to as many as you can, you have two overwhelming feelings.

One is guilt because you have always had so much and they are starving. The other is the urgency to get the food distributed before more of them die. You decide to skip breakfast, lunch, and dinner. That will give you more time to work and provide more food to give.

This all sounds so self-sacrificing, so compassionate. Perhaps you even pride yourself for being so caring. But if you continue this way, after a few days you will not be physically able to pass out any more food. In a matter of weeks you may even die because of the "unselfish" giving of your time, your energy, and your own food. "How absurd," you say. "I would need to take care of myself so I would have the ability to serve the people."

Of course, that makes sense. It is not selfish to pay attention to your own needs. In fact it is your responsibility to keep yourself as fit as you can so that you can serve better and longer. Giving up your food, as in this case, would be irresponsible, both for yourself and for the starving people.

RIGHT MOTIVES

Nourish yourself so that you will have energy to nourish others. Learn to take care of yourself so that you can take care of others.

We hear much about taking care of yourself. Some emphasis is right, some is wrong. If the goal is to serve God and others in a better way, or if it is for your health and growth in Christlikeness, it is a worthy, godly goal.

While ministering in Northern Ireland, we met a vivacious, healthy, elderly woman. As we commented on her vitality, she said her secret was a practice that she has diligently kept through the years. When her first child was born, she began taking an hour-long nap every day. Her purpose was to be fresh with an energetic, cheerful readiness to meet the needs of her husband and children, and to take care of her home.

That nap was not selfish but sensible. Because of it she was personally refreshed so that she could nourish her family with strength and grace. Was she preoccupied with herself and her needs? Was she selfishly looking out for number one? No, she had a higher goal, a higher purpose. She disciplined herself so that she could fulfill the Lord's assignment to her. She did not feel resentful, burned out, trapped, or confined. She had served her family with joy all those years.

Jesus' Example: He Nourished Himself

Jesus took responsibility for His own nourishment. He nourished Himself physically by eating, resting, working, walking. He did not neglect nourishing His body or spirit while He sacrificially gave of Himself to others. He took care of His own needs but did not *selfishly* put the meeting of His own needs first.

Jesus provided Himself with emotional support by collecting around Him a network of friends. He was nourished as He related closely to twelve, more deeply to three, and even more intimately to one—John.

Jesus also received nourishment initiated by others. He allowed Mary to express her love and worship by extravagantly pouring perfume on His feet—costly perfume that one of His accusers said could have been used to feed the poor. He was criticized, but He justified what might have seemed wasteful and didn't accept the shame or blame from Judas (see John 12:1–8).

Don't Worry What Others Might Think

We must not be concerned with what others will think or say about the legitimate nourishment we seek for ourselves. Likewise, we must not wrongly judge someone else's choices or actions (see 1 Corinthians 2:15).

One mother said,

> After a day of office work, I wanted to go running for some relaxation and fresh air. When I mentioned it to my 11-year-old daughter, she said, "Oh, Mom, please don't go. I want you to stay here."
>
> I decided not to go, since she wouldn't be pleased. When my husband asked why I wasn't out running, I said, "Susie didn't want me to leave."
>
> He said, "What does that have to do with it?" She went out to run.

At first the mother felt that to go out to run would be selfish. It was not selfish to get the refreshment and relaxation she needed. Her daughter also needed to learn that mothers need nourishment too.

REACH OUT FOR NOURISHMENT FROM GOD

Our primary source of nourishment for the body is nutritious food. Sometimes it is also good to take a daily vitamin. But that one-a-day pill is not designed to be our primary source of nutrition. We are to eat a healthy diet—and the vitamin is called a *supplement.*

God must be our primary source for soul nourishment, not a supplement to add on after we fill our lives with people or things or even ministries. All too often we try to find satisfaction and fulfillment in these things instead of looking to God Himself as our primary source of soul nourishment.

Though it is good to get *some* nourishment from people and things, we must not look to these as our *primary* source. For example, trying to find primary nourishment in a faithful friend, more pleasant circumstances, a larger house, another gadget, better health, a computer (or a better computer), a job (or a better job), a husband (or a better husband), children (or better children).

Our inner thoughts are, "I'm convinced I would be much happier if I had something more or something different than I now have." So we seek bread that does not satisfy. It does not nourish us where we need nourishment the most—in that God-shaped empty spot designed to be filled with God alone.

Jesus spoke clearly about where His major nourishment came from. He said to them, "I have food to eat that you know nothing about. . . . My food . . . is to do the will of him who sent me and to finish his work" (John 4:32–34).

Jesus frequently slipped away from the crowds that clamored for his attention and "withdrew to lonely places and prayed" (Luke 5:16). He took responsibility for His need for spiritual nourishment.

Salvation Establishes Connection

In order to have this connection with our primary source, we need to come into a family relationship with God our heavenly Father by accepting Jesus Christ as our personal Savior and Lord.

I do that simply by acknowledging that I am a sinner in need of a Savior and that Jesus Christ died on the cross to pay the penalty for my sin. If I open my heart to Him and receive Him, He comes into my heart and life to forgive my sin and to become my Savior and Lord. I become His child. The Scripture says, ". . . to all who received him, to those who believed in his name, he gave the right to become children of God . . ." (John 1:12).

Let me tell you a little story. A few years ago I thought that my housemate, Nettie, and I needed more living space. A house in our neighborhood appealed to us, but we didn't know the owner, only her name.

One rainy Saturday afternoon I knocked on Harriet's door. Since she didn't know me, I told her I was one of her neighbors. She invited me in. Now what was I to do except tell her exactly why I came? "I've been wondering if you have ever thought of selling your home?"

She looked at me and said, "Well, maybe you are the answer to my prayers."

I was encouraged. She showed me through her house, and it seemed to be just what we could use. Then we sat down in the living room.

I said, "I noticed that when I first came in and asked you about selling the house you said, 'Maybe you are the answer to my prayers.' Are you a Christian?"

She hesitated, stammered a bit, and said, "Well, I really don't know. I've wondered and have asked several ministers from time to time, and they would always say, 'Oh of course you are! Why, you've taught Sunday school, you've lived such a good life, and you're a good member of our church.' But I really don't know for sure."

So I asked, "May I tell you my story?"

How I Became a Child of God

When I was twelve years old, I believed that all good, serious Christians joined the church and were baptized. So I joined the church and was baptized, but that didn't give me the peace I was searching for.

I started regular, daily Bible reading, but still this did not give me peace. It wasn't until I was fifteen years old that I came to realize that in spite of being baptized, living a good life, having a Christian mother and father, and reading my Bible daily, I was still a lost sinner needing the Savior.

A song inviting us to come to Christ was sung at the end of the church service one Sunday. I felt every word, heard every question, and I knew what I needed to do. Here is a part of the song:

> Why do you wait, dear brother?
> What do you hope, dear brother,
> To gain by a further delay?
> There's no one to save you but Jesus;
> There's no other way but His way.
>
> Do you not feel, dear brother,
> His Spirit now striving within?
> Oh, why not accept His salvation
> And throw off your burden of sin?
>
> Why not? Why not? Why not come to Him now?
> Why not? Why not? Why not come to Him now?
> —*George F. Root* [2]

The decision was made! I would not leave the church until this issue was settled. When the meeting was dismissed, I went up to talk to the guest speaker. He helped me pray a simple prayer inviting Jesus Christ into my heart and life to be my Savior and Lord.

After the prayer, he asked me if I was God's child. "I . . . guess . . . so," I said hesitatingly. He had me open my Bible and read John 3:36. I read, "He who believes in the Son has everlasting life."

Then he asked, "What do you have to do to have everlasting life?"

"Believe in the Son."

"That's right. Invite Him into your heart and life just as you have done, then you have everlasting life, or in other words, you are God's child." With that explanation he asked me again, "Are you God's child?" Again I answered with uncertainty. He had me read the verse two more times, but still I could not answer with assurance.

So he said, "Let *me* read the verse for you this time, and you watch each word very closely as I read." He read, "He that *feels he is saved* has everlasting life."

As soon as he said that, I realized I was judging according to my feelings, not according to the facts of God's Word. The Holy Spirit at that moment enlightened me. My doubts were gone in the face of God's truth. It doesn't really matter how you feel. Feelings don't change God's facts.

I am so thankful that he stayed with me until the Holy Spirit convinced me of that truth. From that day to this I have not doubted that I was, and am, a child of God, because my confidence is not in my feelings but in the truth of God. Feelings can say what they want. I choose to take God at His word. I am His child.

Harriet was still listening with real interest, so I turned to her and asked, "Would you like to invite Christ into your life?" She wanted to. I helped her pray a prayer inviting the Lord Jesus Christ into her life.

Then I asked, "Are you God's child?" She rather *thought* so. So I took her to John 3:36, just as the pastor had done for me. We worked through it, and she came to see that based upon God's Word she was God's child. A day later I called her up and asked, "Are you God's child?" She gave a resounding yes!

Now my question to you who are reading this book is, Are you God's child? That is, if you were to die tonight do you know that you would go to heaven? If you aren't sure, you can make sure right now by inviting Christ into your life to forgive your sins and to become your Savior and Lord.

The Importance of the Word and Prayer

Why do we need to spend time in the Word and in prayer—to be approved by God or because He says we must? To obligate Him to bless us and cause our day to go "right"? To be able to tell others how much we're "in the Word." None of the above!

A college girl said that she asks the Lord to help her remember to have her quiet time every day, and if she should fail, she asks Him to make her miserable that day. Wrong thoughts! We spend time in the Word because we *need* the soul nourishment that comes from fellowship with the Lord, not to earn anything.

As believers, whether new or seasoned, we need time in the Word in order to be well nourished in our souls and ready for the needs, demands, and stresses of the day. Only God Himself can feed the deepest part of our soul, and we find Him in His Word.

"Your words were found, and I ate them, and Your word was to me the joy and rejoicing of my heart" (Jeremiah 15:16, NKJV).

Do you go to the Word for help in time of need? Have you learned to find soul nourishment through His Word? Perhaps you feel totally overwhelmed with your seemingly unsolvable problems. During these times, our greatest need is to set our focus on the Lord through a verse of Scripture, a quick prayer, a song, a reminder that He is in control and He is good. Let God's Word lead you to Himself for refreshment and nourishment.

The Importance of Applying the Word

Personally I'm not impressed with how much time a woman spends in the Word, or how many years of rich Bible studies she's been in. But I am impressed with how much the Word is in her and comes out toward me, toward her husband, her children, and others in the form of love. Does she yield up her selfish way? Is she compassionate, understanding, tolerant? Is the fruit of the Spirit evident in her life?

Carolyn says that her mother knows the Bible backward and forward. She can quote it readily, and she gives a lot of money to the church and to Christian organizations. But she is selfish, accusing, controlling, hard to live with, and hard for family members to visit with for very long. She has favorites among her children and threatens to take some of them out of her will.

A teenager told about having worked at a Victorious Life conference summer after summer. Some of the women participants attended year after year and raved about the speakers and messages, but when they left the meeting hall, somehow things were never quite right for them. Their coffee was either too hot or too cold, too strong or too weak, or not the right brand. Or their assigned room was facing the wrong direction, or it had the wrong kind of bed in it.

Wherever did the Word go that says, "Let the word of Christ dwell in you richly in all wisdom; . . . singing with grace in your hearts to the Lord" (Colossians 3:16, KJV). The real question is not how much I'm in the Word, but how much of the Word has gotten into me and shows up in my life and relationships in the form of love, joy, peace, longsuffering, and gentleness (see Galatians 5:22, KJV). James 1:22 (NKJV) says, "Be doers of the word, and not hearers [or students of the word] only."

SPIRITUAL FUEL

Barbara and her husband, Rob, have been through one trial after another. For seven years he was unemployed. Once when he did get a job, he soon realized the company was dishonest and he would not get any salary. He had serious heart surgery. She went through cancer surgery and continues to receive therapy, all without medical insurance. They have had to put their furniture in storage and have moved from one kind friend to another for a roof over their heads.

Here's what Barbara wrote recently:

> As we've gone though some very dark valleys these last seven years, I've come to believe that we can just *go* through painful trials or we can choose to *grow* through them. My commitment to spend quality time with the Lord in His Word every day has been my lifeline. The Word has been fuel for my spirit.
>
> Time and again when a piece of bad news comes, immediately the Lord brings to mind many comforting verses I memorized years ago such as:
>
>> He shall not be afraid of evil tidings; his heart is firmly fixed, trusting [leaning on and being confident] in the Lord. (Psalm 112:7, AMP)
>> He knows the way that I take; When He has tried me, I shall come forth as gold. (Job 23:10, NASB)

As these and many other scriptures flood my mind, I realize that my inner calm and peace are a direct result of learning many years ago the importance of putting God's Word in my mind. How incredibly good it is to live with God's words in our hearts. It is not risky to trust an unknown future to a known God. Oh Verna, it is not risky at all!

What has been holding Barbara up through all the trauma of these seven years? What has been nourishing and sustaining her inmost being? Only the Lord, through His Word. And why was His Word so ready and available? Because she has been putting it into her heart for twenty years and letting Him refresh and nourish her each day.

Do you practice going to the Word to get regular nourishment? Remember, our great need is to set our focus on the Lord, and we can do this by spending time in the Word and prayer.

Reach Out for Activities That Nourish

Activities are another way in which we are nourished. You must *do* some things that bring refreshment to you. God gave Adam and Eve each other, but He also gave them a garden to enjoy and meaningful, fulfilling work to do.

There are all kinds of ways we can nourish ourselves. Because we are different people, we are nourished by different activities, which may include visiting with a friend, skiing, snowmobiling, reading, going to a concert, shopping, taking an afternoon nap, helping others, getting an unpleasant or difficult task accomplished and done well, learning new skills, getting a new computer program—of course, anyone who is into computers knows it doesn't always seem nourishing when the program does strange things. But these and many other types of activity all bring a kind of nourishment to us.

Nourishment comes from enjoying what we're doing and from finding meaning and purpose in life. Nourishment brings health to a person. Here are some examples:

- After teaching for several years, a schoolteacher decided that teaching was not really satisfying to her. So she became an on-the-road repair person and began repairing large appliances—refrigerators, stoves, washing machines. She soon realized that she had found her niche in life
- Many people have found their general health is improved through gardening—just being around plants, trees, and flowers seems to provide both physical and mental therapeutic benefits
- A forty-one-year-old widow found nourishment during her time of grieving and lonely hours by polishing up on her musical ability
- A friend spent some hobby time studying about and preparing more nutritious meals
- Some find that giving money or groceries to those in need and giving gifts to encourage others are ways they can reap the reward of personal nourishment

LORD BACON

Perhaps one of the most unusual forms of nourishment was written about in *Reader's Digest*.[3] Here is a short synopsis.

For a year Bette had suffered from agoraphobia, which is the fear of open spaces and crowds. Just going to the local mall could bring on an anxiety attack, so she couldn't leave the house unless her husband, Don, was with her.

Then one day a friend called to see if Bette would like to have a pig, one that adored people. When Lord Bacon was delivered that day and the wire cage was opened, he trotted out, wagged his straight tail, looked around, and headed right for Bette. When she knelt to greet him, he heaved himself up on his hind legs, laid his head on her shoulder, and kissed her on the cheek with his leathery snout. She looked at the pig, and for the first time in a long time, she smiled.

The next morning, instead of dreading another day, Bette was actually eager to see her new pet. Lord Bacon scrambled to greet her and rubbed against her leg—it felt like being massaged with a

Brillo pad. After breakfast, the pig followed Bette into her small home office and settled down beside her desk. Bette found that when she grew edgy, if she reached down and petted Lord Bacon and said a few words to him, she felt calmer.

Lord Bacon disliked loud noises. He figured out that Bette's phone would stop ringing when she picked it up. So if Bette wasn't there to answer the phone immediately, he yanked the receiver off the hook, stood over it, and grunted into the mouthpiece.

Soon both adults and children were stopping by to see Lord Bacon. The children took to calling him "Pigger," and Pigger he became. In Pigger's company, Bette was beginning to be more like her old self—so much so that her father tried to persuade Bette to bring Pigger to a senior citizens' meeting. Bette hesitated.

The next night Don came home with a baby stroller. "What's that?" Bette demanded.

"It's a pigmobile, so you can take Pigger to the seniors' meeting." Pigger loved the stroller.

Bette finally agreed to take Pigger to the meeting—alone. Her nerves tightened as she arrived at the center. She sat in the car, trembling; but as she stroked Pigger, she felt calmer. "I've got to conquer my fears," she told herself. She struggled out, settled Pigger in the pigmobile and wheeled him into the building.

The seniors were intrigued. Bette lifted Pigger to the floor. He immediately singled out the oldest woman and trotted over to nuzzle her cheek. The other seniors broke into laughter and crowded around to pet him.

Later, Bette took Pigger to a nearby nursing home, wheeling Pigger from room to room to visit with the patients. They loved it!

PIGGER'S HERE

On later visits, when Pigger came through the front door in his pigmobile, the call would go out, "Pigger's here!" A commotion would start in the halls—the squeak of wheelchairs, the tap-tap of walkers, the shuffle of slippered feet—as the residents hurried to see him.

The more Bette saw of sick and helpless people, the more thoughts of her own illness faded away. "I used to hate myself," she told Don, "but now I'm beginning to thank God every day that I am me. Pigger is my therapy."

Sometimes when Bette and Don shopped in the supermarket, from the next aisle a child's voice would ring out, "There's the pig's mother and father!" An embarrassed parent would be dragged over to be introduced to "the pig's family."

In one year Bette and Pigger made ninety-five public appearances together, mostly before older people and children. Bette handled each occasion with poise and flair.

Then one day Bette found Pigger lying in his favorite napping spot. He wasn't breathing. Bette has her own theory on why he died: "I think Pigger had a heart so big, it just burst with all that love. He helped me become my old self, and he brightened so many other lives. There'll never be another Pigger."

Warnings About Activities

Activities alone cannot be our total source of nourishment. Some people run from one activity to another, one shopping center to another, one job to another, even one ministry to another, seeking satisfaction or looking for approval.

If a woman is strongly driven to perfectionistic standards in all her activities, she will not find any of them very nourishing to her soul. Though the activity itself may be enjoyable to her, the anxiety, the fretting to do it perfectly—or the fear that she may not be approved of—will rob her of the nutrients that the activity would otherwise have provided.

Likewise, if a woman is more focused on being nourished than on nourishing others and to that end seeks to bring herself joy and satisfy her own perceived needs, she will end up disappointed! Notice what happened to Bette as she brought joy to others. She was nourished by Pigger, but then she reached out to nourish others and found healing in that.

REACH OUT FOR NOURISHMENT FROM OTHERS

We were made for God and for others. While our relationship to God is to be our primary source of soul nourishment and our involvement in wholesome activities is to provide some refreshment, we are not to be isolated human beings satisfied only with fellowship with God and our activities. He made us relational beings. We need to reach out for nourishment from others.

Biblical Examples: Paul and Jesus

As Paul sat in a Roman prison, he reached for nourishment from others. Writing to Timothy, he pleaded, "Do your best to come to me quickly, for Demas, . . . has deserted me. . . . Titus [has gone]. . . . Only Luke is with me. Get Mark and bring him with you." (2 Timothy 4:9–11).

Even Jesus asked His three closest earthly friends to go with Him into the Garden of Gethsemane.

We need people. Much nourishment comes from relationships, and we are responsible for reaching out to others to receive nourishment from them as well as to give nourishment to them.

Self-Care Is Not Selfishness

Many people feel selfish if they consider their own needs. We have already seen that it is not selfish to look after our own physical needs: That is being responsible. The same is true of our relational needs.

Clearly the Bible says that selfishness and self-centeredness are traits we are to deny. On the other hand, Scripture also emphasizes our need for relationships with others. How can I determine whether I am being selfish or am taking responsibility for needed nourishment?

The motive makes the difference. If I am acting solely for my own pleasure or seeking to get something for myself with no regard for the other person, then I am doing wrong. But if I am seeking nourishment so that I will be a better person who will better give glory to God and serve the needs of others, I am being responsible, not selfish. It's not selfish to actively reach out to others (see Philippians 2:3–4).

How to Reach Out for Nourishment

First, we must put ourselves into situations where we have contact with people. We cannot expect others to nourish us if our world is basically the four walls of our home. For the Christian, the church should be our key place to get nourishment, both spiritual and relational. One of our purposes in attending should be to meet people, to nourish them, and let them nourish us. This can happen before and after meetings, in small groups, by working together in outreach activities, and in many other ways.

So often we hear that people are not feeling nourished by others in their church. Joan shared that several people have said they feel like outsiders at her church.

"Just yesterday," she said, "I heard someone bemoaning this. My husband and I have felt the same way, so rather than continuing to complain about it, we decided to do something about it. We plan to invite couples and singles over regularly for a time of fun and fellowship." Joan and her husband are reaching out for nourishment, and at the same time they are nourishing others.

Carla noticed a woman in her church who was fifteen years older than she. Carla admired the maturity, steadiness, and godly wisdom of this woman, qualities she had long desired to have in a friend and mentor.

One day Carla suggested to the woman that she read an article about mentors. As they talked about the article, Carla mustered up the courage to say, "I would really like it if you could be that to me."

Their first weekly meetings were a time to study a book together. As they both began to share some of their inner feelings and struggles, the time became more of a share-and-prayer time, and sometimes, lunch together. These women are nourishment for one another.

Several years ago a friend who lives all the way across the country began to reach out to me for help. "Sometimes," she said, "I feel so intensely my need for nurturing. My husband loves me, but he doesn't know how to nurture me. Sometimes I think I might like to fly out to be with you for a few days, just to be nurtured by you."

Three Cautions When Reaching Out
1. You may try to relate to someone and find that her pegboard is already full:

    *   *Full of people*: She has so many relationships there's no time to add another. You may need to stand back and wait for a change of circumstances
    *   *Full of projects, ideas, causes*: She is too busy for friends. Pray and take some risks

    Keep pursuing relationships. Don't get discouraged and quit. All of us are much more lonely than we care to admit or perhaps even know, so pray and pursue, but do remember:

    *   Some people are more relationship-oriented
    *   Some people are more task-oriented
    *   Some people are unbelieving, skeptical that you even want to be a part of their life

2. Don't expect all your nourishment from your husband.
    Husbands and wives differ emotionally. Some husbands find it difficult to listen to their wives: They don't really understand where their wives are coming from emotionally. One husband admitted that he feels very uncomfortable when his wife wants to share with him on the emotional level. He has no problem with sexual intimacy, but he would rather run from emotional intimacy than take risks.
    One wife shared:

    I am coming to realize that I have different emotional needs than my husband. I want the warm feelings of knowing that someone cares about what I feel and think. I want my husband to provide this, but he either can't or doesn't seem interested. I've come to believe that men are just different emotionally.

There are other areas where my husband finds joy— doing recreational things together, loving one another physically, having fun times with the family. I need to work at improving these things and trust God to help me get some of my emotional nurturing from my women friends.

3. Don't become nourishment-centered.

If there seem to be no legitimate ways to gain nourishment from others, choose to trust God's timing, and in the meantime, to drink more deeply from Him. Choose to be content with what He has provided for you at this moment.

Take Some Initiative

The question we should ask ourselves is, Are we taking any initiative? Are we putting any energy into building relationships, or are we sitting back in our loneliness expecting people to pursue us? We should pursue, not only for ourselves, but for the sake of others who need relationship too.

You may be afraid to pursue because you've been rejected and deeply hurt in the past. You're tempted to create distance between yourself and others so that you will not get hurt again. Reaching out to others does involve taking risks. You will experience some hurt and disappointment, because we live in an imperfect world with imperfect people. I encourage you to be willing to be hurt again.

Choose ahead of time to embrace the hurt and pain. Choose to forgive afresh when necessary and move toward others in love instead of away from them for self-protection. Put some energy into love. Graciously pursue. Don't give up. You need others and others need you.

Putting It All Together

God has made us with a need for nourishment. We need to keep our focus on the Lord as the primary source of our nourishment, but we must not sit passively by saying, "I have God; I don't need people." Reaffirm your God-given need to get emotional and spiritual nourishment from others as well. Choose to take responsible steps of action to find nourishment in legitimate ways. And choose to add some fun activities that will bring it to you.

Take some quiet moments before the Lord to sort through what you've just read. Think about your nourishment needs. Does the Lord have His rightful place in your life, or have you been putting too much emphasis on people or things to meet your needs? What are your sources of nourishment? What refreshes you emotionally and gives you energy? Are you giving out and giving out but receiving very little that replenishes you?

Should you be making plans for how you can reach out to others to be nourished by them? Or have you been thinking that it is selfish to have your needs met?

Thoughts to Remember

Nourish yourself so you will have energy to nourish others. Learn to take care of yourself so you can take care of others.

"Your words were found, and I ate them, and Your word was to me the joy and rejoicing of my heart" (Jeremiah 15:16, NKJV).

Practicing and Journaling

Plan to do something this week just to nourish yourself. Write what you did, how others responded, and how you felt about it.

Part **II**

Freedom from Malnourishment

4

Origins of Malnourishment

God planned that the family would be the primary place for each member to be well nourished physically, emotionally, and spiritually, but sin disrupted the plan. From the time of Adam and Eve right down to you and me today, sin introduced a new principle that has been plaguing us all. Here's what it sounds like: "I want my own way. I can and will make it on my own. I will make life work myself. I must watch out for number one—myself—primarily! I come first! My needs, my plans, my work, my achievement, my pleasure, my reputation, my . . . my priority is *me!*"

The label we put on this is independence, which results in plain and simple *selfishness*. It insists, "I want my way." The result is an environment that does not nurture others, but instead causes them emotional pain.

Judy was sharing how frustrated she was with her own acute sense of emotional neediness. Just that day she had received another deep disappointment in a relationship.

The story came pouring out. She had invited a dear friend from another city to visit her and was eagerly anticipating her coming in a couple of months. Judy was desperately hungry for fellowship and was already planning the fun times they would have together.

Then the news came that her friend would not be able to come. She was devastated and hit rock bottom emotionally.

Off the phone, Judy fell apart and sobbed for several hours. Feeling terribly defeated, childish, and ashamed of herself for being so out of control, she asked herself, "Why am I reacting so uncontrollably to such a reasonable change of plans?" It was then she realized that she was very, very angry at life, but more basically, at God.

She chose to do what Scripture says we should: "Pour out your heart before Him; God *is* a refuge for us" (Psalm 62:8, NASB). She sat down at her computer and poured out her heart to God:

Dear Father:

I'm angry. . . . I have cried and cried until there are no more tears left. Don't You care that I long to be with my dearest friend, the one who understands me better than any other person on earth?

I would ask why I am so dependent, but I already know the answer. Did I ask to be wounded like I am? *No!* I know You allowed it, Father, and I know it's foolish to talk like this to You. But I don't understand why You allowed me to grow up in a home where my Dad gave nothing to me emotionally, my brother used me, the neighbor boys sexually abused me, and my own pastor used me for his own emotional fulfillment.

Did I ask for that? Why me? What good could there possibly be in my having to struggle so constantly with my emotions? The wounds are so deep, and it hurts so much, Father. I am weary of crying, weary of having no one to talk with who is understanding. And I'm angry! Angry at You. Angry at me. Angry that my needs are so great. Angry that I am like I am!

I feel *trapped*. You are the only One I can turn to, yet You seem so far away. I know in my head that You have promised to bring something good out of this. I know that, but I don't *feel* it, and it's hard! It hurts so much! And I want to scream. I don't like being abused and dependent. I don't like being who I am emotionally. I don't like being needy and helpless. Father, why have You allowed it?

Causes of Malnourishment

Judy was from a nonnurturing family. Oh yes, Judy's family of origin was committed to faithful leadership in Christian ministry. But the family did not function as God intended, and she did not receive the kind of nurturing love that God planned.

Time and again she has expressed embarrassment over what she calls her "abnormal neediness." She has asked, "Why am I so needy? So hungry for love?" Even while she asks the question, she gives the basic answer. She came from an unhealthy family system.

Breakdown in the Family of Origin

What makes a home a non-nourishing environment? Remember we have said that, because of sin, everyone since Adam and Eve comes from a family that is not fully functioning as God planned. Because of this, everyone has some deficiencies, some injuries, and therefore some struggles in life. Failure to be nurtured is to be emotionally wounded in one way or another. To help us get a little understanding of the dynamics of Judy's feelings, we are going to look at the characteristics of both a healthy and an unhealthy family.

Traits of a Healthy Family

Let's first take a look at how God intended the family to operate. What are some of the marks of a family that is functioning as God planned it?

Parents are a good example. They show their children how to live by the way they live. God is our example in this, "As children copy their fathers you, as God's children, are to copy him" (Ephesians 5:1, Phillips).

Parents build up their children. They give encouragement, love, unconditional acceptance, and continuing approval—building up, not tearing down.

Parents do not irritate or provoke. "Fathers, do not irritate and provoke your children to anger—do not exasperate them to resentment—but rear them [tenderly] in the training . . . of the Lord" (Ephesians 6:4, AMP).

Parents are respectful. They honor privacy, modesty, and the right to be human and make mistakes for all within the home.

Parents parent *their children.* They take the responsibility to be parents to the children and do not put this heavy burden on any child in the home. It is not the child's responsibility to look after the parent or siblings, but it is the parent's responsibility to care for the children.

Parents defer to one another. There is love and mutual submission between the two parents, and there is harmony in the home (see Ephesians 5:21).

Parents have integrity. "It is a wonderful heritage to have an honest father" (Proverbs 20:7, TLB).

Parents protect their children. They do all they can to protect their children from mistreatment, abuse, and other violations of the person.

Parents are predictable. They stand behind their promises and fulfill them. They can be counted on to be consistently patient and loving.

Parents train their children. They are actively involved in training the children in all phases of life skills. "Train up a child in the way he should go: and when he is old, he will not depart from it" (Proverbs 22:6, KJV).

Parents are trustworthy. They are dependable, and the children know the parents are *for* them.

Parents are free from addictions. They are not alcoholics, workaholics, or churchaholics. They keep themselves from extremes, such as legalism. (Addictions are those persons or things on which we have an excessive dependency.)

Parents do not abuse. They do not engage in any form of abuse: verbal, physical, emotional, or sexual.

Traits of an Unhealthy Family

In contrast, what are some common traits of an unhealthy home? Traits that wound? Traits that cause emotional pain?

Parents are not a good example. They do not show the children how to live. Rather than give their children an example of how life can be lived righteously, their example is negative.

Parents do not build up their children. They tear down the members in the home by failing to encourage them and express love, acceptance, and approval. They shame, blame, and cause others to feel guilty.

Parents irritate and provoke. By their words and actions they aggravate family members and stir up trouble.

Parents are disrespectful. They invade the privacy of others, not respecting their modesty or their right to be human and make mistakes.

Parents abdicate the parental role. Because parents aren't *parenting,* the child takes on the role of caretaker, trying to hold things together and keep peace. Not being parented, the child feels neglected and left on his own, as latchkey children often do.

Parents lack harmony. Each insists on "my own way." Self-concern prevails, and there is conflict.

Parents lack integrity. There is hypocrisy and dishonesty.

Parents do not protect They give and allow mistreatment and violation of the person.

Parents are unpredictable. Their vacillation between anger/impatience and loving care results in confusion: Am I loved or rejected; approved of or not approved of? They cannot be counted on to keep their promises.

Parents do not train their children. They ignore basic training in such things as life skills and relationships.

Parents are undependable. They are either too busy, passive, or absent; and they can't be trusted to be there for the child.

Parents have addictive behaviors. Possibilities include alcoholism, workaholism, rage-aholism, shopaholism, churchaholism, compulsive eating habits, or other extremes.

Parents are abusive. They use any of the various kinds of abuse, such as verbal, physical, emotional, sexual.

These environments are definitely nonnurturing, and they cause wounding. The degree of injury or pain the child experiences is determined by:

1. The degree of malfunction in the home
2. The child's perceptions of that malfunction
3. The personality of the child
4. The frequency, intensity, and duration of the trauma

Keep this list in mind as you read the following illustrations of varying degrees of breakdown in families and its impact on the children. Try to pick out the characteristics that apply in each case.

TIPTOEING ON EGGSHELLS

My mother was an abused child and never felt loved, even to her dying day. My father, also abused, was withdrawn and extremely passive; yet, he enjoyed creating friction. Their marriage was a love-hate relationship. Mom fought to keep all of us under her control—manipulating and shaming us. If my father stood up for himself or one of us, she would angrily shout him down until he withdrew within himself.

We could not relax. There was the constant fear that a volcano was going to erupt any minute. It was like tiptoeing around on eggshells. I spent much of my childhood trying to appease my angry mom and stop the fights between her and dad. I had a strong craving to hear her say, "I love you. You're okay." I worked hard for that, and one big grief of mine is that she died without ever letting me hear that.

What traits of a healthy family were missing in that home?

MR. EXEMPLARY CHRISTIAN

The youngest of five children, I was born into a strict Christian family, devoted to the church. Mother was the piano player and often a Sunday school teacher. Daddy was always extremely involved—deacon, trustee, young people's leader, Sunday school superintendent, head usher. He pretty much ran the place.

Dad was a harsh and domineering man. All of us, including Mother, were afraid of him. He often tried to make Mom look stupid in front of the family. She became his doormat. Dad was extreme in terms of punishment. Welt-raising whippings, withholding meals, knocking heads together, demeaning tongue-lashings, and humiliations were commonplace. Even worse were his "silent treatments," which usually lasted several days.

He might give us the silent treatment during the whole thirty-minute drive to church, or maybe he would stop the car and knock a couple heads together. Then as soon as he reached the church, he was "Mr. Exemplary Christian." But when we were all back in the car, he'd take up right where he left off.

We children were also victims of my father's perverted notion of affection. He insisted on long, close embraces and passionate kisses from his daughters. If we tried to resist, we were punished by his silent treatments. I vividly recall how he would come into my dark bedroom after I was in bed and explain the facts of life in graphic detail.

Mother had little patience with us. I remember a lot of threatening and screaming. She often gagged my brothers by stuffing old socks into their mouths and leaving them in for hours. But Mom was the abused one. Dad was so mean to her.

What traits of a healthy family were missing in that home?

DAD MADE FUN OF ME

My father is an alcoholic. He was raised in an alcoholic home. He cheated on my mother. When I was five, I saw Dad kiss another woman. I hated that. My father was cruel when he teased or corrected us. I grew up thinking I was ugly. He made fun of my bangs as a teenager, always in front of people, and he stared at my breasts.

I tried several times to tell my mother that Dad was touching me in places I didn't like. One time my dad left the house in a drunken rage because I would not sit with him. He left town and planned not to come back. As a result, Mom slapped me all over the bathroom, pulled my hair, and hit my head on the wall saying that I should have sat with him, that he wouldn't have done anything to me, and that I had nothing to be afraid of. Mom was always screaming.

What traits of a healthy family were missing in that home? What deep hurt! Each of these women said her parents were from unhealthy families: alcoholic, abusive, adulterous, abandoning, etc. As adults, these women are all now in abusing situations themselves, but each has a burden to put a stop to this generational iniquity. Each one is determined to do what she can to stop it.

Brothers and sisters can also painfully hurt one another emotionally. When we were very young, I recall my older brother saying, "If I couldn't sing any better than that, I wouldn't try." I believed his evaluation and developed an insecurity about my singing ability, because I continued to run these words through my mind. This was a rather small injury, but it was real and painful.

Other Sources of Malnourishment

Although we are examining how wounding occurs within the family, let's also remember that the home is not the only place of malnourishment. A child may get much hurtful input from his peers, teachers, other significant adults, and from the particular events in his life.

There is the little innocent five-year-old boy who is sexually abused by an older neighbor boy. Or the child who is ridiculed by his peers because of some physical feature or his inability to excel in sports. There are unavoidable losses, such as death or sickness in the family, divorce, or other significant losses.

So when we talk about malnourishment, we include much more than flawed parenting or even sibling rivalry and conflict. Regardless of the source or even the degree of injury, let's look at some solutions, some hope, some basis for healing these wounds.

HOPE AND HEALING FOR THE MALNOURISHED

There was a young boy who came from a home in which God had been honored for generations. In spite of this there was conflict, abuse, and dishonesty in his family. His parents were in conflict with each other. There were a number of boys in the family, but the father showed obvious favoritism toward this young man. Of course, this caused sibling strife. The boy's older brothers hated him, mistreated him, and made fun of him.

You may have guessed that this boy's name was Joseph. In many ways his family was unhealthy (dysfunctional), and Joseph must have suffered much emotional injury and pain through those years (see Genesis 37, 39–45, 50).

Joseph suffered loss upon loss. He lost his mother at a young age. He was his dad's favorite son, but this favoritism and his own claim about God's plan for him drew vicious jealousy and rage from his brothers. They hated him, ridiculed him, and set out to murder him. Instead of carrying it out, however, they sold him for a little bit of money to some traders from another country. Now, at least, he was out of their hair. Then they deceived and lied to their father. Theirs was definitely an unhealthy family system.

Joseph's life continued, but in a totally new and foreign environment. For the next thirteen years, he continued to experience many painful losses, abuses, and abandonment. Separated from his beloved father. Falsely accused of rape. Thrown into prison. Forgotten for two years by the chief butler, for whom he had done a big favor, the one who could have been instrumental in securing his freedom. How did Joseph respond to this?

Do we get any clues from Joseph's responses to life as to what we must do to overcome in our own situations?

Joseph Kept His Focus on God

As Joseph started his new life in Egypt, it is obvious that he kept his focus on God, not on his own pain and abuses—and not on his abusers, the ones who had caused him so much pain. He saw God as the major factor in all his circumstances, and he stated it clearly time and again. He gave God the credit for his wisdom and ability. He was free from pride, bitterness, and resentment; and God gave him favor with people and caused him to succeed. Along with his focus on God, Joseph kept his faith in God. From his responses we can easily see what he believed in his heart about God:

1. *God Loves Me*: God loves me with unfailing love, and He is good and trustworthy

2. *God Is in Charge*: God is in charge of all the events that touch my life. I believe God is bigger than the hurts, and He can heal them

3. *God Has a Purpose for Good*: God has a good purpose and is working all things together for my good, even these evil things

Joseph's primary focus was God—His loving character and His good purpose for his life. Joseph could have focused on the wrongs, pains, and unfortunate blows that family, other people, and "life" dealt him. If he had done this, however, he would have drowned himself in resentment and self-pity (two of the worst enemies of peace). But he did not.

Joseph Forgave His Brothers

Joseph had a forgiving lifestyle. We'll focus here on how he forgave his worst offenders—his brothers—for the wrongs they did to him. Notice, at his first encounter with them, Joseph did not say, "Oh, I'm so glad you've come. I want you to know I forgive you for all of your abuse to me." Although he had a forgiving spirit, he didn't tell his brothers who he was right away.

Joseph was moving toward full forgiveness on his part and full reconciliation between himself and his brothers. Both forgiveness and reconciliation are processes. He was also moving his brothers toward facing their sin, thus giving them an opportunity to repent (see Genesis 42:21). They had sinned against Him. They had done wrong. There needed to be more than a quick "forgiveness" on his part. Covering up someone else's sin is not forgiveness. Ignoring the past, or even excusing or minimizing their wrong toward him, would not bring healing.

EXCUSING IS NOT FORGIVING

Like Joseph, we cannot forgive if we simply excuse or minimize the other person's wrong toward us. We must first acknowledge their sin against us and then *choose* to forgive them. That's clean forgiveness; but it continues to be a process as the memories of former hurts surface and as those hurts may even be repeated. It's not a once-for-all action.

We also need to accept the fact that we have been sinned against. We must neither deny nor even minimize the bad things that have happened to us. We accept truth (the sad facts of our past); but, we also accept grace—grace to forgive ourselves and grace to forgive others. Some think they have forgiven parents or others who have sinned against them, but they have only excused them, thinking, "They did the best they could."

RECONCILIATION

Joseph confronted his brothers. Three chapters in Genesis detail his careful and wise plan. He wanted full forgiveness and reconciliation, and he knew God wanted that too. Forgiveness was his part; but for reconciliation to occur, the brothers needed to face their sinful actions, feel the pain they had caused him, repent, and prove themselves trustworthy. Could Joseph trust them again?

They passed the "trust" test. He accepted them, wept, forgave them, and put his focus back on God and His purposes for them all. Joseph had learned to take responsibility for his own responses, but not for their sin, wrong actions, or attitude. They had been wrong!

After they acknowledged their sin against him, he comforted them with, "Do not be distressed and do not be angry with yourselves for selling me here, because it was to save lives that God sent me ahead of you" (Genesis 45:5).

Joseph was so wrapped up in God's unfailing love and in His good purposes for him that he was able to fully forgive his brothers for sinning against him. He didn't even want them to be distressed or full of anger toward themselves. What forgiveness! What love! Just like Jesus!

The question comes, Would you always confront the other regarding his sin against you? The verse that says, "If your brother sins, rebuke him" (Luke 17:3), needs to be balanced with 1 Peter 4:8, "Love covers over a multitude of sins." So, when is it right to confront? We'll take this up in chapter 10.

Joseph did not excuse his brothers; he faced them with their sin, forgave them, and didn't even want them to be angry with themselves. After they repented, he wanted them to forgive themselves. The succinct statement that Joseph made to his brothers, when they stood before him in great fear, that he would pay them back for their terrible mistreatment of him was, "You meant evil against me; but God meant it for good" (Genesis 50:20, NKJV).

Perhaps you come from an unhealthy family where there was deceit; lying; selfishness; neglect; abuse from parents; and abuse, hatred, and jealousy from siblings or others. Remember, it is not what happens to us in life that is the most significant thing, but it is *our response* to what happens. Joseph had a godly response, and it freed him to be a godly man in a pagan culture.

TAKE JOSEPH'S WAY

There's hope and healing even for those who come from severely malnourishing backgrounds. Joseph, and multitudes since his time, have found it so. God loves you, and He is working out His good purposes in your life and will continue to do so as you continue to trust Him.

I urge you to take Joseph's way:

- Keep your major focus on the Lord—His control, His love for you, and His good purposes for your life
- Forgive those who have wronged you, acknowledging their sin against you and choosing to forgive them

Even if the other person doesn't repent and change, we need to forgive them for our own sake, our own healing, our own freedom. Keep remembering Joseph's confession of peace and victory, "You meant evil against me; but God meant it for good." This statement was a clear confession of truth about his brothers and the event, about God's loving control, and about Joseph's faith in God's goodness and good purposes. As Joseph did his part, God gave the brothers the grace of reconciliation.

One person asked: "What about when you're quite sure the other person had a wrong motive? For example, my grandfather sexually abused me, then he paid my way to a Christian camp. I loved camp and got much from it, but now I realize he probably did that out of guilt and to try to cover his sin. What about that?"

I answered, "Your grandfather may have meant it for evil, but God brought good into the situation."

There is hope! Regardless of the source and the degree of wounding, you can be healed. The foundation of all healing is to keep your focus on God, remember who you are in Christ, and forgive those who have sinned against you.

Take a moment of quiet to think, to let God speak, and to respond to Him in your heart.

Do you need to remove your focus from those who hurt you and focus instead on God, Who is in control, Who loves you more than anyone can, and Who will work all things together for good, to give you a hope and a future (Jeremiah 29:11)? Is there someone in your life you need to forgive? Are you willing to forgive? Are you willing to at least start the process by asking God to give you the grace to forgive?

MALNOURISHMENT FOSTERS WRONG THINKING

Now let's look at some types of hurt that come to us and begin to get some clues as to how those wounds can be healed.

Joy expressed a significant thought when she said, "I read my Bible and pray a lot, but it seems there's something blocking me from experiencing freedom and peace in my life with the Lord Jesus."

Sometimes there are missing nutrients in our lives. This blocks us from receiving all Christ has for us.

One day Nettie and I took our car in to get the oil changed. Later, when she returned from picking it up, she said, "Verna, do you know why the warning light for the oil was on all the way home?"

"I don't have a clue," I said, "but it doesn't sound good to me. I'll call and ask."

"Sir, can you tell me why the warning light for the oil was on all the way home?"

"Well, that shouldn't be. I'll come right out."

What he feared and we feared was true. The man had forgotten to put in the new oil after draining out the old! The warning signal said: "There is no oil in me; I need oil to function. Give me some oil!" (By the way, the distance was short and no damage was done!)

Suppose Nettie had ignored the warning light and said, "There can't be anything wrong with the oil. We just had it changed." The car still looked good on the outside the wheels turned, the horn honked, the doors and windows opened and closed. But something was wrong. A basic nutrient was missing, and soon the motor would have been all locked up and not functioning properly.

Our emotions are also warning lights that signal us when something is wrong and needs correction or repair. We need to give attention to them. They are saying: "Something is wrong; there's a blockage somewhere."

To help us get hold of this, let me explain some significant human dynamics that constitute blockages.

Conscious and Subconscious Parts

Someone has described us like a pear in shape (see Fig. 1). When I drew this diagram in a class, one lady said, "Yes, that looks pretty much like me!"

The narrow top of the pear represents our conscious part. The far greater portion of our personality is the subconscious part of us. This subconscious part has both positive and negative aspects. Many of our good habits operate for us automatically out of our subconscious.

A car that Nettie and I rented had written instructions at the

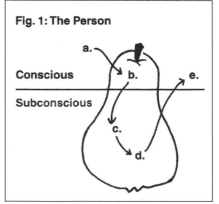

Fig. 1: The Person

Conscious

Subconscious

a. b. c. d. e.

base of the gear shift: *Press brake pedal before taking gear out of Park.* Most of us do that automatically.

We all have a lot of good, automatic habits that spring from our subconscious. But for our purposes here we will try to understand more about the negative subconscious aspects.

A Traumatic Event Injures Me (A)

Because I have been made for a perfect environment that includes people who are trustworthy and who meet my *need* for safety, respect, unconditional acceptance, and continual approval, when a traumatic event happens to me in childhood, I am injured emotionally.

When my God-created needs are not met by parents or significant people in my life, there is injury to my emotions and I experience pain. This pain is much deeper and more lasting than any physical injury.

I Draw Conclusions About Myself (B and C)

When a child experiences emotional hurt, two things typically happen.

1. He has definite impressions and *draws wrong conclusions* about himself and his environment (*b*). Some of his self-depreciating conclusions may be: "I'm to blame. It's my fault. Shame on me. I'm a bad person. I'm unlovable. There's something wrong with me. I can never do anything right."
2. The pain becomes too great and he can't bear it, so he *represses* it. When an experience is too painful to cope with, his defense mechanism takes over, and he stuffs his feelings and wrong conclusions *into his subconscious storage space* (c).

He may deny that it hurts, or deny that it happened. He may even block the painful event out of his memory. Or, if he remembers, he may minimize it—believing it had no damaging effect on him. Or he may deny the other person is responsible for the wrong and conclude there must be something wrong with *him* or it would not have happened.

Now both the pain and the wrong conclusions are stored away securely in his subconscious.

The Subconscious Adds Fuel (d)

Once the pain is stored away, the child's subconscious goes into active duty gathering all kinds of verifying evidence that seems to affirm his wrong conclusions.

These conclusions in his subconscious hidden parts—or "inward parts," as Scripture refers to them in Psalm 51:6 (NKJV)—still control his thinking and behavior on a subconscious, involuntary level. Though the individual is not aware of them, these negative patterns are in control, working against him, often resulting in hate, resentment, and anger toward himself. This works itself out in depression, self-condemnation, shame, blame, guilt.

As Judy did, the child may turn that resentful anger toward God in bitterness and distrust. Or he may turn the anger outward—blaming, criticizing, and not forgiving others.

Flesh Patterns Block Peace and Victory

The impressions stored in the subconscious affect our thinking and acting, and as a result of them, we develop life patterns of wrong thinking and behaving.

Remember, we began to form these patterns of response as we tried to cope with that childhood happening that injured us. At the time, repressing it was probably the only way that we were able to cope with it. But now, as adults, many of these wrong attitudes, perceptions, and habits have become our variety of *flesh patterns* that are buried in our hidden parts, and our tendency is to walk "according to the flesh" instead of walking "according to the Spirit" (Romans 8:4, NASB).

"Don't give the devil a foothold" with your anger toward self, others, or God (Ephesians 4:26–27, Phillips). When we give the devil a *foothold*, these flesh patterns can then become the devil's *strongholds* (2 Corinthians 10:4–5).

Walking according to the flesh, in our thoughts or behavior constitutes a blockage that keeps us from experiencing freedom in our relationship to ourselves, to others, and to God. It becomes a blockage to peace, joy, and victory in Jesus. We become captives of our unconscious thoughts and hidden anger, which we turn inward or outward or upward. We find it difficult to trust anyone, including God. We have been injured and are in need of repair.

We must first become aware of what has happened and what is happening, and of our particular kind of twisted thinking, flesh patterns, and footholds or strongholds of the devil.

A PERSONAL FLESH PATTERN

Not long ago I became painfully aware of something stored away deeply in my subconscious. Two of my very good friends seemed to be laughing at me and ganging up against me. I felt very left out and rejected and became rather quiet.

When Ann and I were alone that evening, she asked me why I was so quiet. So I told her how things had appeared to me all day—that she and Jane were becoming fast friends and were leaving me out. Perhaps it was simply jealousy, but it seemed there was something more I needed to understand.

To my surprise Ann said *she* felt left out and was trying desperately to be accepted by Jane. I was all wrong in my conclusions. When I was able to accept that, we were soon reconciled and I went off to sleep.

During the night this all began to open up before me as I remembered a childhood incident. My brother and I were very good friends. I felt secure in our relationship. We did everything together, until one day some boy cousins came to visit him on our farm. They didn't want me to play with them. Even my brother, my good buddy, didn't want me to join in. I was determined, but they were more determined. To get rid of me, they poured pig slop on me from the stinky slop barrel. I felt terribly rejected and abandoned by them.

As I lay there thinking all this through, it was as if a bolt of lightning hit me. My buried conclusion about that incident had been, "People will be your good friends until someone more interesting comes along. Then, they will try to get rid of you, reject you, and run off with their new friends, leaving you standing alone."

I realized that all through my life I had been unconsciously gathering evidence that this conclusion was true. A number of instances came to mind. I also recalled that for a period of time I consistently had dreams to this effect: A friend would run off with other friends and leave me alone.

This was a special *fear* for me—fear that someone more interesting would take my good friends away from me. I understood that my reaction to Ann and Jane that day was not only jealousy, but it sprang from something deeper—a basic fear of abandonment, a fear of being rejected and left alone, just as I had been that day by my good friend, my brother.

Now I see that the fear of being rejected or left out when someone more interesting comes along is one of my particular *flesh patterns*. I need to realize that when I walk in this fear of rejection or abandonment, I'm walking according to the flesh and not "according to the Spirit," as Romans 8:4 says. I must not excuse it or blame others, but I must face it for what it really is and then *choose* to walk according to the Spirit and not give Satan a foothold.

This understanding has helped me so much to gain victory in my life when this same kind of issue arises at different times and even in different disguises. I realize that the basic issue is fear, not just a symptom of jealousy. That doesn't make it any less sinful. This kind of fear *is* a sin pattern—it is fleshly, not godly—and it must be turned from and then be replaced by walking in the power of the Spirit. This is a process. It takes time and may be continual!

How to Expose Our Hurtful Thinking (e)

How are we going to cooperate with the Lord in the process of bringing our hidden thoughts to the conscious level? We need to humble ourselves, choose to become aware of our wrong thinking, and choose to take responsibility for our thoughts, attitudes, and behavior. We need to *own* our own lives under the lordship of Christ. How do we become aware?

Open Heart to Truth. The first step is to open up all the windows of our soul to the Holy Spirit so that He can reveal "truth in the inner parts." It's only when we know our wrong thinking that we can begin to remove the blockage and be free from the hurtful way. Ask the Lord to put His searchlight on your inner parts and reveal the truth or untruth that is there.

The major ways that He uses to enlighten us are His Word, His Spirit of Truth, and other members of His body. Pray: "Search me, O God, and know my heart; try me, and know my anxious thoughts; and see if there be any hurtful way in me" (Psalm 139:23–24, NASB). Or, O Lord, "enlighten my darkness" (Psalm 18:28, KJV).

The question might come, Do you think we need to go back into our past and dig up everything? No, but we can open our hearts and minds to the Holy Spirit to search our inner thoughts and motives. We must trust God to reveal that which would be profitable for our Christian growth. Always be open and ready to learn from the Lord through whatever "teacher" He has for us, whether it is a person, a circumstance, His Word, or simply His working in our thoughts by the Holy Spirit.

We don't need to be disturbed or discouraged when new issues arise. Just deal with them.

Listen to Others. We learn by reading or listening to others share their discoveries about themselves—their painful experiences, their discovery of wrong thoughts and flesh patterns. Many times the Lord uses their sharing to help us identify painful issues in our own lives. This is one reason why stories of other people's experiences are so important in our learning.

King David was made keenly aware of his sin through the story Nathan told him about another man who had sinned. In this case, Nathan even had to say, "You are the man!" Only then did David see the light and stop hiding his sin (see 2 Samuel 12:1–14).

Biographies are a great way to find out what others have learned. Choose to learn from them. Over and over in the Proverbs we are told that wise people listen to advice.

Be Willing to Share Yourself. We learn by being willing to share our feelings, our doubts, and even our sins with at least one other "safe" person. You will make more discoveries of sin in your heart than you ever thought. "Confess your sins to one another, and pray for one another, so that you may be healed" (James 5:16, NASB).

You will find much help and healing as that safe person extends acceptance, love, understanding, and a nonjudgmental attitude toward you. In the process of sharing we often gain insights about ourselves and what we need to do. Though it was hard for me, it was so helpful in my situation to talk it through with Ann that evening.

In chapter 2, I gave the example of Nancy, who after a year of meeting for counseling said, "Many times when you have problems, they just seem to be stuffed deep down inside and can't come out until you can begin to express yourself. So, if you can just talk out your thoughts in a safe environment, then you can sort through things. Often it becomes clear what needs attention and what you can do about it."

The Need to Change Our Twisted Thinking

Our buried wrong conclusions about how life works, and about ourselves, others, or God, distort our reality thinking. These become our default setting (to use *computerese*) or the lenses through which we perceive life. The deceptive thing is that we think we see clearly, because it is what we've seen all our life. We think distortion is reality, that abuse is normal.

When the Lord begins to enlighten my darkness and reveal truth in the inner parts I come to realize that my thinking is distorted, and I have an issue to deal with.

In the process, there will be some struggles, some tears, fears, and even denials. But when we face the truth and embrace it, we will be moving toward freedom. "Then you will know the truth, and the truth will set you free" (John 8:32).

"It was for freedom that Christ set us free" (Galatians 5:1, NASB). God wants you free from your twisted thinking and your wounded heart. He came to:

- Bind up the brokenhearted
- Proclaim freedom to the captives
- Release those who are bound
- Recover sight to those who are blind. (see Isaiah 61:1–2 and Luke 4:18–19)

Remember it is a process and it takes *time*!

What Do I Do About It?

The question is, Now that I've become aware of the real situation, received a clearer understanding of it, faced it, traced it back to its precipitating event, and have seen some of the twisted thinking and resultant flesh patterns, what am I going to do about it? What is my responsibility? How can I begin to find help and healing?

As I stressed earlier, the foundation is to focus on God and forgive those who have sinned against us. Then I need to begin the process of "Casting down imaginations, and every high thing that exalteth itself against the knowledge of God, and bringing into captivity every thought to the obedience of Christ" (2 Corinthians 10:5, KJV). Or we can express it as "the renewing of your mind" (Romans 12:2).

I need to take responsibility for my wrong thoughts and make a conscious choice to change them. This is a process, not a once-for-all action. It is a walk, a continual capturing of every thought. A continual putting off of old flesh patterns as they come to our attention, putting on the new self, and living as children of light (see Colossians 3:8–10 and Ephesians 5:8).

Satan Will Try to Discourage

If those around you are dispensing shame and blame, you might have to put on earmuffs when your misguided conscience talks to you or when other people or Satan give you false input.

A friend of mine, a deeply committed Christian, has been struggling with various flesh patterns for sometime. Whenever she gets a new insight about a new issue, she takes action. Later, when another issue comes up, it will throw her into another time of struggle. She may then feel discouraged and defeated and think she has really made no progress. This is a work of Satan.

Satan is the deceiver, the liar, the tempter, the accuser. Acknowledge that some thoughts do come from Satan. He puts thoughts in your mind and then tries to convince you that they are yours. You feel sinful and dirty for having such thoughts. The Bible says to humble yourself before God and resist the devil. Be alert to his deceptions, lies, temptations, and accusations. Don't accept them. Resist him and them (see 1 Peter 5:6–9 and James 4:7).

In my friend's case, what is her real situation? She *has* made progress. She is dealing realistically with issues, but there are more issues to deal with. These may be related to a former issue but have a different application.

It is as we renew our minds with truth about God and about ourselves that we will know healing and freedom. This is a continual process. Because of the crucial importance of changing our twisted thinking, the next two chapters are devoted to this process.

Thoughts to Remember

God is in charge of all the events and people that touch my life. I believe God is bigger than the hurts and will heal them. I choose to forgive those who have wronged me.

"You meant evil against me; but God meant it for good" (Genesis 50:20, NKJV).

Practicing and Journaling

Review the traits of a healthy family and put a check by one or two that you need to work on. Write a statement about what you plan to do about it this week.

5

Hurtful, Twisted Thinking

Mark and Diane moved to a different house. Because of the busyness of their work schedule, they were months getting the house in order. One big problem was that Mark wanted to rework the fireplace, which required some wall and roof work. An extreme perfectionist, he wanted to do most of the work himself, although he allowed very little time for it.

After seven months of living in the mess—plastic hanging from the ceiling and plastic covering the furniture that was stacked in the middle of the room, the wall still was not finished. Again and again during those seven months, they talked about it. He promised to work on it, but he never followed through. And still they had a plastic-covered living room.

Finally, they were ready for the stone mason. Mark called to make a date. The mason said yes, he could come out and do it—in about four months!

Inwardly, Diane fumed. She thought of the many things that should have been done differently, but they were undone or delayed because of her husband's irresponsibility. He should have called a long time ago. Sure, he had time to go fishing, but no time to get the family's living quarters in livable condition!

Then she remembered that her greatest need was to set her focus back on the Lord. She began to talk to herself, "God really is in control of this too. He really does love me, so there must be some good that He wants to work out of this experience. My deepest satisfaction could never come from a completed living room!"

Instead of focusing on the disappointing circumstances and her negligent husband, Diane focused on the Lord, His love, and His control. She thought about where real satisfaction comes from. With that came peace. Her soul found rest in God alone. She chose to take her basic nourishment from Him, and she did this by changing her self-talk.

CHANGING OUR HURTFUL THINKING

We need to know how we are thinking and what we are saying to ourselves so that we can intelligently deal with truth and lies, misconceptions, wrong assumptions—all kinds of negative thinking.

General Guidelines
- *First*, we need to become aware of what we are thinking or saying to ourselves
- *Second*, we must judge or discern whether it is truth or lies, healthy or unhealthy self-talk, helpful or hurtful conclusions
- *Third*, we need to own our own thoughts—assume responsibility for them and confess them
- *Fourth*, we must replace them with truth, positive self-talk, or helpful words

Proverbs 18:21 says, "The tongue has the power of life and death," that is, healing and hurting. Proverbs 16:24 says, "Pleasant words are a honeycomb, sweet to the soul and healing to the bones."

The challenge to us, therefore, is to become aware of our wrong, hurtful, twisted thinking and then face it, own it, and commit ourselves to truth.

The ABCs of Our Emotions

Dr. Albert Ellis[1] has developed the ABC approach to identifying our wrong thinking by giving attention to our *emotions*. We have been taught to believe that bad events or the insensitivity of others causes our bad feelings. If good things happen or people treat us well, we feel good—we are happy and content. If bad things happen or people do not treat us well, we are sad and upset. In response, we blame the event or the person, or we try to change the event or person so that we will *feel* better.

Dr. Ellis describes this wrong thinking as:

$$A = C$$

Activating event = Consequences

That is, traumatic events or circumstances in our lives equal or cause our resultant feelings. The circumstances are represented by the *A* (activating event) in our lives. The tendency for us in our culture is to blame these activating events for causing us to act and feel the way we do. These emotional and behavioral consequences are the *C*. Therefore our formula is: $A = C$.

Let's relate this to my experience with my brother and his cousins. I thought their behavior caused me to feel rejected (emotional consequences). That's like saying: *A* (they wouldn't let me play with them) = *C* (I felt hurt and rejected).

My thought was, "If I could get them to include me, my feelings would change." But *A* doesn't determine *C*. Rather my *beliefs* about the event determine my emotional consequences, so the formula should read:

$$A + B = C$$

Activating +	my Beliefs	=	my emotional
event	about the		Consequences
	event		or feelings[1]

My problem comes not from what has happened to me (the event), but from my beliefs (self-talk) about the event—the way I interpret the event. My interpretation becomes my self-talk, either in thoughts only or in audible words. My thoughts, even unconscious thoughts, are what cause my feelings and behavior. Therefore, to change my feelings I don't have to change the event or the people involved, but I must deal with and change my interpretation of and self-talk about them.

Another example of the misbelief that *A = C* occurred when a couple didn't come back to Jean's support group for two successive weeks *(A)*. Jean felt depressed, like a failure *(C)*.

But the *B* (Jean's self-talk) that actually caused these feelings was, "They must not like us. I must have said or done something offensive. They will probably never come back again. I'm a failure. I can't do anything right."

Our thoughts create our emotions. This idea is not new. It is recorded in the Scripture in this way: "For as he thinks in his heart, so is he" (Proverbs 23:7, NKJ). His thoughts determine his feelings and behavior.

Moses: The Two and the Ten

Notice how this is played out in the lives of some Bible characters, Moses and the children of Israel, for example. The Lord told Moses to send some men to explore the land of Canaan and bring back some fruit of the land.

> So they went up and explored the land. . . . When they reached the Valley of Eshcol, they cut off a branch bearing a single cluster of grapes. Two of them carried it on a pole between them, along with some pomegranates and figs. . . . At the end of forty days they returned from exploring the land.
>
> They came back to Moses and Aaron and the whole Israelite community . . . [and] reported to them and to the whole assembly and showed them the fruit of the land.
>
> They gave Moses this account: "We went into the land to which you sent us, and it does flow with milk and honey! Here

is its fruit. But the people who live there are powerful, and the cities are fortified and very large. . . .

Then Caleb silenced the people before Moses and said, "We should go up and take possession of the land, for *we can* certainly do it."

But the men who had gone up with him said, "*We can't* attack those people; they are stronger than we are." And they spread among the Israelites a bad report about the land they had explored. They said, "The land we explored devours those living in it. All the people we saw there are of great size. . . . We seemed like *grasshoppers* in our *own eyes*, and we looked the same *to them*."

That night all the people of the community raised their voices and wept aloud. All the Israelites grumbled against Moses and Aaron, and the whole assembly said to them, "If only we had died in Egypt! Or in this desert! Why is the Lord bringing us to this land only to let us fall by the sword? Our wives and children will be taken as plunder. Wouldn't it be better for us to go back to Egypt?" And they said to each other, "We should choose a leader and go back to Egypt."

Then Moses and Aaron fell face down in front of the whole Israelite assembly gathered there. Joshua son of Nun and Caleb son of Jephunneh, who were among those who had explored the land, tore their clothes and said to the entire Israelite assembly, "The land we passed through and explored is exceedingly good. If the Lord is pleased with us, he will lead us into that land, a land flowing with milk and honey, and will give it to us. Only do not rebel against the Lord. And do not be afraid of the people of the land, because we will swallow them up. Their protection is gone, but the Lord is with us. Do not be afraid of them." But the whole assembly talked about stoning them. . . . (Numbers 13:1–14:10, italics mine).

Notice the self-talk and the resulting emotional feelings in each of the two groups. Remember, all twelve spies were reporting on the same events—the events were the same, but their feelings were different. What made the difference? Their self-talk, their belief systems.

Make a note of the self-talk of the ten and their feelings and the self-talk of the two and their feelings.

Think again of Diane and her response to her plastic-covered living room. What had changed for her? *A*—the events? *C*—her feelings? That is, did she just decide she should be happy instead of sad, more loving to her husband instead of complaining? Or was it *B*—her beliefs, her self-talk?

We need to take responsibility to change our wrong thoughts. Agree with truth that you are not a victim of the event but of your thoughts and perceptions regarding the event, yourself, others, God, and life. Isaiah puts this another way, "You will keep him in perfect peace, whose mind is stayed on You" (Isaiah 26:3, NKJV). This promise is to the one whose thoughts are on the Lord—His character and His promises—instead of on adversities, difficulties, unpleasant people, and circumstances.

Our goal is to bring every thought captive to make it obey Christ (see 2 Corinthians 10:5.) The first step is to become aware of our particular wrong thoughts and flesh patterns. To help reveal some of our wrong thinking, we are going to look at several characteristics that spring from being malnourished.

RESULTS OF MALNOURISHMENT

I could take chapters to describe various common characteristics of the twisted thinking of an adult child who has been malnourished. The range is so great because the degree of malnourishment varies in everyone, and different children react differently to the same situation.

Pam mentioned that her middle-aged, grieving brother recently came from out-of-state for a prolonged visit with Pam and her family. Pam and her brother began sharing together about how they viewed their childhood and upbringing—the joys, the sorrows, the hurts, the concerns. They were amazed at how differently they viewed the same home. Pam saw their upbringing as good and nurturing. Her brother saw the environment as nonnurturing; painful; full of hurts, conflicts, and struggles. They couldn't believe they were talking about the same home and the same parents.

Several common characteristics of one who has been malnourished are:

All-or-Nothing Stance

The malnourished person has little discernment for proper balance. To her/him everything is either all right or all wrong. "If I fail at a point, I'm a *total* failure!" or, "If I'm not going to live perfectly, I won't even try. I'll throw it all overboard. I'll do what *I want* instead."

She prepared a special meal for guests. It looked great and tasted delicious, but the biscuits were dry and slightly burned, and that flaw ruined the whole evening for her. This all-or-nothing attitude manifests itself in several possible ways.

PERFECTIONISM IN RELATIONSHIPS

One manifestation is that the person finds it difficult to believe that when she fails, people can still love her. She believes others can love only an all-good person. She fears losing relationships. "If I don't do something just right, I'll be the cause of ruining this relationship."

She cannot discern the difference between unacceptable behavior and being unacceptable as a person. "I'm either acceptable or I'm not. I can't be partially unacceptable and still be loved."

A mother wrote: "Ten-year-old Jackie came in all disgruntled and in a bad mood. She slid past me—slamming things as she went upstairs—yelling for me to help. I went to help her pull her wet, soggy blue jeans off, over her three layers of socks.

"After I asked her to stop yelling, I told her that her behavior was unacceptable. I explained that she was acceptable but her behavior was not and did she understand the difference? She said an emphatic, 'No, my behavior *belongs* to me so how can they be different?!' We worked at that until she seemed to understand and had calmed down. We hugged each other and soon she was happy and ready to go again."

Another woman was finding it difficult to deal with her daughter's emotions. She felt like a failure when dealing with them, especially in front of me. When I asked her why she was so bent on doing it perfectly, she said she wanted to do it perfectly so that her daughter would not have to grow up and have the same struggles she has. But then she added, "And I want to please you."

"*Who* do you want to please?"

"Well, . . . you." But as she said it, it dawned on her that she really wanted to please herself by performing perfectly before me.

The perfectionist doesn't know how to give herself grace. "I should be better than I am." She feels she needs to do things perfectly in order to be acceptable to herself as well as to other people and to God. God and others aren't as hard on her as she is on herself.

PERFECTIONISM IN TASKS

The perfectionist often feels that she must perfectly complete the task before celebrating or before giving herself any credit. Instead, the perfectionistic needs to learn to celebrate each step of progress along the way.

The goal must not be perfection. To be valid, a goal must be realistic and reachable. Therefore, perfection is not a valid goal. To do my best as a flawed human being, using my particular skills and abilities, is a valid goal. But I must give myself permission to be a human being who will sin, fail, and make mistakes. And it is okay that I'm a human being.

TRUTH OUT OF BALANCE

The all-or-nothing person thinks that denying self means that you should never consider your own needs but always give to the needs of the other person. Anything else is *selfishness*. This one thinks that love means that you give to the other person without any limits, even if it encourages their selfishness. They discount themselves and their needs, believing, "I don't deserve nourishment. It seems so selfish to get it for myself, or even to want it."

A mother got a new car. It was to be just her own. This was the fulfillment of her strong desire to have something that belonged to her alone. But her teenage daughter wanted to use the car as hers—all the time. She persistently begged her mother again and again, wearing her down.

The mother thought that perhaps she was being selfish to want something just for herself. The daughter didn't need the car, she had an older one of her own. I assured her that it is human and right and not selfish to want something that belongs to you.

CANNOT RECONCILE GOOD AND BAD

Another manifestation of the all-or-nothing person is that she has difficulty reconciling good and bad in the world, in others, and in herself. We all need to come to terms with the inevitable fact that there is both good and bad in our world, and there will be until we step on the other shore and find it is heaven. There is pain in our world. Sin has affected everything. Some people can't accept the fact that Christians suffer pain in this world. Why doesn't God do something?

Sin is a fact to be reckoned with. It is the cause of all the grief and pain in this world. There is good and bad not only in your world, but also in you, in your parents, your husband, your friend. And that's okay, and they're okay! Of course, their *depravity* needs to be redeemed.

God says we are incredibly wonderful, created in the image of God, extremely sinful and broken, beset with all sorts of weaknesses, and overflowing with all sorts of talents.

The story in John 8:3–11 illustrates the good and bad issue. Recall when the Pharisees brought to Jesus a woman who was caught in the act of adultery. They were quick to remind Him that Moses, in the Law, commanded that she be stoned.

To her accusers Jesus said, "If any one of you is without sin, let him be the first to throw a stone at her." And her accusers began to go away one at a time until none were left. To the woman Jesus said, "Neither do I condemn you. Go now and leave your life of sin."

Jesus valued the person. Created in the image of God, with potential *dignity*, she was redeemable. Jesus put an "okayness" on her person and accepted both her good and bad parts; but, he told her she needed to face the *bad* part and deal with it. The badness in her behavior, which was rooted in her depravity, needed to be replaced with a new creation.

I recall talking with a friend who felt she had to believe that her dad was actually all good and not bad or flawed in any way. He was emotionally cold, passive, did not initiate love to her, and failed to protect her from some abusive situations. He was legalistic and perfectionistic in his expectations.

"Dad purposely never praised or complimented us children, because he thought it would make us proud," she said. "We understood that performance equaled acceptance. Dad's love was conditional, depending on whether or not we embarrassed him in front of the Christian community. He was a Christian leader and wanted to look good."

To deal with some issues regarding her own struggles, she needed to come to terms with the fact that she was not loved well by her father. He had not given her nurturing love. "He 'loved' you," I said, "but he failed you."

She kept denying this fact by defending him for his lacks due to his own painful background. "He did the best he could." Remember, excusing him isn't forgiving him.

Finally, she came to feel the pain and admit that he was not an *all-good* father. He did some *bad* fathering. He was wrong. Now, instead of blaming him or even excusing him, she needed to forgive him. Then she needed to look for positive things in him.

The fact that people are neither all good nor all bad in their actions is something adult children need to see in their parents. They need to accept the pain caused by the bad parts of the parents or other significant people in their past.

When identifying and acknowledging your hurts, it can be very helpful to fully write out your feelings, either in a journal or in a letter. On paper express your angry feelings. Write what the person did that hurt you and how you felt about it. Share freely on paper, but *do not* mail the letter. Then choose to forgive the person for the pain he or she caused you. *Forgive!*

To summarize the reconciling of good and bad:

1. Give up the denial and face the pain
2. Journal your feelings fully
3. Choose to forgive those who have wounded you
4. Focus on the positive purpose or benefits

Control Issue

A second common characteristic of a person who has been malnourished is the issue of control. When the child's life seems out of control and his world is falling apart, he feels someone must do something. No one else is doing anything, so the child thinks, "I'd better take charge here." So he rises to the occasion and *takes charge*.

My brother and his family had just come from California for a visit with our family and other relatives in Illinois. While we were eating dinner, my sister-in-law said that some of their friends had recently designated a legal guardian for their children in the event of their death. "We've been thinking we should do the same so that if something happened to us, someone would be responsible to take care of the kids. Verna, would you be their legal guardian?"

My mind began to whirl! What a tremendous responsibility it would be to provide for, take care of, and educate four children while teaching school. How would that be possible? So I replied that I would need to pray about that before giving a definite answer, and the subject was dismissed.

Later that afternoon my brother and his wife left their youngest child with us while they went for an overnight visit to other relatives. When I walked to the back bedroom, I found the three-year-old crying his eyes out. Then it all dawned on me. I said, "I bet you don't know where your mommy and daddy have gone, do you." He shook his head. I told him what their plans were and that they would be back tomorrow.

Then I recalled our dinner conversation, and I could feel the pain the little fellow was feeling. I started crying big as I picked him up. When he saw me crying, he immediately stopped his crying and braced up. He had to be strong when he saw that I appeared weak. He had to *take charge*. His world was falling apart! Somebody needed to be strong.

A Child's Mindset

Often a *take charge* child grows up with the mindset: "I must take charge and do what I can to hold my world together or to get it back to normal." As an adult child, this one has a tendency to take control, trying to direct others' lives and solve their problems. She becomes the take-charge person, the caretaker, the fixer, the enabler. Sometimes she neglects taking care of herself because she is so concerned about taking care of others. The real need for this person is to learn to let go and not take responsibility to "fix it."

Lana had a nonnourishing childhood. She became a caretaker and married a man who needed a caretaker. Her sister tells her story.

"Mom died of cancer when my oldest sister, Lana, was just out of high school. Unbeknown to us, Dad told Lana that she was to be 'mother' to the three of us who were still at home. Desperate for Dad's love and approval, she threw herself into the job of mothering. However, all of us strongly rejected her mothering. She was in a very difficult no-win situation. To get Dad's approval she had to 'mother' us, yet we rejected her mothering. She felt that she let Dad down, and she felt utter rejection from all of us. It hurt her deeply. She felt abandoned and alone.

"She married a very dependent man. Their marriage was rocky from the beginning. They entered the pastoral ministry, and no one knew her pain because she covered for her husband, denied her own needs, and became a typical caretaker. Her pain deepened. There was no one to share it with her.

"They were in and out of ministry and in and out of jobs because of her husband's lack of responsibility. He expected her to take care of him, no matter how he treated her.

"In June, at our family reunion, Lana was able to share the rejection she had felt. We all asked her forgiveness and committed our support to her. She has also come to realize that although Dad did not give her what she needed as a child, she is responsible for her own response to him and has chosen to forgive him and to accept him as he is."

A child's learning to take charge might be because:

1. He is told to, as in Lana's case
2. Circumstances seem to call for it
3. The need is inferred by the child, as in my nephew's case

Distorted Views

Another common characteristic of the malnourished is that they develop distorted views of everything—themselves, their circumstances, other people, and even God. In a home where there is little grace, the children begin, as it were, to put on glasses with the wrong lenses. They grow into adulthood wearing these same glasses, perceiving their distorted view as reality. Correct vision comes with grace and truth, and it is freeing. The wrong lenses cause just the opposite: disgrace and untruth, shame and lies.

Even when someone helps us see the truth and dispenses grace, our corrected vision might last only a short time. As time passes or a new incident happens, we automatically switch back to the distorted lens of shame, guilt, blame, inadequacy, failure, rejection. The result of growing up in an unhealthy family is distorted views in several areas.

Distorted View of Self

Unhealthy Shame: Shame is a feeling that I'm a defective person. The person with unhealthy shame is saying to himself: "I'm flawed. Something is wrong with me. I am worse than anyone else. I'll never be normal. I don't even know what normal is.

"I am bad for having boundaries. I am responsible for others. Shame on me for being who I am, even more than for what I do. My wants are not important. I deserve bad, nothing good.

"Spiritual maturity is doing things right all the time, and I don't, so I'm not mature. I'm rightfully embarrassed and ashamed at my childish immaturity."

Invalid Guilt: Shame defines for me the person that I am—defective. My feeling of guilt relates to something that I have done. Whether the guilt is valid or invalid, I believe I have done something wrong.

Some examples of invalid guilt messages are: "I'm to blame for the problem. I'm responsible to see that things go well or to help the other person avoid getting angry. If I fail, I am guilty."

Shame and guilt work together to produce a very low sense of worth, a feeling of being worthless.

Approval Seeker: Because the person with a distorted view of self has a strong drive for approval, she becomes an approval seeker, who will do anything to make people like her. She develops a performance mentality, thinking: "I must perform well so others will like me. I must do what they want me to do in order to gain or keep their approval. I must always have approval from others."

DISTORTED VIEW OF OTHERS

The malnourished person has distorted views of what constitutes acceptance and approval from others. One distorted view is what she *thinks* others think of her. She thinks: "I must not say *no* to other people's requests or they will hate me. I must please others and keep them happy or they will reject me. If others say no to me, it proves they don't like me. People are correct in blaming or accusing me. If others knew how sinful and what a failure I am, they would think I'm terrible."

Another distorted view is what she thinks about others: "Others are responsible for me and/or my behavior. People are selfish if they do not do what I want. Others have it all together in a way that I don't."

DISTORTED VIEW OF GOD

This concerns the belief that people must perform well to have God's approval. It is usually expressed in one of these statements: "God expects me to measure up now. He is impatient with me and my failures and my slow progress. He is disappointed in me that I am not further along than I am. If God says no to me, He doesn't love me and He doesn't want me to have what I want. God is totally sovereign and in control; therefore, I have no responsibility. God is watching to catch me in my mistakes and failures and will punish me in anger."

One person thinks, "God wants me to always deny myself of my wishes and desires."

Another thinks, "God wants me to have everything I want and pray for."

Another, "God wants me to submit to others regardless of what they ask me to do."

People with these distorted views find it difficult to believe in God's goodness and love and that God could be good to her or him. In a healthy family, a nourishing environment, many of these distorted ideas about self, others, and God can be eliminated or corrected.

DISTORTED VIEW OF THE CHRISTIAN LIFE

Malnourished people have false ideas about life and about how the Christian life works. Many Christian authors have written about this. Notice these titles:

- *12 "Christian" Beliefs That Can Drive You Crazy,* Henry Cloud and John Townsend
- *The Lies We Believe, The #1 Cause of our Unhappiness,* Dr. Chris Thurman
- *Self-Talk: Key to Personal Growth,* David Stoop
- *Telling Yourself the Truth,* William Backus and Marie Chapian

Examples of the false, twisted thinking about how the Christian life works:

- "It's not biblical to think about your needs."
- "You shouldn't let your losses get to you like that."
- "My problems are because of some sin in my life."
- "You should have your act together by now."
- "Having God is enough. I don't need people."

- "To feel better, I need to serve others more."
- "A Christian who trusts God shouldn't feel depressed."
- "If my marriage were what it ought to be, my spouse would be meeting my needs."
- "If he loved me, he would . . ."

Blurred Boundaries

A typical outcome of malnourishment due to an unhealthy family system is the lack of proper respect for ourselves and others. This results in having no boundaries; that is, we set no limits on what others can do to us. We feel we have no right to do so.

A child whose person and rights were violated comes to believe she has no legitimate boundaries. As an adult, she may take on a martyr complex, become a doormat, and allow others to do what they want to her. She will feel she cannot say no to them and will become abused or overextended, or both. She may falsely think she is really denying herself—being unselfish and loving unconditionally.

Since this is such a significant problem area for many, we will discuss it in detail in the next two chapters.

How Can We Change These Patterns?

We've talked about four common distortions of the truth that are the normal responses of a child who lacks the ability to think realistically and with maturity. Unless they are corrected, these distortions constitute his thinking patterns in his adult life. And as we said, faulty thinking is a launching pad for the flesh and a foothold for Satan.

What can we do about all of this? How can we change these destructive patterns, these distorted views?

An Open Heart Is a Prerequisite

In the case of each distorted view, there must be a readiness to acknowledge the problem and then offer an earnest request that the Spirit of Truth will lead you into all truth in these areas. You might make your prayer, "Search me, O God, and know my heart; try me, and know my anxious thoughts; and see if there be any hurtful way in me, and lead me in the everlasting way" (Psalm 139:23–24, NASB). Then trust Him; depend on Him.

Commit Yourself to Hard Work

Commit yourself to doing the hard work of exchanging wrong thoughts about self, others, God, and how the Christian life works with truth. This is the process of renewing the mind, taking every thought captive.

Connect with Someone Who Can Help

Then, connect with someone with whom you can talk, think, be honest, and be corrected. We need God and the Word, but we also need others. Women need to connect with other women.

Identify Your Pattern

Ask God to enlighten your darkness; and begin to discuss your thoughts and questions with someone you have confidence in, someone you feel can help you discern reality.

IF YOU ARE AN ALL-OR-NOTHING PERSON

Choose to face both the good and the bad in people, and in your world. Be honest. Give up the expectation of all-good parents, friends, and things in the world. Accept the fact of sin and its influence. Accept imperfection. Don't expect perfection in relationships or in projects.

IF YOU HAVE A TAKE-CHARGE MENTALITY

Face the reality of the situation that seems to be out of control. Realize that God is in over-all control, and deliberately choose to rest in Him. Begin to let go, realizing it is not your responsibility to *fix it* or to *fix them*. Learn to cooperate with and submit to others, when that is appropriate.

IF YOU HAVE DISTORTED VIEWS

When you recognize distorted views of yourself, of others, of God, and of how the Christian life works, pray, "Lord, enlighten my darkness. Make me aware of my wrong thinking about myself, others, and You." Then study the Word to know what God's thoughts are. Commit to renewing your mind and taking every twisted thought captive. Again, to heighten your awareness of your distorted thoughts, discuss them with a trusted person.

If you are open to seeing whether you have false ideas about life and how the Christian life works, I suggest you read some books written by Christian authors who understand and can articulate the balance between our part and God's part in our Christian growth and sanctification (see Suggested Resources). Talk to mature Christians about issues that are unclear to you.

IF YOU HAVE BLURRED BOUNDARIES

Learn what God says about boundaries. Get clearly in mind what belongs to you and what belongs to someone else. You need to know you have a right to have your boundaries respected.

Whenever you become aware of distortions in your own thinking, deal with the pain from the hurts done to you by making sure you have not simply excused but have forgiven those who have wronged you. Commit yourself to discovering and correcting your wrong conclusions and distorted views; then, replace them with truth, because "the truth will set you free" (John 8:32).

All of this takes time—sometimes lots of time—but we're on our way when we see clearly what the real issues are. Take a few minutes now to identify any twisted tendencies in your thought patterns. Do you recognize:

1. Perfectionism in relationships or in tasks, truth out of balance, or an inability to reconcile good and bad (all-or-nothing stance)?
2. A need to take charge or fix people and situations (control issue)?

3. That your reality consists of feelings of shame, guilt, blame, inadequacy, failure, and rejection (distorted view of self, others, God, and how the Christian life works)?
4. A misunderstanding of what belongs to you and what belongs to others (blurred boundaries)?

Are you willing for the Lord to show you flesh patterns that need attention? Will you ask Him to do just that?

THOUGHTS TO REMEMBER

Our thoughts create our emotions. Bad events and the insensitivity of others do not cause our bad feelings, but our thoughts about the event or the other person do. To change our feelings, we do not need to change the event or the person as much as our thoughts about them. "For as he thinks in his heart, so is he" (Proverbs 23:7, NKJ).

"Search me, O God, and know my heart; try me and know my anxious thoughts; and see if there be any hurtful way in me"—and free me from distorted, twisted thinking. (See Psalm 139:23–24, NASB.)

PRACTICING AND JOURNALING

1. What event happened this week that resulted in your feeling sad or happy? What did you say to yourself about it?
2. What is a typical comment you often make to yourself when you feel that you have failed at something?
3. What changes could you make in your self-talk that would cause positive changes in your attitude or feelings?

6

Helping women achieve their full potential.

Dealing with Negative Self-Talk

In the last two chapters we talked about malnourishment and how it can cause twisted thinking and give us distorted views of ourselves, others, God, and the circumstances of our lives. We discussed in detail our pear-shaped conscious and subconscious parts and how the input we get, especially as children, greatly influences our self-talk all through life.

Self-talk means our thoughts or the belief system out of which we operate, consciously or subconsciously. Self-talk, whether positive or negative, can consist of truth or lies, reality or assumptions, valid or invalid conclusions. Our negative emotions often are clues that we have negative, flawed thinking that manifests in negative self-talk.

We would probably all agree that we need to be freed from the tyranny of negative self-talk. It can make us miserable, hard to live with, and less than we could be in our walk with the Lord. Again, the appropriate question is, What can we do about it?

There is a very easy-to-give, brief, biblical answer. In fact, in twenty words we can answer three key questions:

- *What must I do?* Renew the mind.
- *How do I do it?* Take every thought captive and make it subject to truth.

- *What are the results?* A transformed life—changed thinking, changed behavior.

That's it! God has done his part, now you do yours. End of struggles and beginning of peace and victory, right? No, in reality stating the solution is simple, but working it out in life is just plain hard work! And it takes that stuff called *discipline*. We don't like to discipline our thoughts or change our behaviors. We do want the fruit of peace, joy, and self-control, but we want it without effort. I guess we sometimes think that the Holy Spirit should just give us the fruit with no effort on our part. We don't like hard work. We want peace, joy, faith, and contentment handed to us—and we want it now. We don't want to struggle.

WRONG BEHAVIOR IS BASED ON FLAWED THINKING

Let's review our equation, $A + B = C$:

A = Activating event
B = Beliefs or self-talk about the event
C = Consequences of that self-talk: good or bad emotions

Adding D and E to the Equation

Now we need to begin discovering some true, positive statements of self-talk relating to this event. We will label this D—new thoughts and statements of truth. These will replace my negative thoughts, beliefs, and self-talk.

E = new, positive emotions that result from my new thoughts. These positive emotions will replace C, the old bad emotions.

$A + B = C$ must be changed to: $A + D = E$

Betty Jean's Self-Talk Dynamics

See if you can follow Betty Jean's self-talk as she tells her story.

For two years after we moved to Philadelphia to minister to the very poor of the inner city, we had no regular income. It was difficult and really demanding on us spiritually to pray and trust the Lord every day for our daily supply.

One day I walked to the supermarket with thirty-five cents in my pocket. I was going to buy one item. Oh, I needed a lot of groceries, but all I had was thirty-five cents, so I was going to buy the thing I needed most.

As I walked the six blocks from my house to the supermarket, I kept my head down, looking for money in the gutter, on the sidewalks and in the tall grass between the sidewalk and the fence. I was thinking, if only I could find a quarter, a dollar, or even five dollars, I could buy more groceries.

All the way to the grocery store I was praying, "Lord, help me find some money." While I was praying and diligently searching for money, another thing was going on inside of me. I was feeling a deep depression because it was really hurting me to be so poor. It hurt to have to look for money in the gutter.

How Can I Identify with the Poor?

Before we moved to Philadelphia, one thing I had puzzled over a lot was how could I identify with the poor? I knew the Lord was calling us to work among the very poorest of the poor, and I wanted to reach out and minister to them. But how would I avoid being paternalistic or keep from appearing arrogant? I've never been poor.

I grew up in a middle-class family. My parents always owned their own home, and they always had a car or two. We were never rich, but we were always able to pay our bills, buy groceries, and a new dress and even perfume when I wanted.

How could I identify with the poor? I puzzled over that a lot. Even if we voluntarily scaled down our lifestyle and lived as the poor did, voluntary poverty is not real poverty. We don't *have* to live in the inner city. We could move tomorrow. Real poverty is when people are poor because they have no way out.

How does it feel to really be poor? It seemed like an insurmountable problem. I had prayed, "Lord, help me somehow. Do something supernatural to help me minister to the poor. Give me a supernatural compassion for them. I can feel sorry for them, but I can't feel what they are feeling."

THIS IS WHAT IT FEELS LIKE TO BE POOR

This prayer and my desire to identify with the poor came back to me vividly as I was on my way to the supermarket that day with thirty-five cents. As I was looking in the gutter for money and feeling so depressed, suddenly the Lord said to me so clearly in my spirit, "Betty Jean, this is what it feels like to be poor."

It was like a sword in my heart. I thought, "Yes, why yes, this is what it feels like to be poor. Feeling depressed because I'm looking in the gutter for money. Feeling depressed because I don't have enough money to buy food for my family. Feeling depressed because I have no perfume or a nice dress to wear to a fancy wedding. There are some people who have had these feelings every single day of their lives! This is what it's like to be poor."

I BEGAN TO PRAISE THE LORD

Believe me, at that moment I felt poor, and I began to realize that this was God's answer to my prayer. All of a sudden I began to praise the Lord. I said, "Thank You, Lord, thank You," because the Lord was giving me the most valuable experience I could ever have.

The very thing I had longed for, the very thing I didn't know how to get, the very thing that seemed insurmountable to me—what it feels like to be poor—the Lord had given me. I went the rest of the way to the supermarket with my heart singing. I no longer felt depressed about being poor. God had put in my lap the most marvelous experience.

Now I could minister to poor people with some little degree of understanding. Sure, I couldn't feel like those who are poor all their lives, but in a very poignant way that day I experienced what it felt like to be poor. It hurt. It hurt deeply.

The ABCs of Betty Jean's Thinking

What do you think might have been some of Betty Jean's self-talk? Let's take her experience through the equation $A + B = C$ and then change it to D and E.

CONSEQUENCES: *C*

What were the consequences, her negative emotions? Deep concern, embarrassment, anticipation, disappointment, depression.

ACTIVATING EVENT: *A*

What event encouraged these negative emotions? Being very poor, having to trust God every day for daily bread, having only thirty-five cents to go grocery shopping, not finding money in the gutter, not getting her prayers answered as she thought the Lord might.

BELIEFS: *B*

What were her beliefs about the event, her self-talk that caused the feelings? "God doesn't really care about me," or, "Why doesn't He answer my prayers? We moved here to serve the Lord and we have been faithful. Why doesn't He at least provide food money for the family?"

NEW BELIEFS (SELF-TALK): *D*

What were her new beliefs (declared truth) about the event that changed her emotions from negative to positive? "God has answered my prayer—my deepest concern—to help me identify with the poor, the very poor. God has given me the most wonderful gift possible."

NEW EMOTIONS: *E*

What were her positive emotions that replaced the negative ones? Praise, peace, acceptance, thanksgiving, gratitude to the Lord for answering her prayer to be able to identify somewhat with those to whom she came to minister.

Had her circumstances changed? No. What had changed? Only her self-talk, her beliefs.

We Want Life Without Struggle

As we said, to honestly come to terms with and identify our negative self-talk and begin the process of renewing the mind is

hard work. We don't like hard work. We want peace and contentment now—without struggle. Or we think that surely there must
be an easy key to unlock all these treasures, and we begin our
search.

I put it this way in the book *If God Is in Control, Why Is My
World Falling Apart?*[1]

> Today's typical western Christian is searching diligently and
> endlessly to find something to relieve and free him from the
> continual worries and hurts of life. We're always on the lookout
> for a quick fix for our mental, psychological, emotional, and
> physical pain. We go to classes or conferences. We read the lat-
> est book on coping. We talk to numerous counselors in the quest.
> And, if we are serious about our search, we carefully take the
> prescribed steps of action: exercise more faith; apply more dili-
> gence in studying the Word; pray more; spend more time in
> thanksgiving and worship; have more commitment; offer up
> more praise.
>
> Having *more* of any of these good things may still not take
> away my soul anguish, my inner struggle. In brief, we are made
> for heaven. We are designed for a perfect environment, *but that
> isn't where we are now.* Right now we must live for a time in a
> fallen, sin-infested world which is made up of an imperfect en-
> vironment, imperfect people and imperfect relationships.

It's so easy to forget that the pain that springs from these im-
perfections can serve as a warning signal to alert us to something
wrong in our thinking or in our behavior. Something needs our
attention or needs to be corrected so that we can begin to experience health in the soul. Proverbs 16:24 says, "Pleasant words [even
your own self-talk] are a honeycomb, sweet to the soul and healing to the bones."

Do Other Things Need to Be Changed?

Is it only my self-talk that may need to be changed? No, sometimes there are other things, such as boundaries, that need to be
understood and put in place. We take this up in chapters 7 and 8.

THE IMPORTANCE OF RENEWING THE MIND

The world, the flesh, and the devil work against us to continually feed distorted and negative thinking into our mental tape recorder. Therefore, we need to renew the mind by making it accept truth and discard the lies. This is always a battle.

In essence, it is the conflict of the ages: the battle between light and darkness, truth and lies, God's Word and Satan's accusations, the Spirit of God and the flesh, life and death. "Death and life are in the power of the tongue" (Proverbs 18:21, NKJV)—that's self-talk. Choose life!

A Key Truth of Scripture

There are certain bottom-line truths of Scripture that, when understood and believed, become the basis for building positive self-talk. Getting these truths into our minds should be high on the priority list of every believer.

As a friend and I were talking about the importance of our self-talk, Sally said, "Verna, the thing that helps me in my self-talk more than any other is a truth you taught us a long time ago, and it has stayed with me ever since." She mentioned what it was, and I agreed it *is* the bottom line.

In fact, thousands of women have born witness to this fact and have shared how they experience God's "peace that passes understanding" in all kinds of very difficult and trying situations as they rehearse this truth through one succinct statement.

I believe that if you get hold of this concept about God, allowing it to gradually burrow into your subconscious, it will be a solid basis for accepting life—events, people, and even yourself—and thus inspiring you and changing your negatives into positive thoughts, emotions, and behaviors.

THE CIRCLE OF GOD'S WILL

To help us make this truth personal, I like to draw these two circles. The small one represents the will of God. The *X* represents you and me—if we are committed to going God's way. If that is true, we have the wonderful privilege of living in the circle of His will and claiming His promises. One promise is found in Romans 8:28 (NKJV): "And we know that all things work together for good to those who love God, to those who are the called according to His purpose."

THE CIRCLE OF GOD'S CONTROL

The larger outer circle represents the circle of God's control. Every person, every event, every thing—even Satan—is under God's control. Satan realizes this. In Job 1:10, he admitted that God has a hedge around his people. Nothing can touch them except God allows it. God doesn't *cause* evil, but sometimes He *allows* it to touch His children. Even then, for those living inside the circle of His will He will bring good out of the evil or pain, which is caused by our own sin—repented of and confessed—or by someone sinning against us.

JOB'S EXPERIENCE

Please review the first chapter of the Book of Job, and you will quickly get the essence of the situation. Tragedy strikes a wealthy, famous, righteous man who had his "quiver full" with seven sons and three daughters. He had flocks and herds that were "spread throughout the land." He was, in fact, "the greatest man of all the people of the East."

Then one day Satan and the Lord had a talk (Job 1:6–12). Who took the initiative in this conversation? What lie did Satan try to get God to believe? What permission did God give Satan? What limitation?

Satan took all the permission the Lord granted him and set out on his devastating work. He did a thorough job by causing four terrible tragedies (Job 1:13–19)! Only one servant was left to tell of each tragedy. The outcome of it all was that Job's riches—thousands of oxen, donkeys, sheep, and camels, as well as his servants—

were gone. The last report was of a terrible windstorm that caused the house to collapse, killing Job's ten children.

Think for a moment. If you were in a similar situation, what would you do? What would you say? If all your life's savings and means of livelihood were wiped out, what would your self-talk be? Or how would you respond if even one of your children was killed in an accident?

According to our script, when Job heard these reports, he *did* something before he spoke. I suggest that if we learn to do the same, our self-talk will be transformed. Verse 20 says that Job made God his first reference. He worshiped Him. Was his self-talk truth or lies? Positive or negative?

Job's first words were, "Naked I came from my mother's womb, and naked shall I return there. The Lord gave, and the Lord has taken away; blessed be the name of the Lord" (Job 1:21, NKJV).

Job acknowledged God's overall control in these tragedies. But just knowing that truth didn't give him peace or freedom from negative self-talk. It was his response (his self-talk) to the truth that gave him freedom. He could have said, "God is in control and I don't like the way He is doing things! Why, God? Why!" But he didn't say that.

The last verse says, "In all this Job did not sin nor charge God with wrong." In effect, he was saying, God owes me nothing. He's in control and I trust Him—His love, His goodness, His wisdom, and His power. The substance of Job's self-talk was truth in the form of faith and surrender expressed in these words, "Blessed be the name of the Lord." His response was heart surrender and confident trust.

1 TIMOTHY 6:15

There is a verse that wraps this all up in one simple statement, "God . . . is the blessed controller of all things" (1 Timothy 6:15, Phillips)—especially this thing that is touching me at this moment. Rehearsing this verse is a concise way of not only acknowledging that God is in charge but also expressing our acceptance of the situation and our trust in God as the Blessed One, the One to be praised.

This is a tremendous alternative to stewing about the past or fretting about our present problems or looking anxiously into the future. Will you join with Job right now and acknowledge that everything that happens in your life, whether in the humdrum or the crisis, is either directed or permitted by your loving Father, Who is right now wide awake and in control? Whether you lose your job or the company dinner fails, God is reigning, and His reign includes everything and everyone that touches your life.

"God . . . is the blessed controller of all things." I recommend that you memorize this verse—put it in your subconscious and let it come back to you in the thick of a crisis, little or big.

This is positive self-talk at its best—bottom-line stuff! It produces a positive change in the thoughts and consequently in the emotions and behavior. The events in Job's life were tragic, but positive beliefs about the events and about God kept Job from charging God with wrongdoing and plunging himself, thereby, into the depths of despair.

Applying the Formula to "Blessed Controller"

Let's go back to our equation: $A + B = C$. We saw how it worked in Betty Jean's case and in Job's experience. Job went directly from A (activating event) to D (right beliefs) and to E (a heart of trust). A great number of women do the same by declaring, "God is the blessed Controller of all things."

I received a letter from forty-year-old Jessica who said she had been emotionally unstable for twenty years. "My worst disappointment," she lamented, "is being single. I haven't even had any serious boyfriends. And I grew up in a church hearing that 'My God shall supply all your need according to His riches in glory.' I am so disillusioned with God and Jesus. I don't believe He has provided for my needs, and I don't even know if I'm saved anymore. Is God really alive?"

What had she chosen to believe? That "God . . . is the blessed controller of all things"? That "The Lord is my Shepherd, I shall not want"? That God Himself and what He would choose to provide for her was all she needed?

Let's take her through the ABCs. What was her C (the warning signal of her emotions)? She was disappointed; disillusioned with God and Jesus; not sure of salvation, or even whether God lives.

What was her *A* (activating event)? Forty years of being single, without any serious boyfriends.

What was her *B* (belief)? "I really need to be married or at least have a serious boyfriend to be happy or to have my needs met. The church is wrong about God supplying all of our needs. God and Jesus haven't come through for me. They don't do what they promise. If God really cared about me and my needs, He would give me a husband. I don't even know if I'm saved anymore, or whether God really is alive."

What could be her *D* (new, positive self-talk in the form of truth-talk, faith-talk, life-talk)? "I don't need a husband to be happy and complete. Though I greatly desire to be married, I give the demand of this desire to the Lord. I don't *need* marriage. I choose to trust God's love and wisdom to give or withhold, confident that 'no good thing does he withhold from those whose walk is blameless' (Psalm 84:11). I believe He is the blessed Controller of all things. I'll continue to pray and mingle with other Christians— both single and married, but I choose to trust instead of being anxious about the present or future."

What could be her *E* (new emotional response and behavior)? Trust, rest, peace, contentment, new power to handle the emotions and strong desires.

Personal Interpretation of Events

Remember, it is not so much the nature and character of the event that matters. It is my interpretation of the event and what I say to myself about the event that actually puts content, negative or positive, into my belief system. This is true of my childhood experiences as well as the current events of my life.

As you read this true account of Sara, look for the assumptions and inferences about herself that resulted from her own interpretation of the events of her childhood.

I lived with my single mother until I was eight years old. She doted on me and probably spoiled me terribly. When I was seven she married, and my stepfather and I had some very bad scenes. I was never told why I was put up for adoption a year later, but

I assumed it was because I was a brat. I was so afraid of being rejected by my new family that I did everything I could to stay out of trouble and please them. Whenever I did do something wrong and needed correction, I took the correction as rejection.

I internalized every single negative word that was said to me and had extremely bad periods of depression. I tended to feel that I was the cause of everything that went wrong in the adult world around me. It is hard, even now, not to blame myself for everything that goes wrong.

I came to know Christ fifteen years ago and am slowly choosing not to believe some of the negative things that came from my parents during my very sensitive childhood. This is hard to do, because some of those offhand remarks stuck like glue in my mind. With God's Word gradually taking the place of those bad words, I am becoming a healthier person, and God has corrected many of these misbeliefs and healed many of the wounds.

Can you see the ABCs at work in Sara's situation? She could ask, "Was I put up for adoption because I was such a brat? Or were there other problems between my mother and my stepfather that made them unable to care for me?"

Because we tend to feel worthy or not worthy, adequate or inadequate, according to how we *think* other people feel toward us, we need to discover our interpretation of an event. Then we can ask, "Because of this interpretation, what am I telling myself about this event? What entry did I make into my belief system about me, about others, about God?"

ANALYSIS OF SELF-TALK

A mother of three was worried and anxious about what people would think of her for having another child. As you read her story, try to answer:

- Why did she have feelings of shame and disgrace?
- What were her wrong beliefs?
- Where do you think she got those wrong beliefs?
- How were they corrected?
- What is the truth she should focus on and believe?

When I was expecting my fourth child, I often had feelings of shame and disgrace when I was out in public. People would look, and I would think, *What are they thinking of me—pregnant, with three children already?*

Shortly after I delivered I attended the Enriched Living Workshops. When Verna shared on "Child Acceptance," the Holy Spirit zeroed in on me. I knew I had rejected my children and had bitter thoughts about having four children.

The Lord showed me what a blessing and privilege it was that He had given them to me. I admitted my sin to Him and was cleansed. Now I have a whole new outlook on my children. Truly they are a gift from the Lord.

Often it is not easy to recognize and admit what we are telling ourselves. Sometimes we might even need other people to help us realize what we are saying to ourselves; but we do need to get in touch with our inner conversations, our self-talk.

Fighting the Battle for the Mind

For each of us, our belief system has been developing since our earliest moments of life. The world around us has been subtly squeezing us more and more into its own mold (see Romans 12:2, Phillips). But there's a better way, and that is by replacing Satan's lies with God's truth. How do we let God remold our minds from within? How do we take an active role in this battle for the mind?

In my book *Less Stress, More Peace*[2] I give the following suggestions for fighting the battle for the mind.

THE WARNING SIGNAL OF MY EMOTIONS

Heed such emotions as depression, anxiety, worry, anger, and feelings of rejection.

ASK MYSELF, WHAT AM I THINKING?

Hear your self-talk, what you are saying to yourself. If you listen to what you are saying to yourself, you will discover some strong clues as to what is in your belief system. Are you saying self-defeating statements? What are you saying to yourself about yourself, about others, about God, or about how the Christian life is supposed to work?

JUDGE MY BELIEFS

What you hear yourself saying may or may not be true and accurate. It may be an assumption or an exaggeration of the situation. Have you "awfulized" to the point that you can no longer see things as they really are? Then you need to make a judgment—is it a true belief (based on truth and Scripture) or a misbelief. One way you can check this out is by asking yourself, "Am I saying that I must have something different or something more in order to experience contentment and peace?"

TAKE A STAND ON TRUTH

Make a statement of truth and repeat it as needed. Take every straying thought captive, constantly refuting contrary thoughts. Replace lies with truth. The writer of Hebrews affirmed that because God had said, "Never will I leave you; never will I forsake you," the writer could say with confidence, "The Lord is my helper; I will not be afraid. . . . " (Hebrews 13:5–6). This was his statement of faith and truth. We must speak truth to ourselves. And the truth is found in God and in His Word.

Where we have been telling ourselves untruths (literally lies), we need to declare them untrue, state clearly and precisely what the truth is in regard to that situation, and agree with that truth.

REGULARLY FEED MY MIND ON TRUTH

Keep straying thoughts captive and under control by feeding your mind on truth. Bottom line: I must learn to relate this present circumstance to God, stating with confidence:

- God is in control
- He loves and cares for me
- He has promised to work all things for my good
- He will never fail

PLAN A WAY TO RETRAIN THOUGHTS

Continually refute contrary thoughts. This takes discipline. It's the discipline of bringing every thought into captivity and making it obey Christ, making it yield to God's truth (see 2 Corinthians 10:5). It helps to have a systematic method to retrain our wayward thought patterns.

Devise a method to fit your own special need, as Carla did: "Two years ago I fled from a very bad relationship the day before the wedding. I came away with a lot of guilt for letting it go so far and for all the heartache I caused so many people. In the months of readjustment, I had to learn to accept God's forgiveness, or the guilt would have destroyed me. I made a sign for the foot of my bed with the word *forgiven* written on it. I meditated on that until I had finally accepted it as fact."

RELY ON THE HOLY SPIRIT

We should avail ourselves of these other helps, but real change will not take place apart from relying on the Holy Spirit to enlighten and empower us, to bring light to our dark places, and to give us the grace to face the situation and the power to change it (see Zechariah 4:6).

HELPS FOR CORRECTING TWISTED THINKING

God Is the Blessed Controller

Correcting our wrong thoughts is one of my passions. Since teaching the first Enriched Living Workshops in 1969, I have strongly emphasized 1 Timothy 6:15 from the Phillips, "God . . . is the blessed controller of all things." I encouraged the women to learn to say this as a statement of heart surrender and confident trust. They memorized it, took it home, and applied it. Now, nearly thirty years later, women still tell me of the peace they have had in all kinds of really difficult circumstances as they rest in this truth. The book *If God Is in Control, Why Is My World Falling Apart?* is a way of studying these precious truths in depth and sharing them with others.

You Are Very Special

One day in my quiet time I was meditating on Isaiah 40. There the Lord says, "Comfort ye, comfort ye, my people . . . cry to Jerusalem. . . ."

Isaiah's response was, "What shall I cry?" What shall I tell them?

The answer, "Behold, your God!" Let them know more and more of *Who I am* and what I want to do for them, in them, and through them. I want them to know *Who I am* and *who they really are* in relationship to Me. It was in response to this request of the Lord to comfort His people that I wrote the book *You Are Very Special.*

Jan Frank was a victim of sexual abuse. She has come through it and now has quite a ministry to others. In her book *A Door of Hope* Jan writes:

> In the fall of the year, I enrolled in a women's Bible study at our church that was using Verna Birkey's study guide, *You Are Very Special.* We spent five months identifying who we were in God's eyes. Birkey's book pointed out scripture after scripture that showed me I was of value to God—I was chosen by Him and was His "special treasure." Although I had been a Christian nearly twenty years, this concept really hit home for the first time. I saw that, in order to love my husband and my child the way I wanted to, I had to begin to love [respect] myself. This revolutionized my thinking and my actions. I did not realize it at the time but God knew I needed a new self-image. Through His Word and through choices I made daily, my self-esteem improved. I actually began to like myself and could even accept a compliment graciously.
>
> I began to take God at His word and accept His unconditional love for me. . . . At times it became sheer discipline of mind that kept me hanging on to God's truth. . . . The Lord knew I needed to reconstruct the image I had of myself, but I also needed to restore a right image of God.[3]

Most of the time when we're discouraged, anxious, frustrated, worried, or joyless, it is because we have failed to remember who we are and who He is. We aren't, at that moment, really believing Him. We aren't agreeing with Him when He tells us who we are. My desire in mentioning *You Are Very Special* is to give a practical, workable plan to help you actually believe what God says about you and about Himself. God has changed the self-talk of thousands of women through this book. When our self-talk changes, we change.

Input for a Rejoicing Heart

One day I was meditating on Isaiah 26:3 (NKJV): "You will keep him in perfect peace, Whose mind is stayed on You, Because he trusts in You." Knowing what a challenge it is for us keep our minds set on Him, I asked the Lord, "What might we design that would help us as women to 'stay our minds on You' and experience this peace that you promise?" This is how the *Input for a Rejoicing Heart* tape was born. Songs are interspersed with scripture on several aspects of God's character that are vital to our peace—His love, His goodness, and His blessed control. So many have shared how basking in God's love, goodness, and blessed control have dramatically changed their way of thinking. Why? Their self-talk was changed to God's truth.

God's Promises of Peace

The little green book, *God's Promises of Peace,* was intended to encourage your commitment to the God of peace, help you feed your faith with the positive truth of His Word, and give you rest in Him through His promises. There are fifty-two meditations, each emphasizing one phase of peace. You may want to spend a week on each, letting the scripture work its way through your mind to your heart (see Suggested Resources).

CLARIFYING THE THOUGHT-CHANGING PROCESS

Let me say it again: It's not the *event* but our thoughts about the event that create our emotions and affect our behavior. We all talk to ourselves continually, sometimes out loud, but most of the time in the privacy of our minds. The result of this self-talk is always the same: It determines the way we live our lives. "As he thinks in his heart, so is he" (Proverbs 23:7, NKJV).

Let's go back to our beginning question: What can I do about my negative feelings and undesirable behavior? Here again is the brief and biblical answer:

- *What must I do?* Renew the mind.
- *How do I do it?* Take every thought captive and make it subject to truth. "Whatever is true, . . . noble, . . . right, . . . pure, . . . lovely, . . . admirable . . . think about such things" (Philippians 4:8).
- *What are the results?* A transformed life—changed thinking, changed behavior.

Dual Tape-Recorder Minds

Thought changing is a process. It's hard work, and it takes time. It means becoming honest. It means becoming free from distorted thinking (lies) that have controlled you and made you uncomfortable or miserable.

It is as though our mind is a tape recorder that has been recording messages from the beginning of our life. The actual messages given us or our interpretation of them are "recorded" for ready playback. The tape continues to automatically play away in our subconscious, controlling our thoughts and behavior, until what is actually being said comes to our attention—probably through the warning signal of our emotions.

The image of a single tape player isn't quite adequate. That is, if we assume the solution is simply to change tapes, the implication is that we simply discover our negative self-talk, record a statement of truth to counter it, and replace the old tape with a new one. The battle is over and won! No, it is not quite that easy.

The thought-changing process is like having a dual tape recorder in our minds. The picture of the dual tape recorder helps us realize that both tapes—the old and the new—are resident within us, and we have to push the right button.

The tape in the left side is a recording of my distorted, twisted thinking—my all-or-nothing thinking, my assumptions, my exaggerations, my distorted views of myself, of others, of God, or of how the Christian life works. These are areas we have already talked about. We could add more, such as overgeneralization, discounting the positive, jumping to conclusions, negative self-labeling, awfulizing, personalizing, and so forth. This old tape is a commentary on how *they* feel about me.

The possible list of twisted thinking is endless. However, you don't need to memorize lists; you do need to listen to your self-talk and let the Lord help you judge it. Listen to other people as they point out and affirm your abilities. For instance, don't discount your positive qualities and abilities. Learn to listen to and speak truth and positive self-talk.

Here's how it goes. An event happens. My old tape automatically goes into *play* mode. The event activated the play mode. Then I have to take action (responsibility) and choose to push the STOP button on that old recording and push the PLAY button on the new truth tape in the right cassette holder. That's good! And the result is that I feel better.

Then another event happens and my tape player automatically goes back to the negative self-talk tape. Now I have to go through the whole procedure again and again and yet again, until the new tape takes over the automatic response mode to start and play.

Remember my story of my fear that my friends would run off? My old, negative self-talk on my two-tape player went something like this: "People will be your good friends until someone more interesting comes along. Then they will try to get rid of you, reject you, and run off with their new friends, leaving you standing alone."

My new truth tape is fueled by a general statement of faith and commitment that I rehearse before the Lord daily: "For I know [and am becoming more intimately acquainted with] the One in whom I have placed my confidence and am positively certain that the people and the work He has committed to me and that I have committed to Him are perfectly safe in His hands today, and will be each day until the day Jesus returns. This includes the people or lack of them, the opportunities or lack of them, the pains, losses, griefs, and joys. I am Yours and You are good; You have a plan and are working that plan." (See 2 Timothy 1:12, TLB, AMP, Phillips.)

THOUGHTS TO REMEMBER

God owes me nothing. He is in control, and I trust Him—His love, His goodness, His wisdom, and His power. "God . . . is the blessed controller of all things" (1 Timothy 6:15, Phillips).

The substance of Job's self-talk was truth in the form of faith and surrender when he said, "Naked I came from my mother's womb, and naked shall I return there. The Lord gave, and the Lord has taken away; blessed be the name of the Lord" (Job 1:21, NKJV). His response was heart surrender and confident trust.

PRACTICING AND JOURNALING

During the next three weeks, be aware of your self-talk. Fill in the chart on the following page, possibly beginning with C.

We find many references in Scripture to people talking to themselves. Some are giving positive input, some negative. Look up some of these scriptures and notice the self-talk. Choose to memorize one verse. Write it on a card to carry with you. Psalms 14:1; 16:7; 57:7–8; 73; 77; 116:7; Lamentations 3:19–26; Habakkuk 3:17–19.

SELF-TALK CHART

A	B	C	D	E
Activating event	Beliefs: negative self-talk	Consequences: feelings, emotions	Declared truth: positive self-talk	changed Emotions

Part **III**

Free to Nourish
Others with Bold Love

7

Boundaries

When I was Dean of Girls at a boarding high school, a new staff member came to join us. We'll call her Belva. One afternoon I blocked out some time to visit her in her apartment, both to welcome her and to give her some encouragement. But then I remembered that Amy, another faculty member and my close coworker in the dormitory, had known and was a friend to Belva before she joined our staff. I was concerned that Amy might not like for me to spend time with Belva, her good friend.

As I stood in the doorway ready to go, I thought, "What if Amy doesn't like this? If I go I am risking the possibility of her getting angry with me." I hesitated.

Then it was as though the Lord said, "If you do not visit Belva because you are afraid of an angry response, who is controlling you?"

"Well, . . . Amy."

"That's correct. And if Amy is controlling you, that means I am not. If I can't send you to whomsoever I choose, then you are not letting Me be Lord of your life."

"That's right, Lord. I am Yours. I need to be free to minister to anyone You send me to, regardless of the consequences."

Identifying a Control Issue

I gave the situation over to the Lord and went to visit Belva. After about an hour, I came back to the dorm and dropped in to see Amy. She was suspicious and angry and said in a harsh, commanding tone, "Where have you been?" Because of the way the Lord had already dealt with me, clarifying issues and preparing me for this, I paused and said in a calm, low tone, "It's none of your business."

She got angrier and demanded, "I asked, Where have you been?"

After another pause, I said in the same calm, low voice tone, "It's none of your business." She got even more angry and demanded again, "*Where have you been?*"

A third time I said, "It's none of your business." That sounded like a broken record, didn't it?

She finally realized what she was doing and how wrong she was in attempting to control. We talked it through until she calmed down and the issue was settled.

I let her know that I wasn't out to steal her friend, but neither could I let her control me. Then I chose to tell her where I had been. "I really don't mind telling you where I've been. I was down talking to Belva, and I found she really needed some encouragement this afternoon."

Boundary Awareness

This is part of what it means to nourish others with bold love. Amy had overstepped her boundaries, and I was helping her to become aware of this while at the same time drawing a boundary of my own. Notice I did this in kindness and firmness, not out of temper or from an accusing or self-defending spirit, but in simple, bold love.

This was a rather unusual approach, and I would only rarely, if ever, use this method again. In this case, it was right. Amy and I became better and safer friends, and we're still good friends. Her heart was right, and she was willing to talk it through.

Jesus used this same tactic in drawing a boundary for Peter in John 21:19–22. Jesus had indicated to Peter "the kind of death by which Peter would glorify God." Then Peter asked, "Lord, what about John?"

Jesus said, in effect, "That's none of your business, friend. Take care of your own responsibility." His actual words were: "What is that to you? You must follow Me."

What Is a Boundary?

My Property Line

A personal boundary is like a fence around my property that helps me know where my responsibilities begin and end. My *property* is my responsibility, and it includes my person, my possessions, and my rights. It includes what I like and don't like—my tastes, preferences, desires, feelings. My boundary defines what is me and what is not me, what is mine and what is not mine, what belongs to me and what does not belong to me.

Knowing our boundaries gives us a healthy sense of limits, which helps us determine what we will allow and what we won't allow, what we will take responsibility for and what we will not take responsibility for.

His Property Line

Each person needs to identify who owns what, and then each one must take ownership of and responsibility for his own property.

When another person has a self-defeating habit; a negative, critical, controlling, manipulative spirit; or suffers a consequence of unwise behavior—that is their issue, not ours. People's happiness, sadness, beliefs, and choices are their property, not ours; and what they choose to do with that which belongs to them is their responsibility.

They may even try to load some of these things on us, but they are not a part of our property. They do not belong to us. We are not to own them or take responsibility for them regardless of how much other people may try to put them upon us through pressure, manipulation, accusation, or whatever tactics they may try to use. To live in freedom, we must define our boundaries, our property.

His or Mine?

The Scripture says, "Each one should carry his own load," but it also says, "Carry each other's burdens" (Galatians 6:5, 2). So we must discern what responsibility belongs to whom.

I must not try to make others responsible for that which belongs to me. I must discern and own my own responsibilities. My choices, my actions, my problems, my feelings, my happiness, my unhappiness, my struggles, my abilities or inabilities, my pain, my attitudes, my beliefs, and my thoughts are inside my property line. I am responsible for these things.

On the other hand, I am not responsible for someone else's attitudes, beliefs, choices, and actions. My responsibility ends at my property line. There are many times in life when I must decide: Whose side of the fence is this issue on?

We are responsible for whether or not we will allow ourselves to be controlled, manipulated, or mistreated by others. What we allow to happen to our property is our responsibility.

PROTECTING OUR BOUNDARIES

I knew the situation regarding Amy and Belva was a boundary issue where I would need to draw limits to keep Amy from controlling me. I needed to protect my boundaries. When Amy asked, "Where have you been?" I knew she was trying to invade my territory—to tear down my fence and trespass! She was trying to control me. I was faced with the issue: Would I yield to the approval of people or of God?

Others do not own us. We must be free to be controlled by God. We are not to be dominated by others, allowing them to treat us as they want. We are responsible to God for what we allow others to do to us, as well as for what we do to them.

JESUS AND BOUNDARIES

Jesus, Martha, and Mary

We have seen how Jesus responded to Peter by drawing a boundary. Now let's take a look at Jesus with Mary and Martha in the story from Luke 10:38–42.

As Jesus and his disciples were on their way, he came to a village where a woman named Martha opened her home to him. She had a sister called Mary, who sat at the Lord's feet listening to what he said. But Martha was distracted by all the preparations that had to be made. She came to him and asked, "Lord, don't you care that my sister has left me to do the work by myself? Tell her to help me!"

"Martha, Martha," the Lord answered, "you are worried and upset about many things, but only one thing is needed. Mary has chosen what is better, and it will not be taken away from her."

Martha's Property Line

Why didn't Jesus tell Mary to go and help Martha? There was a lot of work to be done. Wouldn't it have been a good thing for Jesus to shame Mary a bit and ask her to help Martha?

Evidently Jesus knew there was a lesson Martha needed to learn more than she needed to get relief from this moment of frustration. Perhaps she needed to own her own problem and take the responsibility for her frustration. Was it Mary's fault that Martha was frustrated? Whose property was Martha's frustration?

Perhaps she was overly committed to having things done her way—the right way, the perfect way! In this case she had a wrong motive and a wrong focus. Did Jesus love Martha? Yes! Did He draw limits on her behavior? Yes. Jesus knew Martha needed truth, and He offered it with grace.

Mary's Property Line

Jesus also protected Mary's boundaries, and in doing that He kept her from enabling Martha's wrong behavior. Evidently Martha's frustration was her own doing, and Jesus knew she needed to learn to take the responsibility for it. She must own her own problem of frustration. Jesus did not let her load it on Mary by blaming her. Mary had a right to sit at Jesus' feet. Martha needed to learn to respect Mary's boundaries and to "carry her own load" (Galatians 6:5).

Even if we suppose that Mary should have assumed more responsibility for helping and did need to be confronted and corrected, that should not have come through shame, blame, humiliation, or accusation.

Perhaps Martha had a tendency to overuse her ability to take charge and was on the verge of an out-of-balance lifestyle. Jesus helped her draw some boundaries for herself and taught her to honor Mary's boundaries.

Think about Martha and her boundaries. What were Martha's feelings, beliefs, choices, actions? These all belong on whose side of the fence? Martha tried to cause Mary to assume responsibility for her frustrations, but Martha's frustrations belonged to her. What might have been some of Martha's self-talk that caused her feelings of frustration with Mary?

The Good Samaritan

Luke 10:25–37 tells of a good Samaritan who had mercy on a man who had been robbed and beaten. The Samaritan sacrificed his time and gave of his resources to help meet the man's needs, but we also notice that he drew a limit. Evidently he had a responsibility in another city, and he went off to fulfill it. When he left, he told the innkeeper that he would be back to check on the man and to pay any bills incurred. However, he again drew a limit. He did not take the injured man home to live with him. We too need to learn to help others, but there will always be a limit to how much we can and should do for them.

VIOLATED BOUNDARIES

Kindly but firmly, we each need to define limits for people who may be violating our person or our property. Sometimes we need to help others honor our boundaries.

We have mentioned that one of the common results of being malnourished is blurred boundaries. A victim of abuse or a person who has grown up in a legalistic environment—home, church, or school—often lacks understanding of what her boundaries are. Her boundary lines are unclear; they are blurred. As a result she finds it very difficult to set proper boundaries. One significant way to nourish others with bold love is to help them draw boundaries.

Malnourished and abused children often think they have no *right* to have boundaries. To them it feels *so selfish.* They tend to continue to let people take advantage of them, and in the process, build up more and more contempt for themselves and for others. These people can so easily feel guilty when they stand up for themselves in any way, say no, or draw limits on others' behavior toward them or expectations of them.

Children raised in unhealthy families have had their boundaries violated time and again. Certainly abuse is a violation, but so is going through the child's personal things without her permission, opening the bathroom door and going in when the child is there, or a father going into a teenager's room when she is dressing. (Of course, an exception would be when the parent suspects drug use and searches for evidence in order to protect the child.)

One lady shared, "At our family gathering there were thirteen people and twelve places at the dining room table. I volunteered to eat in the kitchen." Nobody argued with her as they all began finding a place at the table.

As she sat in the kitchen eating alone, she heard everyone laughing and talking and enjoying one another in the dining room. She was left out and no one even cared or appreciated her sacrifice. She felt hurt, unloved, and unappreciated, and she resented all of them.

"Now," she said, "I realize I allowed myself to be put in this situation and that even my own actions and attitude toward myself encouraged disrespect from them. I felt emotionally abused. Next time, I will protect myself from this kind of thing. We could have set up an additional table so all of us could be together."

Lisa homeschooled three of four children, was a member of the local PTA, helped in the community cancer drive, and was chairman for the Enriched Living Workshops. That's not all. She was also very active in her church as the women's ministry director, organist, pianist, women's counselor, Bible study leader, and on and on. She experienced severe burnout and had to greatly reduce her schedule. It was then that she realized she had neglected her own needs and had failed to draw limits. It was a boundary issue.

Joe was in the Easter drama at church. He did well—even sang a solo, which he had never done before. He got many affirmations and compliments. One person said, "You're *so* good in drama. Where did you get your training?"

After thinking for a moment, Joe replied, "I grew up in a home where I learned to play whatever role they wanted me to play."

Joe's wife remembers that on a single Sunday morning he was Sunday school superintendent, song leader, children's church leader, adult Bible-class teacher, and head of the ushers. At the end of all that, he had to rush back to the sanctuary from children's church to lead in a final song in the worship service. Joe experienced burn-out!

Would you believe he's a brother to Lisa, the lady who burned out from "doing it all." Where do you suppose they got this do-it-all pattern for living? Right! From their parents.

Free to Set Limits

One of the first lessons that dedicated, serving people need to learn is to draw limits. They need to know it is not always wrong to say no, even to ministry opportunities. Joe and his sister had a problem with blurred boundaries as they related to ministry.

However, blurred boundaries affect every role in life, not just ministry or activities. Wives, mothers—people in every relationship situation—need to come to grips with this fact also. It is not selfish to take care of your own basic nourishment needs. You can't nourish others out of a dry tank.

At an early age Glenna was expected to become the *communicator* between her strong-willed, controlling mother and her passive father.

This responsibility to keep her parents happy with one another was a very heavy burden for Glenna. But she longed to please them and to have their approval. To the best of her ability she fulfilled the role they expected of her, but in return she felt only rejection from them. After she married, she was still expected to solve her parents' conflicts, which had increased since their retirement. Her brothers and sister also depended on Glenna as communicator.

Glenna's boundaries were blurred. She found it very difficult to differentiate her responsibility from her parents'.

In her forties, Glenna became depressed. Through counseling, she began to understand just what responsibilities she should and should not own. She came to realize that her parents were responsible for their marriage problems and their own happiness; she was not. She began to draw legitimate boundaries, refusing to step in and take responsibilities that belonged to her parents. As a result Glenna began to receive shame and guilt messages from her mother, and deep anger from her father. But she realized she would have to continually refuse to try to fix them and would need to endure the ever-present pain of her parents' rejection.

The only way another person is going to learn to respect you and your boundaries is for you, at times, to protect that person from invading your territory. Sometimes you need to defend your own rights, so you can be free to do what the Lord wants you to do; and in the process, you'll be teaching important lessons to others. This is bold, but wise, love.

BIBLICAL TEACHING ON BOUNDARIES

Scripture teaches in many ways and places important principles about boundaries.

Free to Limit Carrying Another's Burden

As we discussed above, Paul and Jesus taught that there is a limit as to how much of the other person's burden we can or even should bear (see Galatians 6:5 and Luke 10). Each of us needs to discern what is *not* our responsibility and then let go of it. And we need to let go of our own control and free the other person to have boundaries with us. We will elaborate on this in the next chapter.

Free to Deny Our Own Rights

In 1 Corinthians 9, Paul clearly states that he had certain rights, just as the other apostles did, including the right to travel with a wife and the right to be supported instead of working for his own food and lodging while ministering. But he chose not to claim these rights. His reason was "for the sake of the gospel."

He made the boundary issue clear. Others had no right to deny him his privileges, but he could choose to deny himself what legitimately was his right for the sake of a higher purpose.

I am not to be controlled by any person. I am not anyone else's property. Since this is true, I must asssume the responsibility to *choose* what I'm going to do with me, and what I'm going to let others do to me—boundaries.

Free to Please or Not Please Others

Like many of you, I have chosen to give myself away to my Lord Jesus. Therefore, I am not my own; I belong to Him. I am committed to being a God-pleaser, which means I am free from having to please people. I'm not controlled by the approval of others. I *am* controlled by my chosen commitment to please Christ. In the process, I may sometimes please and sometimes displease people.

Jesus often displeased people. The Pharisees were rarely happy with His replies. The rich ruler went away sad when Jesus told him what he had to do to inherit eternal life.

Paul said, "Am I now trying to win the approval of men, or of God? Or am I trying to please men? If I were still trying to please men, I would not be a servant of Christ" (Galatians 1:10).

Free to Define and Clarify Boundaries

The Biblical truth is that we have the responsibility to set boundaries. We also have an admonition to operate in grace as well as truth. "And, above everything else, be truly loving, for love is the golden chain of all the virtues" (Colossians 3:14, Phillips).

Rather than let another person control me, I will consider my boundaries and his boundaries, and then choose to act for the glory of God and the best interests of both the other person and myself.

I may choose to give the other person the advantage, as Abraham did with Lot; but the point is that my choice is at issue and not the other person's control over me.

Know your own boundaries and rights, but think! You might set a particular boundary with one person, but not in every case. Think and pray through each situation to gain the right perspective. Realize you have the responsibility to choose. Think and pray. Ask, "What is the best thing to do? Am I to give in, am I to deny myself, or am I to take responsibility to deal with the situation in another way?" Then choose. If I do choose to give the other person the advantage, it is my choice. I will not let another person control me or pressure me into doing something I really don't want to do unless I choose to do so.

A woman whose boundaries are blurred because they were violated in a marked way when she was a child said: "One of the biggest releases came when I realized I have this freedom, this right, to think things through, consider what is my responsibility, and decide what choices I should make. But my question is, How do I think it through? How can I know if it is selfishness on my part, or if it is really an issue of boundaries and I need to take steps to protect my boundaries?" I gave her three guidelines.

BASIC PRINCIPLES FOR SETTING LIMITS

Several guidelines for setting boundaries are clearly given to us in 1 Corinthians 10:23–24, 31–33. We can use them to determine whether setting this boundary or allowing this action will be:

1. For the ultimate good of the person himself
2. For the good of the cause; i.e., for the benefit or growth of all persons involved and the benefit of the relationship
3. For the glory of God. Will this action result in growing in grace and Christlikeness? Is it done in love

David Augsburger in *Beyond Assertiveness* states:

When I truly care about you, I will offer confrontation because it will contribute to our relationship and perhaps to each of us as persons. Self-care, relationship maintenance, and care for the other are three valid reasons for confronting. But each of the three must be balanced by equal caring for the other, the other's needs and relationship, and the other's unique ways of expressing caring in return. . . . To care is to be guided by the other's direction of growth[;] although I will choose my responses, I will select my behaviors."[1]

LEARN TO ASK YOURSELF QUESTIONS

If giving in to someone else's request or desire stirs up resentment and bad feelings in me, I should question whether I have made the right choice. Good checkpoints include asking questions like these:

- Should *they* be doing this instead of me?
- Does this reinforce their selfishness or immature dependence?
- Does the principle of loving others and doing things for their good mean that I should *always* give in whenever they want, or give to them whatever they want?

For example, does it mean that Valerie should definitely plan to go visit her mother just to "make her mother happy" instead of getting together with some of her friends? Must she always go against her own wishes and desires in order to please her selfish, controlling mother and keep her from being unhappy?

These are boundary issues. Sometimes it is not for the ultimate good of the person, for the good of the cause (all involved or the relationship), or for the glory of God for you to do what others want. It may just be a means of promoting their self-centeredness and encouraging their manipulation.

Galatians 6:10 (AMP) says, "Do good . . . to all people . . ." It is *not* always best for the other person when we cater to their selfishness and make it easy for them to walk in their sinful flesh patterns. We have to learn that it is not always wrong to say no. In fact, sometimes it is wrong to say yes. Recognize boundaries.

RESPECT YOUR OWN BOUNDARIES

Those who have trouble with blurred boundaries often ask, "Do I ever think of what's good for me? Do I set no limits on my giving as others make demands on me? What about my own need for exercise, health, and personal refreshment? Are these selfish?"

I had to find the answer to those same questions when I was Dean of Girls at the high school. You recall that because I was so fatigued I was responding to the girls with an impatient spirit. That was not a way to show them what Jesus Christ is like. I learned that I had to take responsibility to set my boundary, so I put PLEASE DO NOT DISTURB on my door in order to get some rest.

Was it wrong for me to take care of myself and my needs so that I could more adequately fulfill God's assignment to me in that place? Was it selfish? Did it benefit the girls? Did it benefit me? Did it bring glory to God?

Actually, it was both a gift to the Lord and a gift to the girls. If you are worn out, short of patience, or depleted in spiritual vitality, give a gift to the Lord and to others around you. Put up, in a figurative sense, a *Please Do Not Disturb* sign and get some rest. Your method may be different from mine, but you need to give attention to your priorities and draw a boundary.

INTERNAL AND EXTERNAL BOUNDARIES

There are two kinds of boundaries, *internal* and *external,* and we need to take the responsibility to own our *responses* for both.

Internal Boundaries

Internal boundaries are those that take place on the inside of us against things like lust or self-pity. Setting an internal boundary means taking an inward stand against perfectionism, blame and shame from others, the all-or-nothing tendency, and wrong thoughts—whether they are about ourselves, about others, about God, or about circumstances of life.

Penny asked: "Is there ever a time when you need to draw a boundary on your emotions? I've been going through some rough times lately, and I'm probably oversensitive. Last week a friend I've been really counting on to help me through a crisis responded to me in what seemed to be a cold and uncaring way. Immediately, I began to have very accusing, resentful, and judgmental thoughts toward her. My emotions went wild, and it all generated into a serious case of self-pity and depression."

"Yes," I told Penny, "We do need to draw a boundary on our emotions."

Boundaries on our emotions come in the realm of our self-talk. Penny's thought, "she doesn't care," was self-talk that caused her to feel the emotion of self-pity. What she needed to do was bring that thought captive to Christ and discover what the truth in the situation really was.

Proverbs 25:28 describes a person with no internal boundaries: "Like a city whose walls are broken down is a man who lacks self-control."

JENNIFER'S TEMPTATION

Jennifer is a committed Christian who wants more than anything to honor the Lord in her life. She is devoted to her husband and children and wants desperately to be a godly wife and mother. Her husband, however, is in a time of ambivalence. John is unwilling to pay the price of giving up his own way to really enjoy harmony with his wife. Right now, he is cool toward the Lord, the church, spiritual things, and even toward Jennifer.

"Especially since we moved to a new community," Jennifer wrote, "John doesn't seem interested in going to church or even talking about church, the Lord, or spiritual things. I have felt so alone here. I would like to see us get involved in a good church again. I need the teaching of the Word, and I need people.

"Last night we had a strong discussion about all this, but his rebellion was so evident. I told him my desires and asked what his thoughts were. All he said is, 'You reject me! You won't let me do what I want to do. I can't talk to you.' These accusations are so untrue! I have purposed to give him lots of freedom. Freedom to make expenditures that did not seem wise, but I genuinely gave him the freedom to do as he wished.

"Now, I find myself drawn to other men who look me in the eyes with kindness. John doesn't do that. This is a constant, painful battle. There is a part of me that wants revenge, but I know that's very wrong, and I don't really want any part of it.

"This temptation came to me again recently. As you know, we are building a new home. Since John works during the day, I have a lot of the responsibility to see that the work gets done on a day-to-day basis. The other day, as the foreman and I were talking and planning, he looked right into my eyes and asked a question. It felt so good to have such sensitive attention. On the other hand, I was very uncomfortable. When I explained it to John, there was no understanding communicated. He did not share my burden. All I knew to do was to choose to avoid the foreman as much as possible."

Sometime later, Jennifer was finally able to share what her problem over this temptation had been. "Telling you was so freeing! Before, I always carried it all to myself, prayed about it, and tried to flee temptation; but, it wasn't as freeing as when I talked with you. This is such an intimate issue, and not many people talk about it. Of course, as I told you, I did have the what-does-she-think-of-me-now battle. It helped greatly when you shared that I'm not the only one with this problem, that many wives have the same temptation."

In sharing this burden with me, she found release and a new power to draw not only an internal boundary but an external one also.

HILDA'S DECISION

Hilda's husband was a busy pastor. He was gone all day, and when he came home at night, he would watch sports events on TV. Hilda believed strongly that he should be giving more attention to the children. She felt he was really not sensitive to their need and desire to have more of Dad. It grieved her so, and she felt such pain for the children.

When the church needed a man to help in the music ministry, a committed, gifted, handsome, single young man came from the college in the city. He took a train out for the day, took care of his responsibilities at the church, and then spent the afternoon with Hilda's family in their home.

Hilda wrote, "He was so sensitive and kind to the children—playing games with them, reading to them, talking with them. They loved his attention, and I loved the fact that he was giving them such special attention. He loved them; they loved him. I couldn't help comparing his interest in the children to my husband's seeming lack of interest and attention."

Gradually Hilda's heart began to go out to this man, and she sensed that he was also responding to her. It was a real temptation, though neither had a thought of being unfaithful. When she recognized what was happening, she refused to be in denial about it or excuse herself or blame her husband. Instead, she admitted it to herself and took responsibility to draw some boundaries. First, she took an inward stand against these tempting thoughts and the pull of her emotions. Then one afternoon, when he asked her to walk with him down to the lake, she drew a kind but definite external boundary and said no. Shortly after that, he graduated from college and moved to another community. Nothing further needed to be done.

Sexual temptations are common to women—even to committed Christian women when certain conditions exist. Christian women need to take responsibility to draw clear inward and outward boundaries in their relationships.

External Boundaries

What are the external limits we need to draw? These may be of various kinds, such as time, space, or contacts. In the examples above, we have seen that Jennifer and Hilda set both internal and external boundaries.

Natalie, a committed Christian, found her heart being drawn to a man and his to her. When she realized how very vulnerable men and women are to sexual temptations, she set some strong limits on their contacts. She limited the times and the places and set specific conditions for allowing herself to see him. Then she set some careful, firm, general boundaries for her times of fellowship with those of the opposite sex. Some of her self-imposed rules for fellowship and contact with a man are:

- I will not send the husband a birthday card. Instead, I will send an anniversary card to both of them
- When we have fellowship times together it will always be as couples, and I won't give him any special attention
- I will not meet with him privately. When counseling or talking about my personal things, I won't meet with him alone. I will either ask his wife to be there, or include a friend that I choose
- If I write a letter, I will include the names of both the husband and his wife
- We will never meet for lunch alone
- My goal is to be absolutely free from any means of temptation—for him as well as for myself—or any misunderstanding of my motives by either of them

Natalie was very wise to set some definite external boundaries for herself in relationship to other men. This benefited all those involved and any others looking on.

WARNING SIGNALS

What are some warning signals or indicators that we may not be drawing proper boundaries?

Physical Exhaustion
Burnout that stems from overextending ourselves, taking on more and more responsibilities in our jobs or in serving others. Doing what others want or expect me to do instead of what I feel God wants me to do.

Emotional Weariness
Feeling overwhelmed and unable to concentrate well.

Depression

Feeling down, discouraged, tired, helpless, useless, and hopeless.

Resentment

Toward life, circumstances, job, and others. "I hate life. I don't like my circumstances, but I feel cornered and powerless to change things. I feel I have no real options." Continual grumbling about this, that, and the other thing.

Anger

Sudden explosions of anger over small things or projected anger when the immediate situation or person has nothing to do with the anger.

Inability to Complete Tasks

Finding it really difficult to complete tasks because you can't say no to other things that would distract you and keep you from giving your time and attention to your main task.

Feeling of Being Controlled

Dreading something because you think, "I have to do it," or, "I should do it," or, "They want or need me to do it." The *shoulds* zap my energy. Do you feel that, where relationships are concerned, you are always giving in? Are you giving in to others' tastes, preferences, and desires, and do you feel that your opinions never count? Does it seem that others ignore or discount your ideas, giving you the message that their idea is a better idea, their way is a better way?

Feelings of Guilt, Shame, or Sense of Failure

I'm not doing what I should or what others think I should, so I feel guilty, inadequate, or that I can't ever measure up.

Any of these warning signs should lead us to take a good hard look at our boundaries.

DETERRENTS TO SETTING BOUNDARIES

What are some reasons why I might not draw proper limits or boundaries?

Wrong Thinking

I may think it is not biblical. "Drawing limits is not loving them as the Bible says I should because 'Love bears all things,'" or, "Tough love has no place in Christian behavior. We're to 'turn the other cheek' and be gentle and kind to all," or, "I must not say no to ministry opportunities—that's being disobedient and not using my God-given gifts to the fullest."

Drawing boundaries does not mean that you have ceased loving the person; rather, it is a way of freeing you to give love in a healthier way. You learn to love without resentment or compulsion. Out of freedom of choice you give sacrificial love for the good of the other person.

I tell myself it is selfish. I must not say no to people—no matter what they do to me or desire from me. I must not say no to people who "think I should do it." When I say no, I feel guilty and think, "I should have done that."

I may feel that because they've done so much for me, I owe it to them to do whatever they want me to even though I may be greatly overextending myself.

Fear of Disapproval, Resistance, Withdrawal

I'm afraid of the disapproval of others. Just prior to her grandparents' visit, Joanie called her mother into her room and asked her to look all around and see if there was anything that would not be acceptable to Grandma. Her mother assured her that what she owns is really not offensive and if Grandmother doesn't like it that would have to be her problem. "Yes," Joanie said, "but I want her to like me. If I have something here she doesn't like, she won't like me."

I'm afraid that I will hurt other people if I draw limits on them. Instead of entertaining this fear, I need to realize that even though other people might give resistance or experience pain, if they respond appropriately they will be ultimately benefited.

I'm afraid other people might withdraw from me. If I set boundaries and deny them what they want, they might leave me. I'm afraid that I will lose them. In response to this fear, I need to accept the fact that risking the loss of a relationship in order to ensure the integrity of my boundaries is one element that keeps that relationship strong.

Wrong Teaching

My misconceptions, wrong thinking, and guilt basically come from wrong modeling or wrong teaching from various sources: parents, teachers, books, pastors, and out-of-balance teaching on such biblical truths as unconditional love, submission, denying self, and forgiveness.

Pressure From Others

I get pressure from others to let them violate my boundaries. They may say things like, "After all I've done for you, and you don't appreciate me any more than this."

BENEFITS OF BOUNDARIES

No other person should have power over me to control my behavior and attitudes. Nor should I *let* anyone control me by their attitudes and behavior. We need to know how far we will go and how far we will allow others to go with us. When I learn to take ownership of my own actions and attitudes and what I allow or don't allow other people to do to me or load on me, I become free. Learning the truth about what is my responsibility and what is not my responsibility and learning to draw limits accordingly is a wonderful step toward giving me freedom.

What are some of the benefits (freedoms) that come when we learn to draw proper boundaries?

Free to Follow My Own Choices

Instead of yielding to the pressures of others, I can think, "What is God's plan for me at this time?" I won't be afraid of the person's disapproval. I will be free *not* to fulfill the wishes of parents—like becoming a doctor or lawyer because of parental pressure. This freedom of choice includes the freedom to say no to choices other people impose on me, and instead, to do what I enjoy. This applies to the simple things of daily living as well as to larger issues. If I serve in a capacity that I'm not called to or not fitted for, I rob those who *are* fitted of their opportunity to minister in their area of giftedness.

Sonja was asked to take on a ministry in the church. "Honestly," she said, "I'm very capable of doing the job and have done it before. I realized the need was great, but I was already involved in several ministries that I enjoyed more, and I had no great desire to take this on. The person who wanted me to do it encouraged me to pray about it. I did that and also talked to a friend about it. She helped me see it was a boundaries issue and advised me not to do it if I was only doing it under pressure from someone. I needed to know what the Lord wanted to me to do and what I wanted to do, and I needed to have the freedom to say no. I continued to get pressure, even to the point of implying that if I said no, I might be disobeying God. In the end, I declined and really felt free."

Free to Say Yes or No Without Guilt

Sandra was asked to help out in the children's department at church. She explained, "I was asked to help on Sunday mornings in the summer. When I explained why I couldn't, the gal who asked me to help said those were very valid reasons and gave me a big hug! No pressure! No guilt!"

Sonja's story above is also a good example of this freedom to say no or yes without feeling guilty. This example related to a ministry opportunity, but we also need to be free to say no when someone wants us to engage in bad behavior. On the other hand, we also need to be free to say yes to good behavior, even when it may not be popular or could be misunderstood.

Free to Help Another Toward Maturity

By allowing others to reap the consequences of their behavior, we help them toward maturity. One person wrote: "Jeremy, our close friend, has some serious alcohol problems. At times, we are at a loss to know how to help him. The counsel we received from two different pastors was along the line of tough love: 'Don't let Jeremy move in with you; if he shows up on your doorstep and hasn't eaten for five days, give him a meal and take him to a rescue mission. If he breaks the law, turn him in. If he tries suicide, have him committed. Don't in any way pursue it. Pray for him and be ready to assist him when he hits bottom and really wants help.'

"I have had a hard time with this because it seemed so contrary to love. Now that I have been through the study on boundaries, I see the validity of this approach. Forcing Jeremy to take responsibility for himself *is* loving. By not forcing him to take care of himself but continuing to do things for him before he is ready to admit his need for help, we would only be postponing the consequences, and we would be allowing him to continue in a destructive lifestyle."

All of us have the responsibility to respect and protect the boundaries of others as well as our own boundaries. People are not our property—children, friends, husbands, grandchildren, etc. We don't own them and therefore can't do with them as we please. We must learn to take the responsibility to draw both internal and external boundaries.

When we learn to graciously draw boundaries, saying no when it is for the best interests of all, not only does this give us freedom in so many areas and help us and others move toward maturity, but it also helps love to grow. As others allow me to say no to them, it increases my love and respect for them. All of us need to learn to allow for and receive their no, their limits. We need to know how far we will go, and how far we will allow others to go with us. As we learn to say no to others and also to accept their no to us, we won't be really harmed, though sometimes we might experience pain. But the results are great freedom and an increase of love and respect for one another.

In chapter 8 we'll talk about the consequences of not drawing boundaries, suggest guidelines for setting limits, and discuss further how to draw boundaries in specific relationships and responsibility situations.

Thoughts to Remember

We are free to say yes or no without feeling guilty. Boundaries help us and the other person move toward maturity. "For each one should carry his own load" (Galatians 6:5).

Practicing and Journaling

Continue working on the self-talk chart on page 141.

8

More About Boundaries

Remember my story about visiting my neighbor, Harriet, and asking her whether she wanted to sell her home? She had looked surprised and thought that perhaps I was an answer to her prayers. She showed me through her house, and then we sat down in the living room and talked at length about what it means to be a Christian. Then I returned to the subject of the house.

She explained, "Mother is not happy living in the retirement home. She is very negative, complaining, and critical. She wants so much to move in with me so she'll be happy. Though I can't really afford it, I've thought of buying a bigger house."

Obviously, Harriet felt very guilty for not "making her mother happy," but that wasn't her only problem. When Harriet's mother entered the retirement home, she had turned over most of her assets to them, the arrangement being that the retirement home would take care of her for the rest of her life, providing full personal care, which included an apartment, food, medicines, and complete nursing care. If her mother left that home, she could not get any money back. "I'm not able," Harriet said, "to take financial responsibility for Mother, and my own health is not too good—I'm not very strong. But I want so much to make her happy!" Harriet felt guilty, selfish, fearful, and confused.

After quite a lengthy discussion, instead of talking Harriet into selling the house, I talked her out of selling it—to me or anyone else. I tried to help her see the situation objectively.

"First, you cannot assume the responsibility of making your mother happy. Her happiness is her own choice. If she has chosen not to be happy there, she probably wouldn't be happy with you for long, either.

"But second, it does not seem wise to think of taking her out of that home. You said you don't have the finances to care for her. Plus, you really don't know how long your own physical strength will hold out. What if she came to your home and *you* died? Who would care for her then? Living there, she has the security of being fully cared for for the rest of her life. It seems unwise to make a move."

It all made good sense to Harriet; she had a clearer understanding of her responsibility, and she no longer felt guilty. She did love her mother and showed it by making almost daily visits to see her. She did not neglect or dishonor her mother. She just discerned what really was best for both of them in the long run.

Of course, with this solution I came away with no house. But after a few years, the Lord showed us that He had a better plan to meet our needs. I believe I was sent to Harriet that day for two reasons: (*a*) to help her know how she could become God's child, and (*b*) to relieve her of the guilt of her mother's pressure and help her avoid making a big mistake.

Harriet was experiencing many of the consequences of having inadequate boundaries.

CONSEQUENCES OF NO BOUNDARIES

Frustration

If I don't learn to set limits, I take on responsibilities that are not mine; I try to bear burdens that are not mine to own; and I become frustrated, overwhelmed, resentful, judgmental, critical, bitter, depressed, or defeated.

Loss of Maturity

When I do not set boundaries, I slow or block my progress in maturing in adult behaviors. I get stuck in less mature patterns of responding; I violate my own personhood; and I am not free to act on my own or to think of my own personal preferences, tastes, desires, opinions, and responsibilities.

When I do not set legitimate limits, I also rob the other person of his right to assume his own responsibility, take the consequences of his bad behavior, and choose to change, learn, and grow. We must learn to let others handle the bumps of life. This is all part of the process of maturing.

Loss of Freedom to Make Choices

By not setting limits I end up being either directly or indirectly controlled by another.

The direct controller gives a clear message: "I don't like it when you won't give me your time when I want it, or your money when I need it, or when you won't accept my idea or the job I'm offering you."

The manipulative controller uses guilt or shame tactics, implying or stating, "You don't have time for me, so I'll just sit here and be lonely for the rest of the week." They love to make you feel guilty because they have bad feelings of aloneness, unhappiness, rejection—as though you were responsible for how they feel. Or they might say, "Do you think you really should pass up this opportunity to serve the Lord?"

Not Doing What God Wants

Instead of dealing with God myself to discover what His will for me is, I can be pressured into making choices that are not His plan for me. It could even be that I do not pursue the activity or the profession that I would enjoy, and that God has gifted me for, because I feel pressure from my parents to go a different route. Some parents do put pressure on their children to go out for sports in school and to pursue a certain career—a doctor, a recording artist, a preacher, a missionary.

However, while we certainly should not pressure or push a child into fulfilling our own dreams or unfulfilled desires, it *is* good to visualize several possibilities for the child. Your goal in doing this would be to help the child discover God's plan. For example, a father thought there were two career probabilities for his daughter—nurse or teacher. He provided objects she could use to "play nurse" and some she could use to "play teacher." This gentle guidance, without pressure, did help guide her toward a successful career in teaching. She enjoyed teaching immensely and definitely felt cut out for it.

GUIDELINES FOR DRAWING BOUNDARIES

Do's

- Do identify whose property or responsibility is involved.
- Do describe the limits you are setting; don't attack the person.
- Do take ownership of your property, that which belongs to you—attitudes, beliefs, feelings, behavior. My pain or struggle may not be my fault. It may be coming from something that was done to me; but, it is my responsibility to deal with it now. One person concluded, "I can't blame other people. They may have hurt me, but my response to them is my problem. I am responsible for that part."
- Do address the issue and affirm your stance, but don't attack and accuse.
- Do let people reap the consequences of their own behavior—"Bear their own load" (Galatians 6:5). A friend in Michigan said she tended to clean up after the kids when they didn't do their part. The reason was that when her husband came home, he would lecture them about the mess, and the evening would turn out stressful. She needed to let the kids reap their own consequences.

- Do be willing to hear the other person's no to you.
- Do use easy no's with safe people at first. Start disagreeing in little things where the consequences aren't so great, and only with safe people. After you practice on safe people, then use some "grown-up" no's in tough situations. When you don't *need* that person's love all the time, you will be able to do this.

Don'ts

- Don't take on responsibility that belongs to another.
- Don't let the other person control you.
- Don't try to use limit-setting as a way of controlling the other person.
- Don't flee or fight; face the issue.
- Don't try to defend yourself; simply define the property line or the responsibility.
- Don't try to fix people or things that don't need fixing.

Remember how my brother and his cousins poured slop on me to get rid of me? I made the point of how alone and rejected I felt. As a result of my wrong conclusion, I have developed a wrong flesh pattern that I still need to be aware of today.

One time when I told that story a lady quickly said, "Well, doesn't it help you to realize that your brother was just acting as you would expect children to act. Don't you see that he was just being a child and you have to understand where he was coming from?"

She was trying to "fix it" when it didn't need fixing. It wasn't broken. I'd forgiven him long ago. He didn't need to be excused. He *was* guilty of not loving me properly—even if he was a child. The point I was trying to communicate was something of the relational pain I had felt. The woman totally ignored my point. I wasn't asking her to fix me. I just wanted her to listen and perhaps learn from my experience that feeling alone and rejected had developed into a flesh pattern that I needed to recognize.

Ways to Set Limits

Words

Words are the most common tool for drawing boundaries and setting limits. One illustration of this is the experience I mentioned about Amy and Belva, especially where I gently said to Amy, "It's none of your business." Obviously I used words to draw the boundary.

A friend called for advice. Both she and her husband were frustrated. "My husband's parents," she explained, "are visiting for a few days. Dad likes to look at the kind of TV shows we never allow our children to watch. Do we have any right to ask him not to watch such programs in our home when the children are around?"

My answer was, "Yes, you not only have the *right* but the *responsibility* to protect your children from evil influences as much as you can. Since your husband also feels this way, he is probably the one who should tell his parents. Be gracious and loving, but clearly explain where the lines are drawn, and then trust the Lord for the outcome—good or bad.

"We can't control another person's response or take responsibility for it. Your responsibility is to express the limits you have set for watching TV when the children are around."

Sandy said that she loves to host five-day Bible clubs in her home, but she does not appreciate it when the leader *pressures* young children to make a decision for Christ. She draws a boundary, telling the leader, "You can explain the gospel to the children while they are in my home—please do! But you cannot put pressure on them to receive Christ. Give opportunity, but no pressure." Sandy's words set a boundary.

Physical or Emotional Distancing

Boundaries help us to withdraw when we need to. Myrna's husband was becoming violently angry. She wrote: "What should I do? Just pray? Trust? I'm afraid. He came at me with fists last night, though he didn't hit me. This is the worst it has ever been. I was scared. After he left the house, I called a friend who has some education and understanding about domestic violence. She said violence only escalates and told me I could come to her house if I felt in danger. What do you think, Verna?"

I suggested she gather more information on family violence, pray, and make a plan to take herself and the children to a safe place if the need arose. Then she should calmly share with her husband her awareness of his problem, her fears, and her plan. She should tell him that he must get counsel.

Myrna took the problem seriously. She prayed, made plans for safety for herself and the children, and addressed the issue with her husband. He decided to face his problem and get counsel. They developed a level of communication that had been previously foreign to them. Now they are helping each other with needed changes in their lives.

Peggy experienced emotional burnout. Dealing with a troublesome marriage, PMS, and the continuing insensitivity and accusations of her husband became too much for her. She addressed the situation and told her husband that she was taking the children for a long visit to her mother in another state. "I need to do this," she said, "in order to keep my sanity and receive some emotional refreshment and time for healing."

It wasn't too long before Peggy's husband began to call her, expressing that he was really missing the children. Over time he began to take on a whole different attitude. After two months, she returned to a husband who was ready to work on their relationship, and she was refreshed for a new start.

After breaking our ten-month engagement, my former fiancé wondered if we could still be good friends and keep in touch by writing to one another. I said we could still be friends, but as for writing to one another, I felt that was unwise. We needed to emotionally detach from each other, at least for quite a while; and if we wrote, we would not really be letting go of the relationship. That would not be helpful for either of us.

Time Limits

DEFINE SPECIFIC TIMES OR DUTIES

Carrie said that she and two friends get together weekly for breakfast. They have agreed to limit their time to one hour. Because of the limited and reachable time, they have kept this up for several years.

Sandy said, "I need to limit the amount of time I spend on church projects at home. So I tell myself, 'I will do it between 9:00 and 11:00 A.M. and then I will do my housework.'"

You can also use this tool to set a boundary on thinking about a problem, so it doesn't consume your life. "I will think about this and try to come to a solution between 3:00 and 4:00 P.M."

Della felt guilty for not responding to her mother's hints. "When I was a child," Della said, "we lived on a farm, and we all worked hard and long. I recall that there were times when I had no particular assignment, so would do my own thing, but I would hear my mother sigh or talk about all the work that she still had to do. I would feel guilty for not offering to help, but I knew that if I offered to help, there would be no end to the work and I would have no time of my own. I continued to withhold any offer to help. Mother continued to hint—*code*, we called it, which increased my guilt feelings. But I still did not volunteer to help. I didn't like the coding. I felt that if she would have asked me to do a particular job or had given me a time limit on helping and then released me to freely do my own thing, I would have felt freer to help, and she would have had more help with the work."

REQUIRE A RESPONSE

If you find that someone loves to go over and over the same situation, you might try suggesting a problem-related project for them to complete before you get together again. This will help you to know whether the person is serious about wanting to do something about the matter or if they simply want to talk about it. If they are willing to work at the problem on their own, that is a good indication that your time is probably well invested.

The Scope of Boundaries

We have been dealing with the significance of boundaries in this and the previous chapter. We have discussed some guidelines and ways to set limits. It is also good to consider how we can apply boundaries to specific relationships, responsibilities, and the varied experiences of life.

For Yourself

A big factor in maturing is developing internal boundaries about your priorities for such personal areas as eating, spending time, finishing tasks, spending money, and so forth. Discipline in these areas may be difficult, but it is crucial.

Perhaps you know by experience, as I do, that overextending yourself can lead to burnout, lowered resistance, and proneness to all kinds of diseases.

After attending Linx classes, Sally commented, "I learned that if I don't take care of myself, I won't have the energy or strength to help others. Taking care of *me* is legitimate and important. We all have limitations. God created us that way, and that is okay! I would *never* have figured this out on my own without this class." For the sake of your health you must set limits.

Jenny wrote about her own need for refreshment. "After having had several strokes, my mother-in-law came to live with us. Lydia was very mobile, but she had limited use of her hands and was hardly able to speak. My husband and I both have full-time jobs, but when I was at home I felt I should always be available to her.

"After six weeks of being constantly available, I began to notice that I was becoming impatient with Lydia, my husband, and the staff at my job. I couldn't remember the last time I'd had quality time with the Lord, either. I recall the very morning you said that, in order to nourish others, we must first be nourished. I felt God was saying those words to me! I was starving myself, and my lack of nourishment was affecting others as well as myself.

"I had to make a very hard choice. I told my mother-in-law that I needed time alone on a daily basis. When I was in my bedroom with the door closed, that was my time to be alone with the Lord, to be fed and nourished! She respected my request, and the renewal and refreshment I have received is unbelievable. I am now more equipped to handle what comes along, because I am fed and strengthened."

For Your Relationships

We need to learn to draw boundaries in our relationships with family, friends, and acquaintances. This enables us to love well without enabling others or encouraging their selfishness and irresponsible behavior. As one who was learning to draw boundaries said, "When you are free to draw and receive boundaries with or from others, the result is deeper intimacy—greater connectedness—which is what we all long for."

SPOUSE

A letter came from a wife who had begun to set some boundaries: "Thank you for your counsel and prayers. You were there for me when I needed a friend so desperately. I read the book *Love Must Be Tough,* as you suggested, and began applying the tough-love principles. Within three months I saw my husband move away from the sin that seemed to control him.

"I waited to write you because I had seen him go back into that sin so many times. For seven months now I know he hasn't indulged. But that's not the biggest thing. The biggest thing is now I can see a freedom and peace in his whole life that I've never seen before. He's so different, happy, and content.

"He's the best husband and father I've ever seen. He even got rid of the TV a few weeks ago. The children used to fear him, and they didn't know why. Now there's no fear. They tell me, 'I'm not scared to talk to Daddy anymore.' Marriage now is what I always dreamed it would be. I'm happier than I've ever been in my life. I wanted you to know the tough-love principle did work for our family, and I'm so grateful you shared it with me."

The tough-love principle helped her realize she needed to draw limits or boundaries, which, helped her husband with his problem.

FRIENDS

Sometimes friends or friendships (even helping friends) can demand too much of our time.

A friend shared, "The other day I received a phone call from two friends who wanted to have a ladies day out with me. We've done this several times in the past, and I have to set aside an entire day for the adventure.

"Over the past months I have faced my addiction to relationships, which has resulted at times in my not being a responsible housewife or mother. I am accountable to a godly friend, who has helped me look at that area honestly, and I have realized that I don't have to say yes to every opportunity that presents itself to me.

"Part of the problem has been that I am always looking for fulfillment in friendship, so there is a strong drive to be with others as often as I can. I think that I also use this subconsciously as a way to run away from responsibilities at home. I'm finally seeing that I need some boundaries, not only to control my addiction but to fulfill my responsibilities in the home for the benefit of my family.

"All this was running through my mind as I considered how to answer this ladies'-day-out invitation. In addition, our house is full of unfinished redecorating projects that need my attention. It was agony to actually say no to my friends.

"Finding that there were legitimate conflicts on all of the possible dates, I told my friends that I couldn't go. But I also explained that I needed to protect my time right now because of all that needed to be done here. I was amazed and grateful that the Lord had helped me set a boundary on responding to please my friends. After getting off the phone, I felt so *adult*—I had set some limits in terms of priorities in my life and had not just responded emotionally."

CHILDREN AND PARENTS

In this section, we focus on the problem of adult children whose parents are controlling, abusive, or who simply try to make their children feel responsible to solve the problems between the parents.

For example, Bobbi, after much frustration, came to realize that she was not responsible for her parents' conflicts, for their happiness, or to solve their problems as they expected her to. She began to discern what was and what was not her responsibility and to draw legitimate boundaries as to what she should and should not own. Though it was difficult, she chose not to take responsibility to try to fix their many problems. She realized that she had been enabling immature behavior on their part and that their problems belonged to them, not to her. Bobbi learned to draw boundaries with her parents.

PARENTS AND CHILDREN

What about the boundary needs of parents as they relate to their young children?

Children need to know they have both limits and responsibilities. Setting limits helps them know exactly what they are and are not responsible for.

A friend observed a child asking his mother for cookie dough for breakfast. His request was granted. Later, the child stated that he did not want to take a bath that day—wish granted! The mother was afraid to say no to the child for fear of losing his love. The child was learning poor habits, instant gratification, and how to let his wishes and desires control him. He also lost respect for his mother, who could not say no to him.

Knowing that there is a limit to what is expected of them in regard to their assigned work helps children exercise responsibility and yet still have some time for their own creative outlets.

One mother discovered that nagging her children to be responsible did not work. "Each morning I awakened my three grade-school boys an hour before it was time to leave for school. Most of the hour I spent encouraging them to 'Finish your egg . . . Hurry . . . Make your bed . . . Hurry . . . Feed the dog . . . Hurry.' During the last fifteen minutes this barrage included several announcements of the small amount of time left. To my frustration, the boys were still five or ten minutes late most of the time.

"After I attended the workshops, I became aware of the destructive effect nagging has, as well as the importance of teaching responsibility. Obviously, my early-morning reminders fit the description of nagging. Since I was hurrying enough for all of us, why should the boys assume any of the responsibility?

"I shared my insights with the boys and stated a new policy: During the hour before school the only reminder would be an announcement of departure time when it arrived. All three boys were late to school the first morning, but it hasn't happened again. The first hour of the day has become quiet and pleasant, with each boy attending to his own responsibilities and often having time for other brief activities."

This mother learned to draw limits on the responsibility she would take for her children's prompt arrival at school, and what responsibility she would expect them to take. She was helping her children mature into responsible adults.

For Your Responsibilities

YOU AND YOUR WORK

Perhaps your boss wants you to work overtime, even though it means you will be neglecting your family or your other responsibilities or interests. Or perhaps he wants you to take on more work than you can possibly handle in the hours given. Maybe a fellow employee was slack or negligent in his work and your employer wants you to take up the slack for him. Possibly you just feel someone is taking advantage of you.

Often when Laura would bump into Melanie in the hall at work she would ask, "When are you going to do my cash reporting for me?" Cash reporting was Laura's job, but Melanie was her back-up for vacations and sickness. Because Laura got tired of doing the job every day, she repeatedly asked Melanie to do her work. Understanding boundaries, Melanie did not capitulate to Laura's nagging requests to do work that was not her responsibility.

YOU AND YOUR CHRISTIAN MINISTRY

Perhaps ministry boundaries are the toughest of all to draw because the ministry opportunity may seem so great and may never return. Our impression is: "This is the Lord's work, and it feels so good to be involved."

Clarifying our boundaries helps us draw the line on our own behavior when we have gone beyond our limits to expend ourselves in serving others. There are times when we need nourishment ourselves instead of more activity or more ministry.

In mid-June I received an e-mail inviting me to go with a ministry group to Moldova. They were to leave in mid-July for a three-week-trip. The leader assured me that some alumnae of my workshops in the area would help with the expenses. What a wonderful opportunity!

Now the question surfaced: Should I go? Was this an opportunity that the Lord was opening up? I love to minister to those with less access to Christian teachers, and my way would be paid. One of my counselors said, "Go for it. You may not have another chance." But I didn't feel free to accept the invitation. Why? Because I had a strong prior commitment to finish writing a book. This meant that I had to draw a difficult and undesirable (to me) boundary—both internal and external. Internally, I had to draw a boundary on my desire to always respond to a ministry opportunity, especially to a country where women have few opportunities for Christian growth. Externally, I had to disappoint both the friends who were looking forward to helping financially and the person who was taking the group.

At one of the workshops, a woman named Sally said, "I limit my church ministry involvement so that it doesn't involve my weekends or my evenings. I want to be free to spend time with my family, and I don't want my ministry activity to become a point of resentment with my husband or the children. I haven't always been that smart! I figured it out through trial and error over twenty years! I'm a slow learner!"

YOU AND YOUR CHRISTIAN ACTIVITIES

Norma was homeschooling her children, attended a weekly Bible study, had weekly meetings for discipling other women, was dealing with PMS, and needed to give special attention to her relationship with her husband. After praying about it, she dropped the Bible study group. She was beginning to develop some boundaries.

Of course, doing nothing is no more right than doing everything. The key is *balance*. Jesus exemplifies that balance. He took time for personal rest, time to eat, time to speak to the Father, time to visit with friends. However, sometimes—even when He was tired—He *chose* to be with the people. Choosing to act is different than reacting.

YOU AND YOUR HOBBIES

Hobbies come in many forms: computers, genealogy, television, reading, gardening, crafts, photography, shopping, going out to lunch, and more.

A lady in Michigan greatly enjoyed creative artwork on her computer. It was such fun to get new programs and learn new techniques. She did find that she was spending quite a bit of money on this hobby, but she was sure it could even generate income for the family. However, her husband was providing very well for the family. They didn't really *need* added income.

As she got more and more into the computer work, she began to neglect the home. She didn't cook proper meals. At lunchtime the children had to shift for themselves. The house was a mess. When the children were fussing or in need of her attention, she was irritated and unkind toward them.

"Sometimes," she admitted, "the children are such a bother to me because they keep me from doing what I really enjoy. Many times I wish I didn't have them. I guess I shouldn't have had them in the first place."

That was a hobby that desperately needed a boundary!

One of my friends finds that her interest in tracing her family's roots can be very addictive, consuming far too much of her time.

She can easily neglect her primary responsibilities: homekeeping, meal preparation, devotional time, family time. Hobbies *can* be addictive, and they need to be held within boundaries.

For Effectiveness in Your World

"We need to put a limit on the time we choose to spend a certain way or with a particular person," my friend Sally affirmed when we discussed the need for boundaries in every aspect of our life. "Setting limits can help us stay focused on what God wants us to do, instead of on what everyone else wants us to do.

"The goal of my life will be achieved if, at the end, Jesus comes and holds me and looks into my eyes and says, 'Well done, Sally, I'm so proud of you.' For that to happen I need to say no to what He doesn't want for me and yes to what He does want. Boundaries help me do that."

WHY TAKE THE RISK?

Is it worth it to take the risk of drawing boundaries when we will sometimes face challenges for doing so? Yes! Remember why you are doing it.

For the Good of the Cause

One cause would be the relationship or the situation.

A friend said that her daughter tried to diligently apply the biblical principles that related to her as a wife—accepting her partner unconditionally, yielding her rights to the Lord, submitting to her husband. But things in their marriage became worse and worse. Finally, it deteriorated so much that they got a divorce. What went wrong?

The daughter failed in the area of boundaries. She did not understand how to balance these truths, so she became more of an enabler than a helper. She lost the respect of her husband, instead of gaining his respect by setting some limits. For the good of the marriage (the cause), she should have drawn some boundaries. When the challenges came, she would have been able to meet them in a nonthreatening way.

For the Good of the Other Person

Why did Paul give the command to the people in the Corinthian church to expel the immoral brother? Ultimately, this action was for that brother's own good, that he might suffer some consequences, see the error of his way, and return to fellowship in the Lord (see 1 Corinthians 5).

Shirley's husband drinks a lot, and he has many other addictive behaviors. Shirley has confronted him numerous times, and he always graciously "repents," but then he doesn't do anything to get the help he needs to change. Soon, he is back into the same old patterns of abuse, neglecting his responsibilities, and using her money to maintain his addictions. Now Shirley has given the ultimatum: If there is no change, she will move out on the last day of the month. Shirley needed to draw a boundary long before this, for her husband's own good.

For the Glory of God

Of course, the primary reason for drawing limits is for the glory of God to be seen in the situation and in the people involved. To help determine whether that will be the outcome of the boundary we intend to set, we can ask a key question: Will setting a boundary in this case help the people involved grow toward maturity, and will it improve relationships?

EXPECT SOME RESISTANCE

We should expect some resistance when we own our responsibilities, begin setting boundaries, and say no. We can expect people to react in some way when we begin to do things differently, because our change in behavior will undoubtedly affect them. We may get a negative reaction. That's all right. We do not have to let their reactions control us, stop us, or influence our decisions. Allow others to have their feelings and their reactions, but continue to calmly and kindly draw the proper limit.

If people are accustomed to controlling us, they won't want the system to change. If people are used to our saying yes all the time, they may be frustrated and start grumbling and accusing us when we say no. If people are used to our taking responsibility for their problems and feelings, they may try to make change difficult for us so that we will renege. That's normal; they don't want their system upset. If people are used to controlling us through guilt and shame, they may increase their attempts to make us go back to the old way. That's normal. We can take some resistance—but not abuse.

Do you recall how Bobbi's parents expected her to solve their conflicts. For years she tried hard to accommodate them and fix them. However, when she learned that this was not her responsibility and began to draw boundaries, she was in deep trouble. When she refused to intervene to solve problems, her mother brought heavy pressure on her through manipulation and unkind, guilt-producing words. Her father expressed deep anger. When Bobbi came to realize that the responsibility for peace in her parents' marriage was theirs, not hers, she chose to quit being their caretaker. In doing this, she had to withstand some strong resistance and endure the terrible pain and hurt of parental rejection.

Was there a happy ending to this? Yes, a couple of years later, when her parents began to assume responsibility for their own "property," their relationship with each other and with Bobbi improved.

Resistance may show itself in several ways:

They May Vent Their Anger on Me
I must set limits on allowing people to vent their anger on me. I cannot control what they will do, but I can tell them, for example, "You can scream for about one minute. If you don't calm down after that, I will leave the room (or the house)."

They May Try to Load Me with Guilt Feelings
Others often want you to feel like you are destroying their lives by setting limits. Process the negative self-talk. Talk to someone about what they are saying to you. Let an objective person help you sort out the truth.

They May Use Physical Force

You may need to call 911. Sometimes that is the most loving thing you can do, if your boundary of words is not respected. If you are dealing with a person who will only listen to consequences, let him experience the consequences.

They May Use "Spiritual" Pressure

My righteous indignation is stirred when I see how some people misuse or abuse truth and cause other people to suffer as a result. I call this spiritual/emotional abuse, and it results in spiritually/emotionally battered people. The perpetrators abuse by stating or implying their expectations of what others should or should not do, and then they make those people think this is *God's* expectation of them, when it really isn't.

The victim is battered, which manifests in a sense of confusion, guilt, frustration, and a feeling of failure: "I can't measure up." This leads to discouragement and sometimes disillusionment. Instead of being ministers of encouragement and reconciliation, the abusers are ministers of discouragement and confusion. Satan loves this. It's his heyday, and these people have given him an advantage in someone's life.

We are not responsible to communicate the specific will of God in unclear areas for anyone else. I cringe when I hear, "The Lord told me," or "The Lord revealed to me" that you or I should do thus and so, especially when it is a very absurd thing. Yet the claim is God told them to do or to say a certain thing. Or there is the guilt-producing question, "Do you think Jesus would do that?"

Charles did not want to hear his wife's suggestion that they needed better communication. When they heard of a possible idea that might help, he used the "spiritual" protective shield: "That's not biblical!"

One weekend at a seminar in Idaho, the couples were given a list of fifty typical, unspoken desires that husbands and wives have of each other. The homework was to privately check off the areas they felt they should work on as a couple, each deciding which one was the most important to him or her, and then talking about it together. Charles's wife was overjoyed that at last they had an assignment they could do together—one that might move them toward more understanding and communication.

When she shared her anticipation of doing this project together, he immediately said, "It's not biblical. We aren't going to do it." She was exceedingly disappointed, but to him the case was closed. He used "spiritual" pressure.

A lady at one of the workshops wanted some counsel regarding a difficult situation with a relative. Even though she felt her approach to confront her relative would only cause greater trouble in already strained relationships in the family, and even though it didn't make sense to her, she *knew*, "The Lord told me to do it." As it turned out, her confrontation made the situation even worse. When she related the story in detail, she still insisted, "The Lord told me to do it, and it was His will." Since she had asked for my counsel, I had to start with the fact that I really didn't think God would tell her to do something that was obviously so unwise.

HONOR OTHERS' BOUNDARIES

Be Willing to Hear "No"

I need to give others the freedom to say no to my requests. When I respect the boundaries of others, I am able to be a more loving person.

"Six months ago," Sara wrote, "I was offended—in fact I was just plain angry—when my supervisor, who had assigned a job to me, was too busy to answer some questions about the project. My inner thoughts were, 'What do you mean, you don't have time to answer my questions? This is *your* project and I need your input.' Now I didn't really care that much about the project, but I did care a lot about the relationship. That's why I was so sensitive about his response to me.

"As I continued to work on the project, I was also learning more about boundaries, and our relationship was becoming more secure. I realized that he does like me, that I'm acceptable to him. Now, I'm not so offended when he draws a time boundary because he's in the midst of working on something else. Since I know I'm really acceptable in his eyes, I can ride the waves and wait for the project to be done in his time, not mine."

For quite a long time, Reba and I were planning to go to a women's conference in another state. Because we lived in different parts of the country, we hadn't been together for quite some time, and both of us eagerly anticipated this time of renewed fellowship. Our registrations were paid, and the motel was reserved weeks in advance.

Shortly before the event, Reba's husband announced that the church board had planned and paid for a getaway vacation for just the two of them. That's right—it happened to be the exact same weekend as our get-together. Though she didn't want to, she had to tell me no and cancel our plans. She was genuinely sorry and we were both very disappointed. I had to *hear* her no, even though I was very disappointed. I shared my feelings honestly with her, but I also said that I would accept the change of plans.

We must give the other person the freedom to say no to us. We must be willing to hear no as well as say no sometimes.

However, some people will not hear no, as this story illustrates.

As my friends will tell you, I have a lot of fun keeping my age a secret. One day after I had told my "age story," a lady in the audience came up and said, "I really want to know how old you are."

Smiling, I said, "That's something I don't tell."

She got more serious, "I really want to know."

"As I said, that's my secret."

"No, I really want to know."

"That really is my secret." She would not hear or accept my no.

The question is, when someone says no to me, do I think *they* are bad or *I* am bad, or am I just sad or mad? I need to learn to be willing to graciously hear another person's no.

Help Others Draw Their Boundaries

Sometimes we can help others draw boundaries by not hearing, or allowing, their yes when we know they are doing it out of self-imposed pressure and blurred boundaries.

Ruth and I were working together on a project. I asked if she could call to get permission to use copyrighted material. She said that she would. As soon as the words were out of my mouth, I remembered she was extremely busy that day. So I asked, "Do you really have the time?"

"Yes, I will do it," she said.

Ruth wanted to help, but she didn't need one more thing in her busy day. I knew she had a hard time saying no, so I helped her with a boundary.

"Ruth," I explained, "this project is my responsibility. You don't need to feel guilty about not helping. You've already done your part."

USE GODLY WISDOM IN SETTING BOUNDARIES

We have been discussing the significance of setting limits on our behavior or another's behavior as it affects us. It is so important to understand boundaries and to have boundaries in all the varied relationships of life—for our own health and growth, for the glory of God, and for the other person's good and possible growth.

A warning is in order here. We must be discerning and careful not to try to set limits:

1. Prematurely
2. When they are unnecessary
3. When we need to hear something the other person is saying about us or our behavior
4. When we need to choose to deny ourselves a right or privilege for the sake of the relationship and for the glory of God

We need the discernment of the Spirit to know which sins, slights, or misunderstandings to cover (forgive) and which we need to address for the glory of God. My motive should not be my own comfort or to "get it off my chest" and load it onto the other person.

It is also important that we don't go to extremes in drawing boundaries—being either too passive or too aggressive. Make love your overall guideline, remembering that "love is the golden chain of all the virtues" (Colossians 3:14, Phillips). Ephesians 4:2 says, ". . . bearing with one another in love." The Phillips paraphrases that, ". . . making allowances for one another because you love one another."

When it is necessary or wise to draw a boundary, do it in a spirit of love and kindness. Be firm, yet affirming. Candace's story will tie together much of what we've been saying about boundaries.

Candace begins, "I was raised in a Christian home, where our parents gave selflessly to others. I automatically believed that is what dedicated Christians should do, give until it hurts—and then give more. Give until your back breaks and then give more. That to me was the Christian way of life. Even after I was married and had a family of my own, if anyone had a need, I was off to meet it. I had many talents, and of course, felt God needed every one of them. I couldn't get enough of always, always doing something for someone else."

Candace homeschooled her four very active children and was involved in community activities and a multitude of church activities—music, teaching, women's ministry, counseling, and general helper-of-all! But that wasn't everything. Whenever a need arose, people both in the church and community would say, "Well, Candace can do that, let's ask her."

Candace said, "How can I possibly say no. God wouldn't want me to say no. Besides, He has given me the gifts and the ability to do these things.

"Then a single mother with two children came to our church, and she needed a place to live. My husband and I decided to invite them to stay with us for a short time. That was the capstone on my stress! It was constant confusion. Our plan had been to help her out for three or four weeks, but it ran into ten months!

"The hardest thing was that for all of our giving of ourselves and our resources, she gave only bitterness in return. Her attitude was that since we were God's provision for her, why didn't we give her more?

"Slowly, I began to see that our giving her everything was not what God wanted for her or for us. Through talking with my sister-in-law, I finally realized that God wanted me to confront her in a tender, loving way and not just keep doing and giving. She needed to begin taking care of herself. Only after I was totally exhausted emotionally and physically was I able to come to that point. That was very, very difficult but very necessary for her as well as me. It was only when I took this step of obedience to the Lord and began saying some no's that I started coming out of burnout.

"The bad part of having that serving-serving mentality as a way of life was that I drastically neglected myself. There was just never any time for me to relax or do things I enjoy. I thought that was the way it should be. I believed that the way to please God was to please others, to constantly serve, serve, serve!

"Of course there is only one end to that way of living—exhaustion. After years of taking on way too much, I found myself with way more than I could handle, even with God's strength.

"When I finally listened to what God was saying to me, I came to realize that I was doing all of this out of pride and selfishness—because I got so much applause from others. I proudly thought it was something I could do for God, not necessarily what God wanted me to do. Once I jumped off the bandwagon and realized that God wanted me to take time for myself, I was able to put my feet up and spend long periods of time with Him, not just a few snatched minutes here or there on my way to doing this or doing that.

"I was totally physically and emotionally exhausted from the constant do, do, do, do; and it took many months to recuperate and to get my energy and my joyful spirit back. I praise God that He's brought me to the place where I can freely and with no guilt say, 'No, I really can't do that. God has given me plenty to do, and I'm to do that and to do it well.'"

Perhaps your boundaries are not as blurred as Candace's. Even so, we will all do well to check on our boundaries from time to time. Are there some small no's you need to practice with safe people?

Thoughts to Remember

Identify and take ownership of your property, but don't take responsibility for that which belongs to another.

"Am I now trying to win the approval of men, or of God? Or am I trying to please men?" (Galatians 1:10).

Practicing and Journaling

1. Continue your work on the ABC chart (page 141). Fill in for the third week
2. Write about a time when you didn't draw a boundary and you should have. Describe the situation and what you could have done differently
3. What is the major reason you hesitate to draw boundaries?
4. What are the consequences when you don't draw limits?

9

Conflict Resolution

The boundary issue is often a source of conflict between people. Not all conflict, however, is a boundary issue. There are at least seven basic sources of conflict between two people in various relationships: marriage partners, parent and child, friends, roommates, workmates, church workers—any two people made of flesh and bones and descended from Adam. Therefore, the first step in resolving conflict is to discern which issue is at work at the moment.

SOURCES OF CONFLICT

Crossed Boundaries

Many conflicts are over boundaries not respected; that is, crossed boundaries. Someone crosses over into my territory and violates my boundaries. They expect things of me that are really not my responsibility. Or people might demand things of me just to make them happy or comfortable. They use my things without my permission. They tell my secret to another, betraying my confidence. They do not respect my person or my property. This brings conflict between the two of us.

One of my friends didn't hesitate to open my purse to get something of mine that she wanted to use. However, I felt my purse was mine and that my privacy there should be guaranteed! She couldn't understand that. Weren't we good friends who trusted each other?

Yes, we were and we did, but there are limits even to the privileges of good friends. This caused some mild conflict, until I addressed it. She chose to honor my boundary and the conflict was resolved.

Someone might read another's mail or go into their computer and read their e-mail without their permission—A crossed boundary.

Sometimes children hear their mother telling things about them to her friends that they don't want her to tell—A crossed boundary.

A friend shared with her friends and family something about me that I had confided in her. I felt betrayed. She had crossed my boundary.

Polly was thrilled that her son had accepted Jesus as his Savior. The next morning she was telling one of her friends about it, and to her surprise, just then the son came through the room. He heard her, registered disappointment, and the mother wondered why.

Locked Wills: The I-Want-My-Way Stance

Many conflicts arise simply because each wants his or her own way and insists on holding out for it.

For one couple, it all started with assumptions not discussed. They had bought a new home that had an extra bathroom. He said nothing, but thought, "Now this bathroom will be a good one for me to use just for myself." She, also saying nothing, thought it would be very convenient for her use in caring for the children.

After they moved in, it soon became evident they had different viewpoints concerning this bathroom. He thought, "This bathroom is mine!"

She thought, "This bathroom is mine!" and she was not going to let go. Without saying anything, she left her hair equipment around just to give the clear message: "This bathroom is mine!" And the battle of the bathroom raged silently on.

Just at that time she attended the workshop. On her way home, she presented herself to the Lord with an attitude of openness and surrender, "Father, I really do want more harmony in our home, more oneness. If I have any blind spots, anything that is hindering, please show me. Is there anything, Father?"

The Lord said, "The *bathroom!*"

"The bathroom?"

"The *bathroom.*"

"Okay, Lord, if it must be the bathroom, it will be the bathroom."

When she got home she took her things out of the bathroom and really cleaned it up, wondering if her husband would even notice. "Lord," she said, "even if he doesn't notice, that's okay. I'm doing this for You." She gave up her way, her expectations, her resistance—no conditions attached.

He came home. Went past the bathroom. Didn't even notice. But it was okay; she had taken care of that. Sometime later she went to use the bathroom and saw a note, "This bathroom looks really neat. I like it! Your lover."

In surrendering the bathroom to the Lord, she gave up her *right* to have it her way. They were each determined to have their own way about the bathroom—locked wills, the I-want-my-way stance. It took one of them giving up that selfish way to begin to see the conflict resolved. This proved to be a giant step toward building harmony in their home.

Unspoken or Wrong Assumptions

Two different people will have two different viewpoints. That is natural, but the difficulty comes when I assume that the other person is thinking as I am thinking and that I know what she wants and what she is feeling or thinking without asking her. Thinking this way, we each build our own assumptions. Many times these are inaccurate, negative, and relationship-destroying assumptions. These wrong assumptions result in wrong conclusions, misunderstandings, misjudgments, resentments, hurts, alienation, suspicions, and distance in relationships.

"What shall I do?" Pauline asks.[1] "I can't trust my husband another day. I have enough evidence to convict a saint.

"First, I have this bill from a hotel in the Poconos for two guests, signed with my husband's signature. I've never been to the Poconos. Then I have a room key for a motel that I found in my husband's drawer. I've never been near that motel. Obviously he has!

"Last week, when I was visiting my mother in Chicago, I called home at 8 A.M. A sweet feminine voice answered the phone. He had a woman there at eight in the morning! I hung up without a word. What more do I need to prove that he's playing around?

"Three strikes and he's obviously out, if Pauline chooses to use the evidence to establish guilt."

What will Pauline choose to do? What would you do if you were in her situation? Pauline could be quiet and build resentment. She could immediately blow up in anger, accusing, judging, and threatening. Or she could ask some questions to find out how accurate her assumptions are. Actually, her husband could explain everything.

The facts were: "The bill from the hotel was from the forgotten ski trip Dad and son took last January. The motel key was left in the guest room by a visiting friend who had carried it off absent-mindedly and left it in the bureau drawer. The early morning feminine voice? Just a babysitter who came in early so the kids wouldn't be alone while dad was off to a 6 A.M. business breakfast."

When people assume that others should know what they are thinking or that their decisions should go unchallenged, they do not take the time to discuss things with others, and there is a clash! A moment of truth! A conflict!

Unfulfilled Expectations and Personalization

In a sense, wrong assumptions and unfulfilled expectations are similar and are often linked together. But there is enough difference to separate them and consider each as an independent source of conflict, especially when personalization—the conclusion that it is about me—comes into the picture.

The bathroom story illustrates this combination of unspoken assumptions and expectations—but without personalization being a major factor.

Very often we have unrealistic, unspoken, and even sometimes unconscious expectations of the other person. When the other person fails to meet our unspoken desires, we feel hurt, disappointed, put down, devalued, or frustrated. And an element that makes it even worse for us is that we tend to personalize about the situation; that is, I conclude that the event is a statement about me and especially about how the other person feels about me. That creates internal conflict, often results in emotional distance, and frequently breaks into open conflict!

When we have certain expectations of others and they do not follow through according to our expectation, we are greatly disappointed, and we conclude, "It's about me and their feelings and thoughts about me." The dashed hopes, disappointed expectations, and the personalization result in misunderstanding, resentment, accusations, guilt, and shame. These can only lead to emotional distance, inner turmoil, and outward conflict.

HE DOESN'T LOVE ME ANYMORE

Mary's strong complaint was, "My husband comes home late from work every night."

"Why do you think he does this, Mary?" her mentor asked.

"It's obvious! He comes home late because he doesn't love me anymore, and he doesn't want to be with me." Mary felt neglected and unloved.

Mary expects her husband to come home from work on time. When he doesn't, she takes it personally. This is a clear case of Mary's unspoken expectations of her husband that have not been fulfilled, and she has concluded by his behavior—his coming home late every night from work—that this makes a statement about her. To her, this behavior reveals his estimate of her. "He doesn't want to be with me; he doesn't love me." With that conclusion, of course, she feels neglected, unloved, angry, and bitter.

When Mary was asked if there could be other reasons for his continual lateness, she insisted this was *the* reason. Her mentor persisted in encouraging her to think of other possible reasons. Very reluctantly she came up with several: Perhaps he has a lifestyle of always being late. Perhaps he is a workaholic who wants to work long and hard to feel good about himself or to gain the approval of his supervisor. Or perhaps he has poor boundaries and lets his boss take advantage of him—expecting him to work overtime. Getting some other possibilities out in the open helped Mary to see that her sure and certain conclusion might not be the right one.

Certainly, some situations may need to be addressed, such as workaholism or neglecting to make time to be together. But when my focus is on *me* and what I think his behavior says about how he feels toward me (without discussing it), the situation doesn't get better. Rather, my feelings are hurt; I feel inadequate, unloved, rejected, awful; and conflict between us only increases. Almost without exception, however, when we think of several other possible reasons for the person's behavior, we begin to see that perhaps we have been building our thoughts and feelings on wrong assumptions.

Instead of personalizing, we need to stop, think, and ask ourselves, Is what the other person did or said a statement about me or about him? Is it a statement about what I am like or what he or she is like? Or is it a little of both? Develop the practice of thinking of several other possible reasons why the person is behaving the way he or she is.

I Personalized His Rudeness and Disrespect

In her younger years, Susan had felt that she was quite a competent nurse—knowledgeable and experienced in her field, with a love for her patients. Now after twenty years of being away from nursing, things had changed so much. Different techniques, equipment, and medications—all so unfamiliar to her now. She felt very inadequate. She worked hard, studied, took in seminars, and asked questions when she was unsure. Still she felt inadequate and very vulnerable.

Susan tells her story: "It happened that the specialist I worked for, though an excellent doctor, was very impatient, never affirming, and quick to make fun of me in front of other nurses and the patients. I was not only embarrassed, but it confirmed my thoughts that I was just not adequate for the job. I was a bad nurse. For a couple of years, I constantly felt inept. Then I gradually came to realize that he treated all the other nurses in the same harsh way. Daily, I would hear him put down even our most skilled, up-to-date nurse/supervisor—a precious gal and an excellent nurse.

"Finally, one day it dawned on me that his comments and behavior aren't primarily about me, they are about him. Yes, there are areas that I continually need to grow in, but he definitely had attitude and professional ethics problems. When I came to terms with what belonged to him and what belonged to me, I no longer personalized his behavior and comments. I was free to acknowledge that it was his problem and refused to own it myself."

Even if we are treated badly, we don't have to take that as a reflection of who we are. Susan came to realize that her doctor/supervisor, though he seemed to have little respect for her, had little respect for other nurses as well. She just happened to take the brunt of his rudeness and disrespect at times. His behavior is a commentary on who he is—a person with little respect for others.

Keep in mind: What other people say or do says much more about *them* than it does about you. How you react to them, though, says something about who you are. When the other person fails to meet our unspoken desires, we feel hurt, disappointed, put down, devalued, or frustrated. If we don't begin to communicate about it, the situation will create internal and sometimes open conflict!

Broken Promises

One wife shared that her husband was forever making promises that he did not fulfill. "Many times these promises relate to what he plans to do for or with me or the family. Each time I think, 'He means it this time and will surely fulfill his word,' but lo and behold, he doesn't. Then my hopes are dashed. I feel devastated and extremely disappointed. Again, I have to go through the painful process of readjusting my expectations.

"We've talked about this many, many times. Usually he is sorry and makes a new promise, but then he fails to follow through on that. He has good intentions, but after twenty years, I've learned that the only way I can cope with this is to give up my expectations and pray and hope that perhaps it will be different sometime."

Broken promises can bring conflict, distrust, uncertainty.

Conflicting or Blocked Goals

Another common source of conflict is when each person has a different goal—an unspoken or even an unconscious goal. Each assumes he can reach his goal unhindered by the other. Again, this is only assumed, not discussed. Each proceeds ahead to accomplish his individual goal until their goals clash. Then one or both feels frustrated, slighted, taken advantage of, not cared about, hurt, angry. The smooth path to accomplishing their goal has been blocked.

A blocked goal is when something has happened that hinders my getting to my goal, my agenda. This may be a clash with another person's goals, or it can be an event that has blocked me. Angry feelings usually indicate a blocked goal. We may react by venting our anger in a temper flare at the situation or by trying to strike back at the person who has kept us from reaching our goal. When anger occurs, ask, What goal of mine is blocked or is in conflict with another's goal?

Sometimes after arriving home from a speaking trip I would have things I wanted to do—some were not urgent, but they were things I was excited about getting into. Nettie, my house-mate and coworker, and I did not share with one another what we were thinking or planning, we simply went about doing our own thing. Then, she would come to me wanting some help with a business problem or a decision that required lengthy discussion, and I would feel frustrated and would sometimes express it in unloving ways—like the "Christian" silent treatment. I felt my time wasn't my own, and my goals weren't important. I know she felt the same way whenever I tried to involve her in projects that she hadn't planned for that day.

Finally, we learned that the source of this frustration was our conflicting goals, which we had failed to talk about. We had simply assumed we could involve the other at the time we wanted. We learned a very simple solution. Now we try to ask, "What do you plan to do today? Is there anything you want me to be involved in?"

CLASHING GOALS

"Yesterday," Ann wrote, "I carefully set some specific goals to do a number of special things to show love to my family: (1) do my teenager's laundry (she's been doing her own for the past two years),(2) make both the girls' beds—just for a love surprise, (3) go to the grocery store, (4) write letters, (5) clean up the kitchen, and (6) spend time preparing a lovely supper for the family. In the morning, things were going very well, and I got much accomplished.

"At 12:30, my husband came in as I was unpacking the grocery bags. He announced that a staff member was coming over in fifteen minutes for a difficult confrontation session. Would I help? I thought, 'If I do that, my goals will certainly not be accomplished. This session could take hours. How can I make the special meal I was planning for the family—or even an ordinary one?'

"I shut down! Of course he noticed how quiet and unresponsive I was. Under the pressure of my wrong response, he decided to have the session on his own.

"Our goals had clashed. His goal was to get through the counseling session with my help. My goal was to get all six things done. I really would have been happy to give him time for the counseling session, but he had not told me ahead of time when to expect it, and I had already planned a very full day. It's the surprise factor that is so hard for me to handle. I feel that he thinks his goals are more important and that mine don't count. I get so frustrated when he always wants me to help him complete his goals, because he never helps me complete my goals."

Have I Been Sinned Against?

A seventh possible source of conflict is that I have been sinned against.

"When Prince Charming came along," wrote Rae Ann, "I was delighted. He was a dedicated Christian, a pastor's son, always active in Christian ministry, which is also my heartthrob and commitment. We married, but I can't say that we lived happily ever after, serving the Lord with joy.

"The fifth year of our marriage began years of discovery for me. Time and again I found things hidden. At first I made very little of these pornographic pictures and magazines. When I mentioned it to him, he confessed and repented; I forgave him and believed in him again. I tried hard to be the kind of wife I should be to him. But there was more discovery, more 'repentance,' and more guilt and blame for me.

"After three years of this happening time and again, I began to feel hopeless and suicidal because our marriage was falling apart. We had tried everything. We talked calmly, we yelled, we argued, but there was no lasting change in his behavior. Finally I became desperate and spilled out all my suicidal feelings. He was scared. It was better for a while, but soon I discovered more pornographic material and again addressed it. He always had some way of blaming me, and insisted that I was overly critical, had unrealistic expectations, and just needed to accept him as he was. I always thought, 'This must be my fault. I need to give more to him sexually—and I tried to.'

"From day one, I carried all of this inside me. I would tell no one. I was willing to end my life rather than reveal to others what was going on. I guess I thought I was protecting myself as well as him. I didn't want people telling me that I had made a mistake in marrying him or that if I had been the right kind of wife this wouldn't have happened. I secretly wondered if God was punishing me for some reason. Also, I was afraid revealing this might ruin his Christian testimony. People loved his Bible teaching and his ministry.

"When suicide thoughts began to plague me again, I went to a counselor. For one whole year, we talked about my anger problem but never about my husband's addiction. The counseling did help me identify some of my needs, but I got more and more depressed as I became more aware of how deeply his lifestyle was affecting him and our relationship.

"I lived with this secret and all the pain, confusion, and depression for seventeen years. Then one day, while having lunch with a friend, I mentioned there were some serious problems in our marriage. She listened empathetically, but quite immediately asked if she could ask a very pointed question. The question was, 'Is he involved in pornography?' and I answered with a brief but honest, 'Yes.' That was the first time that I had shared with anyone. That was a turning point for me, because I felt my friend accepted me, supported, and comforted me. She gently but firmly urged me to get some professional help from someone who had training and experience in counseling for sexual addictions. I searched until I finally found a psychiatrist who specialized and was experienced in this field. I made an appointment and then approached my husband saying, 'I've made an appointment with a doctor who specializes in sexual addictions. Either we can go together, or I am going alone.' He chose for us to go together. Sam entered into a special program for sexual addicts, both group and individual therapy.

"Even though he kept saying, 'This group therapy isn't for me,' he stayed with it for a year. The counseling was working for him, but it did nothing for me or our marriage.

"Again, feeling very depressed and extremely hopeless, I was about ready for suicide when a friend recommended a counselor for *me*—not for our marriage or my husband's problem. She was a godsend. It was the first time a counselor had validated me and my feeling that things were not right with my husband. Her counsel was so different than the standard, 'You must spend more time together.' I needed her validation and clarification. Sam was willing to pursue marriage counseling again when he began to see a change in me.

"Through this counseling I was beginning to understand more about boundaries—what was and what was not my responsibility. Then I began to share my needs and set limits as to what I would and wouldn't do or allow. I came to realize that I had spent years trying to see that he didn't get angry and trying to take care of him, so that he wouldn't be unhappy and go back into the old habits.

"I came to realize I needed time to separate—not divorce, but to take a time out. When I told him, he said, 'Where are *you* going to go?' This was his usual pattern—to see to it that he was comfortable. He's very self-centered.

"Of course, some didn't understand why I needed to move out. One great support was my Bible study group. Though they had no knowledge of the addiction, they trusted my judgment and supported me. That was a big help.

"As I spent this separate time, I began to feel more empowered to cope with life and the situation. I needed to learn to let go, not worry about him, and not take any responsibility for what he was doing or how he was feeling. I had to come to realize that my happiness and my sufficiency was in the Lord, and not in him.

"Why did I choose to move back after ten months? Sam told me that he listened to a taped message on self-pleasing and said that he had had a life change. I didn't believe him. He said that from now on the Lord was going to be first in his life, and then me. I told him I needed to see some evidence. 'I'm not going to move back until you see our pastor and tell him your whole story. You need to admit your adultery to someone in authority who could do you damage. After you do that, then I want us to say our marriage vows over again. We need a new marriage. I don't want just one more promise. I want evidence that this change is for real.'

"On his own he called our pastor for an appointment. (That was different!) Sam told our pastor his whole story and took the full responsibility for his behavior; he didn't blame me or anything else. Not until that happened could I be convinced that it was for real this time. So, after that time with our pastor and our renewed wedding vows, I was willing to move back in again.

"Two years have passed and we are doing great! Obviously, there are still some struggles, but this is better than we have ever had it. I found that identifying the problem, getting him to a place of being willing to get help, and then actually finding someone who understands both of us and has some solutions is a long process. For us, it took years."

REVIEW SOME SIGNIFICANT POINTS

Notice a few of the very significant points this story brings out. Rae Ann's sense of needing to keep the secret was so strong that she considered suicide rather than telling. For one year she would not tell her counselor about the addiction. She had feelings of guilt and shame for his problem. She needed validation and also a willingness to see her need for changes. She had to be confronted by a safe friend. She needed some time of separation, so she shared that with her husband and moved out for a time. She made some conditions for him to meet before she would move back home. She had been deeply sinned against, and the healing process took a long time.

Analyze the Conflict

Become Aware

In attempting to understand and work toward a resolution to conflict, my first step is awareness. My negative feelings are key to realizing there is conflict. Pay attention to the emotion; admit, "I feel angry." If I'm feeling angry, frustrated, hurt, disappointed, or resentful, this is my clue that there is a problem somewhere. I should give attention to these emotions and ask myself, "What is wrong? What am I feeling? Where is the conflict?"

Identify the Issue

Attempt to discern what is actually going on—how do I feel and what are the real issues? Do I feel hurt, angry, violated, resentful, disappointed, hopeless? Ask yourself questions to find out what your feelings are and where they are coming from.

Discern which of the seven common sources of conflict is the basic cause of the conflict—crossed boundaries, locked wills, unspoken or wrong assumptions, unfulfilled expectations, broken promises, a conflict of goals, or have I been sinned against?

Think back to a time when you had a conflict with another person. Which of these seven possible issues was it?

Wrong Ways of Responding in Conflict

Four Typical Wrong Ways of Responding*

When we feel angry, hurt, disappointed, or frustrated, we typically respond in one of four wrong and ineffective styles: passively,

---

* Material on "Four Typical Wrong Ways of Responding in Conflict" has been adapted from the book, *Speaking the Truth in Love* by Henry Virkler, Ph.D. Book is available from Dr. Virkler and may be ordered by sending e-mail to HVirkler@aol.com or by calling (561) 845-1934.

aggressively, passive-aggressively, or manipulatively. There is a fifth and proper response style, which we will talk about later. First let's get an understanding of these ineffective response styles:

THE PASSIVE RESPONSE STYLE

Some of the ways we respond passively are:

- We fail to express our disappointment or hurt
- We say yes when we really want to say no
- We allow others to make decisions about our lives with which we disagree

Passive people may try to stand up for their desires or needs, but they do it so timidly that others readily coerce them into doing things their way. They sacrifice their own wishes, feelings, and desires in order to be accepted by others. They consider the other person's thoughts and feelings as much more important than their own.

In short, the passive style says: "I value you, but I don't value me."

At first, passive people tend to feel okay about themselves because they believe they're acting in a Christian manner—turning the other cheek, denying self, and returning good for evil. However, they may be frustrated and depressed because other people don't consider their feelings and make adjustments to accommodate them.

Recall the lady who, at a family gathering, volunteered to eat in the kitchen while all the rest had a lot of fun together in the dining room. As she sat alone, feeling left out, she began to resent all of them, but she didn't say a word about it. Later, she said, "Now I realize I allowed myself to be put in this situation. Next time, we will do things differently. I will protect myself from this kind of thing. We could have set up an additional table so all of us could be together."

The passive person must realize he has *chosen* to let others override and intimidate him. No one can intimidate you without your choosing to let them.

THE AGGRESSIVE RESPONSE STYLE

We respond aggressively whenever we try to reach our goals in ways that do not respect the needs, feelings, goals, or desires of others around us.

These aggressive behaviors say: "I value me, but I don't value you."

Aggressive behavior is often an angry response to having a goal blocked by someone else. Some of our goals that may be blocked by others are:

- Arriving somewhere on time
- Completing a task without being interrupted
- Being approved of, affirmed, and agreed with

Usually the purpose of an aggressive response is either to punish the person who has blocked us from reaching a goal, or to intimidate that person into withdrawing the action that blocked us. Aggressive behavior includes name-calling, belittling, blaming, interrupting, insisting on having the last word, or more severe forms—such as physical violence.

THE PASSIVE-AGGRESSIVE RESPONSE STYLE

This includes characteristics of both the passive and aggressive styles. It usually begins when we allow someone to do things that bother us, or when we fail to tell someone he isn't doing what we expect. Eventually the irritations build up and begin to come out in ridicule, sarcasm, or silence, designed to punish. The response may even slip out several hours or days *after* the situation occurred.

Christians frequently use the silent treatment, which is intended to send a very powerful message: "I don't like something you've done, and I'm withdrawing from you to show you how much I don't like it."

The passive-aggressive attitude is: "I don't value me, and I don't value you."

THE MANIPULATIVE RESPONSE STYLE

A fourth conflict response style is manipulation. Whereas, aggressive people use angry threats and intimidation, manipulative people use more indirect means. They create fear by stating or implying that something bad will happen to the person they want to manipulate, or even to the manipulator, if they don't get their way.

For example, a manipulative mother would not tell her daughter directly what she desired, but would cry, "I don't know what I'm going to do with you," or, "You're going to drive me crazy!"

A father who had left his family told his ten-year-old daughter that he would return to the family if she got straight A's in school.

Manipulation may take several forms:

Comparing: "Any Christian who really loves the Lord would/ wouldn't . . . Any good husband would/wouldn't . . . Why can't you be like your brother/sister/kids at church?"

Sarah recalled her mother saying one Sunday after church, "Sarah, I wish you would sit nicely and listen in church like Gina and Iris do." But Sarah knew that usually those girls *didn't* sit quietly and listen most of the time, but she herself did. After many years, Sarah still remembered her mother's words of comparison because they hurt so much, and they were really inaccurate.

Children quickly learn to use the same manipulative strategy: "I wish you were like my friends' parents. They let them . . ."

Guilt-producing statements: "After all I've done for you, how could you do this (or fail to do this) for me? . . . If you really loved me, you would . . . If you don't quit doing that, you'll drive me crazy/make me commit suicide/etc . . . God won't love you if . . ."

One woman shared that she felt manipulated or shamed into helping with the work at home by hints, sighs, and comments, "I'm so tired and have so much work to do yet." It would have been so much better if her mother had assigned a certain amount of work, with the understanding that when the daughter got that done, she was finished for the day or morning and could do her own projects.

Dwelling on negative details: Emphasizing details that place the other person in an unfavorable light. For example, a husband who wants his wife to change her behavior can rattle off a list of things she does inadequately, without noting any of the positive things she does. The wife thinks she must give in to his demands, since she is performing inadequately in so many other areas.

Whining: People will often give in to the whiner because they want to be free of the noise the whiner makes. Because it works, some people continue this method throughout life.

When I taught middle school, one of my students would come up, and in a whiny voice, ask a question or make a statement. I knew he needed to break this habit, so I discussed it with him. Then I told him what I would do to help him become aware when he was doing it. I said I would not answer him when he used that voice; I would hear him as soon as he changed his voice tone. I followed through on the plan, and he improved.

The manipulator, like the aggressive person, operates from the position: "I value me, but I don't value you."

Application of Wrong Response Styles

We've discussed four wrong styles of response. Now let's take a look at an exchange between a mother and her teenage daughter, Julie, and see how each response style might work out in this situation.

THE PASSIVE RESPONSE STYLE

MOTHER: "Julie, I would like you to clean up your room. We'll be having company this evening and . . ."

JULIE (interrupting): "My room is perfectly fine! It's just as picked up as any of my friends' rooms are!"

MOTHER (quietly and a little timidly): "Julie, you have dirty clothes lying on the floor and under the bed. Your bed isn't made, and there's a wet towel . . . "

JULIE (interrupting again): "Well, if you don't like my room the way I keep it, why don't you do something about it? You don't have anything to do while I'm in school anyway!"

Julie abruptly goes to the family room, slamming the door as she leaves. She turns the stereo on at a deafening volume. Mother decides to straighten up Julie's room so that she won't be embarrassed when company comes.

Although her mother's first statement sounds somewhat confident, Julie knows from past experience that she can easily intimidate her mother back into the passive response.

Mother *invites* Julie to intimidate her by: (1) talking softly and timidly, (2) allowing Julie to interrupt her and end the conversation without correcting her, and (3) cleaning Julie's room for her.

THE AGGRESSIVE RESPONSE STYLE

Julie's responses to her mother illustrate the aggressive response style. Julie was aggressive by: (1) not caring to consider why a clean room was important to her mother, (2) interrupting her mother twice, (3) leaving the conversation abruptly before her mother finished, and (4) blocking her mother out by playing the stereo.

Aggressive behavior can result from having a goal blocked by someone else. Julie's goal was to not have to clean her room. Her mother's request blocked that goal and Julie became angry.

THE PASSIVE-AGGRESSIVE RESPONSE STYLE

If Julie's mother had been passive-aggressive rather than passive, she might be frustrated by Julie's messy room, but rather than talk with Julie about this directly, she might express her frustration in any of the following ways: (1) being less friendly toward Julie—without telling her why, (2) failing to do some of the things she normally did for Julie—without saying why, (3) not allowing Julie to take part in some activity—without telling her why, or (4) discussing with other mothers how irresponsible Julie is.

THE MANIPULATIVE RESPONSE STYLE

What might Julie's mother have done to try to manipulate her into cleaning her room? (1) Compared her to one of her friends, spelling out how the friend always keeps such a neat, clean room, company or not; (2) tried to control her with guilt, "Since I've done this and this, can't you at least clean up your room?"

In addition to being ineffective in relationships and not solving the problem, these wrong response styles tend to disrespect the person and destroy a proper sense of worth. The passive person feels she doesn't count, lacks control of her life, and has low feelings of worth. The aggressive person may feel good temporarily because she got what she wanted, but then she realizes she has lost a relationship and feels lonely. The passive-aggressive person sees how his weakness and wrong behavior wound and alienate others, and he doesn't feel good about himself. The manipulative person rarely feels good about himself, because he knows his methods are unhealthy and unfair.

THE JESUS WAY

There is a right response style that is healthy and freeing for both people involved, and it can be a very significant factor in resolving the conflict.

The first four ways of responding that we looked at are *reacting* instead of *choosing* to act righteously—the *Jesus way*. The Jesus way is to think, then choose how to act—not simply to react.

Consider Jesus' Way

I see Jesus responding to conflict in three basic ways, depending on what the occasion required:

BOLD POSITIVE ACTION AND SPEAKING TRUTH

When necessary, Jesus took action for righteousness'. At times He boldly moved in to correct wrong behavior. Jesus' confronting of the merchants and money changers in the temple is perhaps the most graphic record of Jesus taking bold positive action to confront wrong behavior. John tells the story.

He made a whip out of cords, and drove all the animals and the men selling them out of the temple area. He scattered the coins of the money changers and overturned their tables. "Get these out of here! How dare you turn my Father's house into a market!" (See John 2:13–17.)

Jesus was *acting* from controlled strength, not *reacting* with a temper out of control. He was acting in behalf of righteousness, not from a desire to get His own selfish way.

At another time, Jesus boldly and assertively confronted the Pharisees and denounced their practices. He called them hypocrites six times and then went on to say they were blind guides, blind fools, snakes, and vipers (see Matthew 23:1–39).

Why did He speak so boldly and clearly to these people? They were spiritual abusers—spiritually abusing the people by perverting and misapplying truth. Jesus was free to nourish even the Pharisees with bold love! Sometimes that meant strong confrontation. But before we leave the scene, let's hear His heart of compassion for these same people: "O Jerusalem, Jerusalem . . . how often I have longed to gather your children together, as a hen gathers her chicks under her wings, but you were not willing" (v. 37).

Jesus spoke strong truth, but with a heart of love.

Chosen Silence

Another response of Jesus to conflict was silence—chosen silence. The Bible says: "Who, when he [Jesus] was reviled, reviled not again . . ." (1 Peter 2:23, KJV). And, "He opened not his mouth . . ." (Isaiah 53:7, KJV).

This was not a silence of fear, nor the silent treatment, nor seething silence. At times He chose to be misunderstood without giving any explanation. He chose silence from a position of strength.

Speaking Truth in Love

This style is so typical of Jesus. He distinctly spoke the truth with a heart of love, clearly addressing wrong thinking and wrong behavior. He cared enough to confront the issue with love. He was free to nourish with bold love!

When Jesus said this, one of the officials nearby struck him in the face. "Is this the way you answer the high priest?" he demanded.

Jesus replied, "If I said something wrong, testify as to what is wrong. But if I spoke the truth, why did you strike me?" (John 18:22–23)

Remember when Mary poured expensive perfume on Jesus' feet and Judas accused her of being wasteful and tried to shame her? Jesus became Mary's "defense attorney" and helped her draw boundaries. See how He nourished both of them with bold love.

"Leave her alone," Jesus replied. "You will always have the poor among you, but you will not always have me" (John 12:7–8).

The Jesus style/way actually says: "I value you, and I value Me."

Follow the Jesus Way

Not only does Jesus model in His life what our response should be, but Scripture also commands that we follow the model, "speaking the truth in love" (Ephesians 4:15). That's the Jesus way.

When someone wrongs us and the situation is not corrected, our fellowship with that person is hindered. We tend to isolate, become cool, and draw away from that one. Instead, the Bible says, "If your brother sins against you, go and show him his fault" (Matthew 18:15).

It is true that sometimes the other person won't hear or admit wrong. In that case harmony cannot be restored, but you are free if you have taken care of what is your responsibility. The Scripture says, "If it is possible, as far as it depends on you, live at peace with everyone" (Romans 12:18).

However, there is a need to face the situation and address wrong behavior that destroys relationships or damages the person. For such an occasion, the Scripture says we are to speak the truth in love. Let's give attention to these three instructions one by one.

First, Speak

Much anger and conflict comes because we do not speak. Instead, we make assumptions, have unspoken expectations, or even misread body language. The result is that we stuff the bad feelings, build resentment, and create distance.

We should respect the person enough to talk about issues that destroy healthy relationships. We should care about God's glory, the relationship, and the person's growth. Care enough to confront—to speak.

SECOND, SPEAK THE TRUTH

Be honest. If you are too busy to do that "one more thing" someone is asking you to do, say so.

In speaking the truth in love, sometimes we can simply say no. At other times, give a simple statement, "I would really prefer not to spend Saturday morning shopping." But frequently, it is good to give the reason for your preference. Giving the reason could give the person more understanding, and he can give you more consideration.

When there is a conflict in goals, share your goal without anger and explain why this goal is important to you. Try also to find out the other person's goal. Then attempt to work out a compromise that is acceptable to both of you. If a compromise cannot be reached, denying yourself and deferring to the wishes of the other may be the only answer—except in situations that involve moral decisions.

Choosing to defer to the other is very different than being so passive or so discounting of yourself that you can't say anything but "have it your way." Lovingly deferring is acting out of strength and personal choice rather than out of weakness, fear, intimidation, or a lack of boundaries.

THIRD, SPEAK THE TRUTH IN LOVE

As you speak hard-to-hear truth, use grace. Have a loving, affirming attitude. Affirm their efforts, good intentions, or understanding. Choose to value the other person's feelings, rights, and goals. Galatians 6:1 says that to help restore someone from a fault we must come to him in a spirit of love and meekness, not pride.

Dumping or unloading our anger on someone is not the way of the cross. Our goal should be never to take out our wrath on, assault, hurt, or punish someone. Rather, we are to confront them with a desire to benefit them.

My reason for approaching the person is to reconcile and solve the problem, not to be punitive or wrathful. Therefore my manner should be calm and kind, but clear and definite on the issue. Say things like, "I'm really bothered by this, and I want us to work this out."

Speaking in love is reflected not only in the words but also in the voice tone. The old saying is so true: "It's not what you say, but it's the way you say it." Tone can often be offensive and unloving, and it communicates our attitude of heart. One day a little girl asked her mother, "Mommy, could we take you to the doctor and get your voice fixed?"

Statistics say that 38 percent of what we communicate is communicated by our voice—tone, tempo, volume. "Ho-o-one-e-e!!"

We can speak in a warm, gentle, confident voice or in a cold, harsh, stern voice tone. A voice that is too soft communicates a lack of confidence and suggests you are easily manipulated or intimidated. A voice that is squeaky or whiny will not command respect. A harsh, loud, demanding voice will usually turn people away.

A lower-pitched voice is associated with confidence and strength and is quieting. A higher pitch suggests anxiety or insecurity and is disquieting. The voice tone is an essential element in speaking the truth in love.

Applying the Jesus Way

The speak-the-truth-in-love style, or the Jesus way, is the ability to courageously express our thoughts, feelings, desires, and goals in such a way that we will show love and respect for the other person and his thoughts, feelings, desires, and goals. It includes the ability to say no to requests that conflict with your priorities, as well as the ability to defend yourself against wrong accusations.

A REPLAY OF JULIE AND HER MOTHER

To put before us a positive, helpful example, let's replay our scenario between Julie and her mother. This time Julie's mother takes the Jesus way, speaking the truth in love.

MOTHER: "Julie, I would like you to clean up your room. We'll be having company this evening and . . ."

JULIE (interrupting): "My room is perfectly fine! It's just as picked up as any of my friends' rooms are!"

MOTHER (with gentle firmness): "Julie, you are not to interrupt me when I'm speaking to you. The issue is not what your friends' rooms look like. The issue is that your room is not acceptable *to me* in light of the fact that we will be having company this evening. You have dirty clothes lying on the floor and under your bed. Your bed isn't made, and the wet towel lying on it has made your sheets and blankets all wet. I want you to clean up your room and bathroom to my satisfaction before you do anything else this afternoon."

JULIE (exasperatedly): "Oh, Mom! Terri was coming over right after school, and we were going to the mall. Why do you have to be so unreasonable?"

MOTHER (normal tone of voice): "I don't think it's unreasonable to expect you to clean up your room each day. You know you are to do this before leaving for school each morning. If you had done these things then, you wouldn't be needing to now. Also, you know we have a family rule that you are to check with your father or me before making plans with your friends. I'm sorry if you and Terri are frustrated about not being able to go to the mall this afternoon, but you wouldn't be in this difficulty if you had observed our family rules."

JULIE (pouting tone): "Why can't you just close the door to my room when the company is here?"

MOTHER: "I could, but that wouldn't change the fact that you have dirty clothes to put in the wash, a damp bed that needs changing, and at least forty-five minutes of work to get your bedroom and bathroom looking presentable. It's not just for company's sake that we keep the house picked up. The family has to live here seven days a week. Your father and I have made a joint decision—we believe it is fair and reasonable to expect each family member to do a share of keeping the house attractive and picked up. You and your friends may not agree with our rule, but while you *live* with us you must abide by our rules. You may either try to call

Terri now and reschedule your trip to the mall, or you may wait until she gets here and tell her of your change in plans then."

JULIE (recognizing that her mother is not going to change her mind): "Okay."

The Jesus way respects and values the other person and does not devalue self. We want to develop and grow in following the Jesus way—speaking the truth in love! As we speak hard-to-hear truth, we must do it with grace. This means having a loving, affirming attitude and choosing to value the other person's feelings and rights. This is the foundation we must build before we confront someone about an issue that needs to be dealt with or corrected.

THOUGHTS TO REMEMBER

Keep in mind that what other people say or do says more about them than it does about you. How you react to them says something about you.

Speak the truth in love. Love is patient; love is kind. Make allowances for one another because you love one another. (See Ephesians 4:15, 1 Corinthians 13:4, and Ephesians 4:2; Phillips.)

PRACTICING AND JOURNALING

Think through and evaluate your conflict areas:

1. With whom do you tend to have the most conflict?
2. Which one of the seven typical sources of conflict initiates your conflicts most frequently?
3. What is your most typical wrong response to conflict? How do you feel you can change that?

10

Confrontation

Jana led a Bible study for mothers of young children on Tuesday mornings. Six weeks into their study, she noticed one of the ladies seemed to avoid her. Jana felt it was important to see if she could resolve the problem.

"Rita, I'm not sure if my perception is right, but I feel you're uncomfortable when I'm around. You seem very open with others in the group, but if I approach, you stop talking. Have I done something to hurt or upset you?"

Rita stepped back and folded her arms, "Well, not upset maybe . . . but I'm definitely disappointed with you. In fact, I'm not sure I want to continue this study."

"Oh Rita," Jana spoke kindly, "I would be sorry if you stopped coming. Can you be more specific? What have I done to upset you?"

"I'm not upset! I just don't think I can respect you as a Bible teacher, especially concerning parenting subjects."

"Have I taught something you disagree with or find in error?"

"Error?" Rita exploded, "Why, you're a hypocrite, Jana! Every week you present yourself as a source of wisdom and guidance for us poor, struggling mothers."

"Well, Rita, I don't see myself as any kind of expert. Do I come across in a superior way? I don't have all the answers. I'm still growing in parenting too, and I'm constantly noticing my own weaknesses."

"Weaknesses! What an excuse to cover your sin! I saw you last week at the grocery store with your son. You went right past me in the produce area and didn't even say 'hi.' Then your son tried to climb out of the cart, and you shoved him back into the cart. The way you yelled at him, I bet the whole store could hear you! What an incredibly bad testimony! I was ashamed—and to think that you lead a Bible study on mothering!"

Jana spoke calmly, "I'm sorry I didn't see you in the store. I would have welcomed a 'hello' from another adult. I don't remember the exact incident you saw, but I do know I struggle with being impatient with my son—especially in the grocery store. I really do need to improve in my mothering skills, and I see our group as a chance to learn how to do better. When Pastor Larson and the women's ministry team asked me to lead this study, I wasn't sure, but I said I was willing to try. Do you feel they made a mistake?"

"Well," Rita spoke harshly, "when I told Pastor Larson what I had seen in the store, he as much as said you don't really have the spiritual maturity to handle this job. It's just that you have a personality that other people like, so they follow you. If you truly cared about others as our leader, you would've at least picked up the phone and called me last week while my husband was out of town. I know you knew because it was on the prayer list."

"Rita, I sense the hurt you feel I have caused you. I can imagine how lonely you felt with your husband away. I'm sorry I missed the chance to be your friend by calling you. I hope you'll give me another chance."

As Rita turned away, her parting words were, "Don't count on it. I don't think you have what I need in a friend anyway."

It may seem hard to believe that this was an actual encounter between two women. Jana had sensed a breach in fellowship and took the initiative to attempt a reconciliation the Jesus way. Her attitude was humble, open to correction, not self-defensive or accusing. She even admitted her own faults. She kept asking good questions to encourage Rita to share just how she really felt about her, but the situation was not resolved. It takes the two people working together to be reconciled, and Rita chose not to understand, love, or forgive. The Bible says, "If it is possible, as much as depends on you, live peaceably with all men" (Romans 12:18, NKJV).

THE IMPORTANCE OF CONFRONTING

The word *confront* can be a heavy word, and it can be both misunderstood and misapplied. Perhaps the expression *address the situation* will clarify what we mean by confronting. Webster says *address* means "to use skill and tact in handling situations." That's speaking the truth in love.

Let's think of the word *confront* as "addressing the situation in love, using skill and tact." David Augsburger, in *Caring Enough to Confront,* calls it *Care-fronting.*[1] Care-fronting expresses both the caring and the confronting. We must discover care-fronting ways of giving both truth and love.

Conflict in relationships simply happens. In itself it is neither good nor bad, right nor wrong. Conflict is normal and can even be beneficial to the relationship. It can also be very painful and devastating, depending to a large extent on *how* we work through our differences. In his preface, Augsburger writes: "It is not the conflicts that need to concern us, but how the conflicts are handled. The frontal impact of our coming together can be creative, strengthening, and growth producing. If, that is, we do not choose the cold hostilities of rejection, insult, and affront."

The concept of boundaries (chapters 7–8) encourages us to be responsible for our own feelings, attitudes, and reactions. You cannot *make* me angry, discouraged, disgusted, or depressed. These belong to me. When I realize what is my responsibility and my property and what belongs to the other person, I am free to choose to respond in understanding ways, but also to address situations that need to be addressed—courageously and with love.

In choosing to speak the truth in love, I put an end to the blame or victim game and get on with the real issues. I ask myself, "What is the loving, responsible thing to do?"

David Augsburger defines Care-fronting: "Confront by saying what you really *want.* Care enough to say what you really *feel*" (italics mine). One example he gives is when you are criticized and feel rejected. The tendency is to sulk or brood over the hurt. Instead, you could say, "When you criticize me like that, I feel rejected. I hurt. I usually run. But what I really want is to feel close to you. And I want your respect."[2]

Say how you really feel and what you really want. This is caring enough to confront, addressing the situation with skill and tact, speaking the truth in love. When we're cut off by another's offending words, silent withdrawal is not the way to go. It is self-defeating, relationship-damaging, and is not the loving thing to do.

David Augsburger urges us to care enough to confront, working through our differences "by giving clear messages of 'I care' and 'I want'. . . . I want to stay in respectful relationships with you, *and* I want you to know where I stand and what I'm feeling, needing, valuing and wanting." And I would add, care more for the person and the relationship than for the issue and for winning, or even settling for peace at any price.

He Never Had Time to Listen

One wife had this creative way of sharing her feelings and needs: "Sometime ago I had a problem getting my husband to spend time with me. He is a physician, often comes home late, and really enjoys being alone. It seemed he never had time to listen to me or hear the concerns of raising our two sons.

"One night as we were getting ready for bed, I asked him how long he allotted his patients for an office visit. 'Fifteen minutes,' he said.

" 'And how much do you charge them?'

" '$60,' he replied.

"I went to the closet, took out my purse and quietly and calmly handed him $60, asking for fifteen minutes of his undivided attention. I talked; he listened. Then he advised, 'You need to send your husband in. He really needs to listen to you more.' Now, months later, he not only asks me to share with him my concerns, but seems to know when I need to talk with him, and he suggests it first."

This dear woman could have sat passively by when she needed to address the issue concerning their two sons and have her need listened to.

Perhaps you remember the illustration of the family that went for a friendly walk. Twelve-year-old Susie started sharing a recent thrilling event with Dad, when all of a sudden he left to give a child a push on the swing. Disappointed and hurt, Susie looked up at her mother and said, "Mom, Dad isn't interested in me."

Mother acknowledged the hurt and said, "You must tell your dad about how you feel."

With mother's encouragement, Susie addressed the situation with her dad. He responded and began listening and showing interest again. Mother knew we must care about the relationship enough to risk telling the other what we need.

"My husband and I finally learned that confrontation within our marriage was very, very important," Peggy wrote. "It is so easy for both of us just to sweep things under the rug. If someone is hurt or something goes wrong, sweep it under the rug. Don't bring it up. Keep peace at all costs.

"Instead of confronting it's so easy just to hide my feelings and try to forget the problem by going off and doing things for others. This just creates more distance between my husband and me. To lovingly confront, one must risk some conflict, misunderstanding, and hurt at first; but, it can result in a deeper oneness. Marriage oneness does not happen unless we face and share the real issues with one another. We learned that even though it hurts, we have to sit down and talk it out. Then we can build a strong relationship together." Now they care enough to confront.

Many conflicts are resolved by my giving up my selfish way. On the other hand, many issues are much more critical. Some can be handled on the spot, speaking the truth in love. Others need more prayer, thought, and perhaps advice from others, as Proverbs suggests:

> For waging war you need guidance, and for victory many advisers.
> (Proverbs 24:6)

Make plans by seeking advice; if you wage war, obtain guidance. (Proverbs 20:18)

The principle is: When you get into the heavy stuff, get some helpful advice from people who are experienced in this field.

GUIDELINES FOR CONFRONTING

Remember, when we use the word *confront*, we mean addressing the situation in love—deeply caring for the relationship and the person. Let's consider some general guidelines for how and why we should confront. Some of these will apply to all situations; some will not be necessary for the less involved, less critical situations. You will need to discern which guidelines to use.

Decide Why You Need to Confront

To determine whether or not the situation is one that calls for confronting ask yourself, "Why am I confronting?" It should not be to dump or unload your anger just to try to make you feel more comfortable. Nor should it be to lambaste others and put them in their place, or punish, tear down, and get even.

Again, ask yourself the three significant questions: (1) Would it be for the good or growth of person; (2) for the good of the cause—to move toward more healthy relationships; (3) for the glory of God—for righteousness?

After you have identified the real issue, ask the Lord to help you answer these questions: Will confronting help resolve the issue? Is this important enough to be addressed? What will be the probable long-term results? (There are times when you may realize a confrontation would have no potential for good, so you should not pursue it.) Will failure to address the issue damage the relationship? Will it cause you to withdraw from that person out of hurt? If so, then take the initiative and try to resolve the situation according to Matthew 18:15–17. The results of confronting may not be pleasant, but this may be a necessary step to healing.

If you sense that confronting is not that important or has no potential for healing, what should you do? If the conflict is due to an unrealistic expectation and personalization on your part, make the proper adjustments. Lower your expectations or think of other possible reasons for the behavior rather than taking it personally. If the conflict is due to a wrong assumption, ask an appropriate question to find out if your assumption is wrong. Pursue the truth. If the conflict is due to your selfishness—you simply want to hang on to your goals, your agenda—let go and move toward the other in self-denying love. Or you may decide this is simply an occasion when love should cover it.

This process of letting go of unrealistic or self-centered issues or wrong thinking, and then replacing that with worthy thinking, will free you from anger, or else greatly diminish the anger, frustration, and disappointment and help you handle the conflict in a healthy way.

If you decide your issue is an important and legitimate one to confront, plan how you will lovingly do that.

Choose the Right Time

Carefully consider the right time to confront.

It should be after you have identified and clarified the real issue. The seven typical sources of conflict (chapter 9) will help.

It should be after I've examined my own heart for any fleshly motives that might be causing my hurt, anger, or disappointment, and after prayer and determination to walk in the power of the Spirit.

It should be after I know assuredly that this is God's way and time for me to address the situation, and after I have cooled enough to do it with grace and truth. I need to take the emotion out of it.

Confronting should be done before the issue grows too large. A wife thought that to be submissive she should meet all her husbands sexual demands. For years it was "sex on demand." She hated being taken advantage of, but she cooperated. Finally, she came to the point of not wanting to touch him at all, or even sit close to him. Their relationship became a love-hate relationship.

How much better it would have been if she had cared enough to confront; that is, if she had addressed the issue at the very beginning, instead of seething with resentment all those years.

Study How to Confront

Take responsibility and the initiative to address the real issue as Jesus teaches:

> If you are offering your gift . . . and there remember your brother has something against you, . . . First go and be reconciled to your brother. . . . (Matthew 5:23–24)

> If your brother sins against you, go and show him his fault, just between the two of you. (Matthew 18:15)

PAUL'S WAY

Paul gives a clear pattern for confronting in 1 Corinthians 11:2, 17–34.

1. *Affirm them.* Paul writes, "I praise you for remembering me in everything and for holding to the teachings, just as I passed them on to you" (v. 2). Paul praises before he confronts. Commend what you can before addressing what needs to be corrected.
2. *State what is wrong.* "In the following directives I have no praise for you, for your meetings do more harm than good" (v. 17). He states clearly and specifically what is wrong and spells out the consequences.
3. *Give illustrations.* "In the first place I hear . . . there are divisions . . . "(v. 18). "It is not the *Lord's* Supper you eat, . . ." but *your* supper—each man for himself (v. 20). You are guilty of sinning against the body and blood of the Lord, and for that there is judgment. There are bad consequences for it (vv. 27–32). Implied: I love you too much to see you suffer those horrible consequences.
4. *State how to correct the wrong.* It is the *Lord's* Supper not *your* supper! If you are hungry and need to eat, eat at home.

Jesus said, "Do this in remembrance of me" (vv. 23–25). You aren't thinking of Him, but yourself. You are drinking unworthily. If you keep on as you are in your behavior, there are consequences you will not want. I want you to be delivered from those consequences because I love you! I suggest you change in these two areas (vv. 27–34).

5. *Expect accountability.* "And when I come I will give further directions" (v. 34). Paul seems to be implying that he will check on their follow-through on his suggestions, and then give any further instructions necessary.

Paul took responsibility to address wrong, especially in his "family," his territory of responsibility. So must you in your family—with your children, and with the adults too. And not just in your little family, but in the big family—the family of God—as well.

Let's follow Paul's model: (1) affirm, (2) state clearly what is wrong, (3) give specific illustrations, (4) state the change you desire, (5) follow through by expecting accountability.

In minor issues, it is not necessary to go through all five steps; but always, where you can, *affirm* the person before bringing up the area of wrong or the desired change. For example, in the conflict of goals that Nettie and I discovered we had on Saturday mornings, it was not necessary to go through all five steps. We simply needed to identify the problem and design a workable solution.

PREPARE YOURSELF

A second principle on how to confront is to prepare yourself for the event. The following will help in doing that:

1. *Check your manner.* Confronting must be done in love. Very important! The Scripture gives us such a clear summary of the attitude or manner we should have when we confront.

> As, therefore, God's picked representatives of the new humanity, purified and beloved of God Himself, be merciful in action, kindly in heart, humble in mind. Accept life, and be most patient and tolerant with one another,

always ready to forgive if you have a difference with anyone. Forgive as freely as the Lord has forgiven you. And,
above everything else, be truly loving, for love is the
golden chain of all the virtues. . . . [even the virtues of
setting limits and addressing situations]" (Colossians
3:12–15, Phillips).

Confronting in love demonstrates that you care more for
the person than for the issue.

2. *Be wise—Pray.* The Scripture says we are to be "wise as ser-
pents, and harmless as doves" (Matthew 10:16, KJV). Realize that some of these suggestions will be much more effective when you're dealing with a responsive person. However, you will need more carefulness, thought, prayer, and
perhaps counsel when dealing with a very defensive or non-
responsive person.

3. *Plan where to confront.* Confronting is something you do in
a safe place, usually a place of privacy. Sometimes, however, it should be done in a public place, for safety, if the
issue is critical and the other person tends to be angry. Sometimes you will sense "this is the moment"—that the time
and place have been planned by God.

4. *Be alert to sidetracking.* When you attempt to lovingly address issues, some people may try to sidetrack you. Be fore-
warned and choose in advance to stick to your position. Be
alert to some typical ways they use to sidetrack you.

They might deny that they have any problem. They
might make excuses for their behavior. They might say
you're the problem. "You're just too sensitive. You always
get so angry!" They might take the *poor me* position expecting you to back off: "I can never do anything right. I
always do everything wrong."

Plan to stand your ground—even if you may sometimes
sound like a broken record, as you calmly repeat over and
over the line that clearly defines the real issue. You may

recall that I did this with Amy when she repeatedly asked, "Where have you been?"

To each strong question, I simply and calmly said, "It's none of your business," until she gave up her control mode. Then we were able to talk about where I had been.

5. *Enlist support from the family of God.* If you have always been one who gives in to controlling people, you will probably need a support system. Find one or several people who will pray, give guidance, or be present with you when you confront. They can help you feel safe, validated, and understood. That support should come from the family of God—your new family. The Bible says to strengthen the knees that are feeble and the broken limbs. We need support. (See Hebrews 12:12.)

PREPARE YOUR WORDS

Carefully think through ahead of time what the real issue is and what you want to say. You will want to include at least four things: (1) affirm the person with whom you feel a conflict; (2) describe the specific behavior that causes you frustration—giving illustrations; (3) share your feelings in response to it; (4) state specifically how you would like for the person to change.

Remember to affirm first, then follow with the other three items. Augsburger gives these examples.

"When you come home an hour late in the evening without a call, it completely disrupts the dinner hour for us all, and I feel angry and mistrustful of your other promises. . . . I want a phone call as soon as possible after you become aware that you will be more than a half-hour late.

"When you criticize me in front of others, it touches something very painful for me since I was shamed frequently as a kid, and I feel like hiding. . . . I am open to hear[ing] your criticism in private. Just ask for a time, and I will be available."[2]

Then affirm the person generously and be very light on criticism if they slip back to old behavior patterns occasionally. Remember, change takes time.

1. *Make I statements.* When you describe the behavior that causes your frustration, make *I* statements rather than *you* statements. With *I* statements you can identify your feelings without accusing the other person; whereas, *you* statements seem to cast blame on the other person. "When you do . . . , I feel hurt," is much easier to receive than "You make me angry when you . . ." Avoid any words that sound like accusing and blaming. Avoid the typical overgeneralizing statements that include *always* and *never.*

2. *Write it out.* In the most critical issues, it is good not only to prayerfully think through the issue, but prepare your script ahead of time, as the prodigal son did. He didn't know what his father's response would be, but he assumed the responsibility to initiate restoring the relationship. As Jesus directed us in Matthew 5 and 18, whether you're at fault or the other is at fault, either way, take the initiative.

   The prodigal son thought through the issues and planned his specific words: "[I will] say, 'Father, I have sinned.' I was wrong. [Affirming his father was right.] 'I am no longer worthy to be called your son; make me like one of your hired men.'" (A statement of what he expected.) He didn't get to fully carry out his plan because of the eagerness of his forgiving father to have the relationship restored. Nevertheless, he prepared his script (see Luke 15:11–32).

   Write out your script, fully expressing your thoughts and feelings—but don't send it. Let it rest for a while, then read it again and revise it as you see fit, praying for guidance and discernment.

3. *Get some help.* For very serious or long-standing conflict, I would also suggest some careful and prayerful study before attempting the confrontation or preparing the final script. Ask for the Holy Spirit's clear direction. Read some helpful books, such as James Dobson's *Love Must Be Tough; Speaking the Truth in Love* by Henry Virkler; *Caring Enough to Confront,* or *When Caring Isn't Enough* by David Augsburger.

In addition to reading helpful material, find a trusted friend or counselor with whom you can share your thoughts, your script, and your plans. Let him or her help you discern the wisest approach. Ask for reactions, insights, and suggestions for deletions or rewording.

4. *Make your approach.* If your thoughts about the situation do not change after several days and you have carefully edited your script, and perhaps have let a wise counselor read it and check it for you, ask the other person to agree to a time when you can talk over a concern that is on your heart.

In the meantime, go over the script several times so that you have the important points clearly in your mind. Then share with the other person your thoughts and feelings about the situation. To keep the conversation natural, don't use your notes. On the other hand, you could choose to read the script if that seems more fitting and you prepared it for that purpose.

BALANCING THIS TRUTH

There may be numerous reasons why we fail to confront. For one thing, it is easier not to cause ripples; so we say, "Peace at any price." Or our passive nature may be the reason. Our conscience and other people congratulate us for godly maturity, loving care, and self-denial, when actually we are bowing to our passive ways and not taking responsibility. Another reason might be that we think to confront it is not biblical. We misunderstand the scriptural teaching of self-denial, submission, yielding our rights, etc. We think we should just be patient, loving, forgiving, prayerful, and wait—no matter what the issue.

Consider the Consequences of Not Confronting
If the situation calls for confrontation and if I do not follow through, everyone loses out on the best—God, the other person, and me. I build up resentments and create distance in relation-

ships. The other person is denied the opportunity to see some blind spots and to change. This situation would not bring glory to God.

Remember Pauline, who told about the woman's voice on the phone, the mysterious motel key, and the charge on the Visa bill? What would be the consequences if she had continued to say nothing to her husband, but instead built on her wrong assumptions, and suspicions.

Her response was to address the situation in love as soon as it occurred. She shared with her husband in a nonaccusing way that she was confused: "I'm puzzled by this bill, Dear. I don't recall what the Pocono trip was about," or, "I just found this key to a strange motel. I'm wondering how it wound up in our house?"

There were no accusations, no blaming. She simply addressed the situation in love, checking out what was puzzling to her. When she showed respect for her husband's point of view at the same time that she was checking out what was puzzling her, she was building her trust in him. This gave him opportunity to share the truth, help her to be free from relationship-destroying attitudes, and to build closeness instead of distance.

"It was important to me that the lawn be mowed," Marge related, "because I was the one who had to trudge through the high grass to hang up clothes, and I was the one to greet visitors who walked around our high grass. I lived with this problem day in and day out, yet my husband didn't want me to mow because he felt it was his job. It needed it to be done twice a week, but he would frequently let three or four weeks go by.

"I refrained from nagging and tried to apply the principles of denying myself and giving up my expectations, but I still found myself getting irritated and pressured. Then I began to realize that I was totally ignoring the important principle of lovingly confronting and addressing the issue.

"Now the problem was how could I share with him in the right manner, without nagging. I had no idea how to begin. Then one night he said, 'What's the matter?'

" 'I feel so pressured,' I explained.

" 'What can I do to take the pressure off?' I mentioned about the grass and explained why it was so important to me. He said he never saw it from my viewpoint and didn't realize it was so important to me. The grass got cut, but more important, I learned to share."

By way of contrast, from the beginning of their marriage, Alberta's husband was addicted to pornography. She kept his secret and kept forgiving him again and again. After thirty years, he was still unwilling to get help, still unrepentant, and they were divorced. This caused hurt to both of them and tremendous hurt, confusion, and frustration to the children.

Our question here is, are there consequences that could have been avoided if Alberta had addressed the need much earlier and tried to get help for herself and for her husband? By confronting him and addressing the issue in love perhaps, with the church's help, the story might have been different. Possibly the marriage could have been healed and the divorce avoided. We don't know how things *might* have been, but we do know that many times addressing little and big issues and learning and growing together reap wonderful results.

Ask: Is This a Time for Silence?

Confrontation is sometimes crucial. On the other hand, there is a time for silence. This could be a silence of rebuke through a simple look, like the time Jesus just looked at Peter after Peter had denied Him. Sometimes it's a silence of self-control where you say nothing, but simply deny yourself. Jesus "was reviled, yet he reviled not." Or it may be a silence of wisdom when there would be no benefit in speaking. Or a silence of surrender. Jesus committed Himself to God; there are times when we need to do the same. (See 1 Peter 4:19, NKJV.)

Not all conflicts will be resolved as, for example, in the stories of Jesus and the rich young ruler, or Rita and Jana. However, sometimes we still need to take the risk to care enough to confront by identifying the need and addressing it with skill and tact.

We need the Holy Spirit's discernment and often the counsel of wise, godly people to know when to, as the Bible says, "Go and show him his fault" (Matthew 18:15); "Restore him gently" (Galatians 6:1); "Correct, rebuke and encourage" (2 Timothy 4:2). It is clear that there are times when our Christian responsibility is to show the person his fault—not ignore it, deny that it is there, hope it will go away, or think that time will make it better. We need to address the issue. If we do not, we may build up resentments and misunderstandings, creating distance.

On the other hand, we are not to be out lambasting people all the time—correcting error. Balance is the key. Go back to our three guidelines: Is it for (1) the good of the cause, (2) the good of the persons, and (3) for the glory of God? Also, ask yourself, Is this a time to respond in silence?

THOUGHTS TO REMEMBER

Affirm before confronting and "be merciful in action, kindly in heart, humble in mind" (Colossians 3:12, NTMB).

"If your brother sins, rebuke him, and if he repents, forgive him" (Luke 17:3).

PRACTICING AND JOURNALING

Paul uses five principles in confronting (see p. 228). In minor cases, one may not use all five principles; but always affirm before addressing the situation.

Write how you recently addressed an issue, big or small, and what the results were.

Part IV

Nourishing Others
Through
People- Helping

Final peper

Be a People Helper

In our travels for the Enriched Living Workshops we have had contact with many skycaps and bellmen. As a bellman at our motel in Wichita was working hard and cheerfully to get our twelve bags into the car, Carol said, "You're a good packer!"

Smiling broadly he replied, "Well, thank you, ma'am. I've been doing this a long time, but I don't hear that very often."

With those simple words Carol was a people helper, encouraging that man who seldom heard any words of praise or appreciation. He was serving us, but Carol in turn served him by speaking that word of encouragement.

The expression *people helper* is a good use of words, because all of us can and should be nourishing one another by being helpers of one another. The Scripture is full of reminders to think of, encourage, love, exhort, care for, pray for, and strengthen one another.

> Each of you should look not only to your own interests, but also to the interests of others. (Philippians 2:4)

> But encourage one another daily, as long as it is called Today . . . (Hebrews 3:13)

> . . . there should be no division in the body, but that its parts should have equal concern for each other. (1 Corinthians 12:25)

Confess your sins to each other and pray for each other. . . . (James 5:16)

But I have prayed for you, Simon, that your faith may not fail. And when you have turned back, strengthen your brothers. (Luke 22:32)

Dear friends, let us love one another, for love comes from God. (1 John 4:7)

I have chosen to use *people helper* instead of *counselor,* since the word *counselor* tends to limit our helping to times when we can sit down and give counsel. It might even imply to some that they need to fix people or live up to a self-imposed counselor image. For others, *counselor* can be a scary word: "Who, me? Oh, I could never be a counselor!"

The word *mentor* can also be scary to those who feel inadequate or not well equipped. To others it might wrongly imply superiority. However, *mentor* is a good word if we understand it to refer to a person who has a servant heart and functions in a servant position. Many of us who aren't counselors can be very effective mentors. All of us can be people helpers. Whatever our label, we are all to "serve one another in love" (Galatians 5:13).

THE MINISTRY OF RECONCILIATION

People helping people is what life is all about, whether it takes the form of encouraging, mentoring, or counseling. In fact, God's whole redemptive purpose is wrapped up in the word *reconciliation.* "God was reconciling the world to himself in Christ. . . . And he has committed to us the message of reconciliation" (2 Corinthians 5:19). God has a plan to use each one of us in the ministry of reconciliation. He wants each of us to be reconciled in three basic areas and to help others find reconciliation in the same three areas:

- With *God*: Restoring harmony with God through Christ.
- With *self*: Finding personal harmony, reducing inner conflicts, experiencing peace.
- With *others*: Knowing harmony with others, improving personal relationships.

Our Goals in People-Helping

Our goals in people-helping all relate to these three areas of reconciliation, and Scripture presents us with the guidelines for those goals:

- To lead others into inner *peace*—the peace of forgiveness of sins and acceptance of self and circumstances (see Romans 5:1; Colossians 3:15)
- To encourage them to increasingly *know God,* and thus be able to trust Him more (see Psalm 9:10)
- To give them guidance toward more satisfying *relationships* with others (see 1 Peter 3:8–9)
- To help them find a place of personal *usefulness* in the cause of Christ by ministering to others (Matthew 5:13–16)

The overall goal in helping any individual is to communicate hope, that he might more courageously and confidently face daily life with its trials and struggles. Our God is a God of hope: "May the God of hope fill you with all joy and peace as you trust in him, so that you may overflow with hope by the power of the Holy Spirit" (Romans 15:13).

God gives hope to His children through a sense of His presence (see Exodus 33:14), through the numberless promises in His Word (for example see 1 Corinthians 10:13), and through His gracious, generous provisions—including loving, caring, and understanding members of His church body (see Philippians 4:19).

We need to communicate that hope and encourage others to "hope against hope" as Abraham did. When hope was dead within him, he went on hoping in faith, believing that he would become "the father of many nations" (Romans 4:18).

Finding Our Ministry

All of us have a deep desire to have a meaningful ministry that gives purpose to life. We want to know we've made some impact for the kingdom as we've passed through this life.

One workshop alumna shared her frustration as she searched for her ministry:

> So many of my friends who are walking with the Lord have shared with me that they have a "ministry." One works with prisoners. Another ministers in song. Others have a ministry with young people.
>
> As these women shared with me, I began asking, Where is my ministry? The more I searched, the more discouraged and frustrated I became. One day I sat down with a friend and said, "Do you know where I might find the ministry that God has planned especially for me?"
>
> He very simply said, "Oh yes. It's in the Word. The Word says that you have a ministry in your home with your husband and children."
>
> His words were like a revelation to me and a light came on! Just as a man called to preach spends time preparing his sermon or a woman called to sing, spends time in rehearsing, I too began putting much more time into my home. I have tried to make it more attractive. When my family comes to eat, the table is pretty and the food is tasty. I have also found I have the ability to create clothes for my children from scraps. This has been so fulfilling and such a blessing to me!
>
> I began putting into practice the things I learned in the workshop because I wanted to fulfill to the best of my ability the ministry God gave me. In all of this I give glory to God and praise Him, as our home is becoming more of a heaven on earth. This is my ministry for now!

Although a wife and mother may have other ministries outside her home, it is important for her to realize the significance of her ministry in the home. This is a very vital place of personal usefulness in the cause of Christ in ministering to others.

A mother who came to the Enriched Living Workshops when her daughter was young, learned some principles from the Word on parenting and began changing her ways. She noticed a definite difference in the children's responses and attitudes. Twenty years later she and her daughter came to the workshop and told me their story. The daughter emphasized several times how very much her mother had changed in her ways of dealing with them.

"What a difference it made in our home, and now I am using these same principles in training my children."

That mother's ministry goes on and on.

This illustrates only one area of ministry—the home. But people-helping opportunities are around every corner. My prayer as you read these next four chapters is that you will be sensitive to the gentle prodding of the Holy Spirit as you look for ways you can nourish others by being a people helper.

THREE SIMPLE WAYS TO BE A PEOPLE HELPER

You can become a people helper—an encourager—in your ordinary, daily living encounters and casual sharings. My neighbor purposed to look for at least one blessing from the Lord each day and then share it with at least one other person. It was such an encouragement whenever she would say, "May I share my blessing for today with you?" Then she would tell of a verse that had helped her or an answer to prayer or a kindness shown to her. This is one way of people-helping, but there are a thousand-and-one other ways.

One mother shared, "I have learned that when living with teenagers, I should not pry, nag, or 'bug' them. I should just provide a comfortable communication climate, being pleasantly present and interested in them. This is the foundation of our relationship." Though she may not recognize it, this woman has found a very important way to be a people helper in her home.

Another woman told how a simple "Good morning" led to a very special result. "At my job I always made it a point to say good morning to the girl who worked in the cubicle next to mine. One day I found a bunch of daisies on my desk. She had brought them for me just because I always said 'Good morning' to her! This led to a friendship and eventually she received the Lord as her Savior [friendship evangelism]. It's amazing what a simple 'Good morning' can lead to when you take the time."

People want to be noticed and valued! Our actions and attitudes—as well as our words—can be ministers of encouragement, comfort, cheer, and love.

Beyond the casual daily contacts with the grocer, waitress, neighbor, or repair man, you can plan specific help for the people in your sphere of influence. There's no better place to start than in your own family. Then, as time allows, reach out to others to be a people helper in a variety of ways. There are three simple ways we can all reach out.

Affirm the Self-Worth of Others

Look for opportunities to affirm the self-worth of others.

Give A Sense of Belonging

One mother has a unique way of reminding each child of her love. "I have devised a secret code with each of my two children to show and remind them that I love them. When we are in a crowded, public place or when I am busy with friends, we use *our signal*. My six-year-old boy and I share a wink; my ten-year-old girl and I share an 'OK' sign.

"One day, as I pulled into the schoolyard, it happened to be recess. As I got out of the car, my little boy came running across the playground, smiling from ear to ear. He stopped at the edge of the playground just long enough to give me a big wink, then he ran back with his friends. What a neat feeling! This has become very special for me and the children, and it has strengthened their sense of family belonging."

A woman who worked outside her home wrote: "I have a job during the day, but many of my friends are at home with their children. I have a habit of calling them during my coffee breaks. Often, I won't have specific things to say, just, 'Hi, I was thinking of you.' I call most of my friends at least once a week. They have said the calls really bless them and encourage them. And it gives me a real boost to continue my day's work."

Encouragement! "He who refreshes others will himself be refreshed" (Proverbs 11:25).

One mother found a unique way to let her middle daughter know she was a special person in the family: "We have three girls and a boy. My oldest girl noticed that I gave more attention to the youngest girl than to the middle girl. There are many reasons for this, of course. She was the youngest and demanded more from me. My middle daughter also seemed very independent. I have heard of the 'middle-child problem,' and I thanked my daughter for her insight and for sharing this with me.

"Now I call my middle girl 'Stuffin.' I explained to her that she is the good stuff in the sandwich. Now she knows when I call her 'Stuffin,' she's the yummy in-between!" How encouraging!

"Pleasant words are a honeycomb, sweet to the soul and healing to the bones" (Proverbs 16:24).

GIVE MEANING AND PURPOSE TO THEIR WORK

Recognize successful ministering when you encounter it, and put value, meaning, and purpose to the person's efforts. At the end of one of our workshops in Portland, I greeted the lady who had been making the coffee for all the breaks.

"I understand you've been making the coffee for several years now."

She said cheerfully, "Yes. . ." probably wondering what I was getting at.

I said, "That's quite a ministry! It's not only an enjoyable treat for the ladies, but it's a refresher. As they are refreshed physically they are more receptive spiritually. So you have really had a vital ministry."

Encouragement! Affirmation! Help them to see far beyond the work involved and realize the value of their efforts.

Teach Responsibility and Skills

Learning to take responsibility and develop new skills helps us have a sense of worth.

One mother tells, "Our eleven-year-old son and fourteen-year-old daughter are supposed to make their own beds every day. But getting them to do this had become quite a hassle. Then I started surprising them once or twice a week by making their beds—even picking up clothes and hanging them in their closets. During the past year, they have expressed their appreciation for my help more and more. Now they are doing very nice things for me. 'Mom, I'll vacuum the stairs for you.' They help with the dishes without being asked. I am always careful to thank them for their help and let them know I appreciate their thoughtfulness; and they do likewise to me. Yes, now they take pride in keeping their beds made and their rooms clean. Taking that responsibility has boosted their sense of worth."

Another mother wrote:

> One problem area I have had is in teaching my daughters to cook. I would just rather do it myself to get the job done faster. After attending the workshop, I realized I was not fulfilling my responsibility to them by not training them for this important duty.
>
> We decided it would be good for them to take turns every other Saturday and plan, buy for, and prepare the evening meal. It's amazing the cooperation and interest they show in doing this. They make their favorite foods and desserts and sometimes create new dishes or try new recipes. Most of the meals are delicious; although I'll have to admit we have also eaten foods that were burned, too spicy, or raw in the center! This was a learning experience for everyone, and it encouraged my daughters' interest in and preparation for responsibilities they will have when they leave home.

Affirm Their Worth in Discipline

Correcting a child in firmness and love affirms his worth. When he is corrected with anger, insults, criticism, and harshness, his spirit is wounded and his sense of worth greatly diminished.

Though he will test the limits you set for him, the child really wants to know if you care enough about him to control him. Thus, when he is corrected in love, his worth is affirmed.

Develop a Listening Heart

One of the most vital ways you can be a people helper is to develop a listening heart. We will amplify this subject in the next two chapters, but because of its importance, it merits a mention here. Casual contacts may turn into listen-and-help sessions. Learning to listen actively to family members and friends is often the key to a warm relationship, as this person discovered: "I realized that I had the weakness of dominating conversations and not really listening to the other person. The Lord spoke to me that I wasn't being as attentive to others as I should be. One person in particular had been suffering because of my lack of attentiveness.

"One evening, as I was visiting with this friend, I made a conscious effort to really listen to what he was saying and to encourage his sharing by asking questions. He shared his interests, goals, and feelings for several hours without my ever doing more than asking a question. Several weeks later he shared with me that he enjoyed our conversation that evening so much. He said, 'You always have such creative input!' And all I did was listen."

Anita, the family talker, decided to discipline herself and not do all the talking at dinner one evening. Instead, she planned to encourage her children to share, and she would listen. She asked each of the four children some questions about their day. "I couldn't believe how much each one shared. It was really fun. Some were slow in sharing, but then they were used to my talking and not giving them opportunity."

"Even a fool is thought wise if he keeps silent, and discerning if he holds his tongue" (Proverbs 17:28).

Direct People to Places of Help

Another good way to help people is to guide them to places of inspiration and help. Share with them the sources of growth and inspiration in your Christian life—a book, a cassette, a Bible study, a seminar. We all grow in such a wide variety of ways. Share these with others as you perceive that a need in their life could be filled.

One workshop participant sent our *Input for a Rejoicing Heart* cassette to a missionary friend in France. Her friend wrote back: "How I have enjoyed that tape you gave me, Liz! I don't know how many times I have listened to it carefully and prayerfully. Now, I have begun to memorize the Scriptures."

Another woman shared how she encouraged others to come with her to the workshop. "I attended the workshop three years ago and learned more about myself in those four sessions than I could have imagined. I felt great hope that my life and home could be improved. And they were! In fact, it was so meaningful that I began working hard inviting my friends to go to this year's workshop with me. I'm so excited! Now, one week from today, I'll again be at the Enriched Living Workshop and with me will be many friends whom I have encouraged to attend. What a joy to share with them something that has meant so much to my own growth in the Lord." If you have a class that has been a means of growth for you, invite someone to benefit with you.

James Freeman Clark, from the past century wrote:

> Each soul has its own faculty; it can help in some way to make the world more cheerful and more beautiful. This it is which makes life worth living. If we are living only for ourselves, our own amusement, luxury, advancement [and we can add in today's world, pleasure, possessions, position, power and prestige], life is not worth living. But if we are living as co-workers with Christ, as fellow-helpers with God . . . then our lives are full of interest. This gives sweetness and strength to all our days."[1]

PREREQUISITES FOR PEOPLE-HELPING

Basic to helping another is that the people helper develop and maintain a good relationship with the one helped. Without a connection that includes a relationship of goodwill and confidence, the person's real problem will not surface, nor will the advice given have any value or even be heeded. If this essential relationship is to be built, there must issue from the helper genuine humility, empathy, interest in, and love for the individual. These qualities will be communicated in several ways.

Be Willing to See and Admit Your Faults

Be willing to "confess your faults" to one another (James 5:16). We have to develop the ability to say, "I was wrong," or, "I'm sorry, will you forgive me?"

"Search me, O God, and know my heart; try me and know my anxious thoughts; and see if there be any hurtful way in me, and lead me in the everlasting way" (Psalm 139:23–24, NASB).

If we have not learned to honestly acknowledge our own wrongs and accept responsibility for them by admitting them and, when necessary, asking forgiveness, it is easy to project a better-than-thou attitude or an I-am-never-wrong spirit. It is very difficult for a spirit of understanding, love, and forgiveness to come through to others when these attitudes are present; and it is difficult for others to freely share with us. "Humility comes before honor" (Proverbs 15:33).

A couple told how they had learned to humble themselves: "My husband and I realized we both came from homes where our parents were 'never wrong.' So, we thought parents had to stand their ground, never admitting a mistake, or they would 'lose face' with their children. We reviewed the effects this attitude had had on us and our children. We decided that if parents are never wrong, then no opportunity to forgive ever arises. Consequently, resentments build between all family members, and the result is unhappiness for all. My husband and I decided we would muster our courage and admit to our children our wrong reactions and actions. That took great courage.

"I had the first opportunity. I had screamed at my son for misplacing the car keys when I was ready to go on an errand. Then I discovered that he really hadn't misplaced them—I had! I took my tearful, resentful ten-year-old aside and told him I was wrong. I asked him to forgive me. He stood there in amazement. Then, out came the resentment bottled up in his short life. I agreed with him. He was absolutely correct about my past errors. I was amazed at the things he remembered. After he had released his pain, he put his arms around me and said, 'Mom, you do love me. I forgive you.' We both cried with a joy and love for each other that was never there before.

"Later, my husband had an opportunity to admit his wrong. Our children have now learned to forgive each other and themselves, because God taught us it isn't terrible for parents to tell their children when they are wrong."

The apostle Paul said, "I don't mean to say I am perfect. I haven't learned all I should. . . . " (Philippians 3:12, TLB). We all would have to say that's true of us too. But do we really believe it, and do we know wherein we are imperfect? Are we aware of our flaws? A lot of people around us—our friends, spouse, child, coworker— know what they are, as the couple above discovered.

Let's Talk About Blind Spots

Our faults, which we often do not easily see or admit, are blind spots in our awareness.

"For twenty-five years of marriage," one wife shared, "we had nothing but unhappiness, and yet I didn't know why. My husband and I had the poorest relationship and virtually no communication. Every time I tried to converse with him, after a few sentences he would spew out an answer and storm off. I would sit there trying to figure out, What did I do? What did I say? But I could never find the reason for his reactions.

"Through the workshops I began to realize that maybe I did have some blind spots. I began to pray as David did in the Psalms: Lord, reveal to me my secret faults. Then my eyes began to open to the fact that I was damaging our relationship and cutting off communication by my attitudes.

"I came across to him with superior attitudes: *I always think of it,* making him feel incompetent. *I'm always right,* which slammed shut the conversation. *I already knew it,* which made him feel inferior and stupid. *I have the best way,* which lowered his self-esteem.

"Now that God has revealed these things to me, and I'm beginning to correct them, you wouldn't believe the change in our relationship and the communication between us. We are even discussing spiritual matters, and he was never interested before."

While we may be unaware of the areas in our personality that hinder our relationships, they do need to be exposed and dealt with and *not* excused on grounds of temperamental weakness, environmental weakness, or difficult circumstances. It is only fools who "despise wisdom and discipline" (Proverbs 1:7). The *Life Application Bible* explains it this way:

> One of the most annoying types of people is a know-it-all, a person who has a dogmatic opinion about everything, is closed to anything new, resents discipline, and refuses to learn. . . . Don't be a know-it-all. Instead be open to the advice of others, especially those who know you well and can give valuable insight and counsel. Learn how to learn from others. Remember, only God knows it all.[2]

What are some of the faults or blind spots (attitudes and ways) that can damage our relationships? The following mindsets and behaviors illustrate some of them:

I Always Think of It

I pose as a person who does or should always think of everything. "Oh, I should have thought of that," or, "Why didn't I think of that?" The other person might think, "I must be incompetent," or, "She is superior to me."

I'm Always Right

I reflect this in a harsh, strong voice tone and critical, condemning manner. The other person thinks, "You are never wrong. It's useless to try to discuss it."

I Already Knew It

I let people know I always have the answers, have already heard the news, already know that spiritual principle. "Well, if you would just . . . " or, "What you need to do is, . . . " or, "Don't you remember I told you that?" or, "Oh, didn't you know that? I underlined that in my Bible a long time ago."

The other person thinks, "I didn't ask your advice," or, "I'm inferior," or, "She must think I'm stupid," or, "I must not be very spiritual."

HARD TO PLEASE ATTITUDE

I have perfectionistic standards. Gifts or kindnesses of others are not appreciated, and I like to point out where something hasn't been done perfectly. Or, I never use a gift you've given, or I ignore and reject you. Or, I make you feel you should have done something additional. The other person thinks, "Nothing I do is quite right. It's impossible to please you."

I HAVE THE BEST WAY

I let everyone know (in subtle ways, of course) that my ways are best. "This is how you're supposed to do it," or, "Well, if you'd just follow my instructions and do what I tell you to do. . . ." It might be how to open the jar, make the bed, fold the towels, drive the car. The other thinks, "Don't you think anyone else can do anything? Please let me try some of my own ideas."

SHAMING

I say things "just for laughs" telling others of the "stupid thing" the someone has done. The other person feels embarrassed, stupid, shamed.

"Our nine-year-old son was eating grapes. Instead of putting his seeds in the garbage can, he absent-mindedly threw them on the floor. My first response was a loud rebuke, 'Don't you know better? You know you don't put the seeds on the floor!' Immediately I was sorry. I did apologize later, but he was hurt."

No doubt the child could use some correction and instruction, but not a put-down or shaming, as the mother's voice tone indicated.

THE MOTHER HABIT

I give advice or instruction to someone who should be able to care for himself. The other thinks, "Why do you always have to instruct me? Don't you know I'm grown up?"

The loudspeaker in the subway blared out, "Hold on to a handrail or post. This vehicle is about to depart." A couple in their early sixties had gotten on. She sat down; he stood by a post, but did not hold on. Upon takeoff, he jostled a bit. The wife scolded, "Don't you believe people when they say to hold on to the handrail?" After the subway stopped and was ready to start again, she instructed, "Now hold on there."

OVERLY TALKATIVE

I dominate time together with continuous talking. I don't give others a chance to speak by asking questions, listening to them, and giving them some talking space. The other person thinks, "She's not interested in me. I'm not important."

A DEFENSIVE MANNER

I get angry, accuse the other of a wrong, or justify my own actions when someone points out something that I could improve or do a better way. The other person thinks, "You always misinterpret me," or, "I can never point out a possible improvement that you could make without your taking it personally."

A CRITICAL, COMPLAINING SPIRIT

I criticize the small flaw or thing left undone rather than focusing on all that is good or has been done well. The other thinks, "I can never do anything right or anything to please you. I hear only the criticism."

A daughter told her mother, "Mother, you are always sighing." The mother thought she was all wrong, but then wisely gave attention to it and found her daughter was right. "I was complaining all the time."

Manipulation or Control

I try to manipulate or control others through my moods, silent treatment, anger (verbal and nonverbal), guilt, talking, or asking endless questions. The other person thinks, "What have I done to displease you? Please tell me," or, "Why, don't you let me talk and not ask so many questions."

Discover Your Offensive Actions/Attitudes

Be willing to see and admit your faults. Honestly ask the Lord to show you any blind spots in your relationships with others. There are a number of ways you can discover what these traits are.

By the Prodding of the Holy Spirit

Be sensitive to the prodding of the Holy Spirit in your day-to-day contacts with others. Having asked the Lord to help you see your weaknesses and blind spots, pray, "Search me, O God. Enlighten my darkness. Reveal truth in the inward parts." (See Psalm 139:23; 18:28; 51:6.)

The Holy Spirit often helps us become aware of what we have done wrong, as this mother found: "After my son had washed and dried his hair I said, 'Ugh, your hair looks flat.'

"His response: 'No, it doesn't.'

"My response: 'Yes, it does. It looks awful.' Then what I'd just done hit me." The Holy Spirit made her aware of her harsh, unkind words.

By Knowing I've Caused a Reaction

The reaction of the other person may cause you to sense that something is wrong. When this happens, ask yourself, "Have I done something to cause this?" At a workshop a young wife shared these comments about her reactions: "This week I have come to realize how much I have been hurting my husband in the two years that we have been married. I have constantly complained about his not making enough money. I nagged him with my wild ideas and dreams of moving into a much bigger and better home.

"I didn't know how much of a pest I was until one day I saw the look on my husband's face when I said, 'But we need money.' He looked like a small child in a man's shoes. It was then that I finally realized how I had hurt him, and I asked him to forgive me."

A young mother became sensitive to the reaction of her boys: "Our boys, were having a drink of Koolaid. They spilled it again. After many sessions of cleaning up the spills, I finally let loose and really growled. Their faces dropped, and immediately I was aware of what I had done to them. I am thankful that I now realize what these unkind remarks do to our children and to my husband."

BY SOMEONE POINTING IT OUT

One lady shared, "My friend and I were listening to a speaker who said that sometimes parents compare their children unfavorably or talk about one child in a praiseworthy way and comment that another is much more difficult. My friend nudged me and said, 'You do that with your children.' I was surprised and later asked her for some examples. When she gave several, I realized she was right. I was so grateful that she helped me become aware of this blind spot."

BY INQUIRING, HOW CAN I IMPROVE?

Ask, "How can I [as a mother, wife, friend, or coworker] improve?

Give people opportunity to share their evaluation of you. In an evaluation questionnaire, you might include such questions as:

1. Do you feel I wait until you are through talking before I have my say?
2. Do you feel I respect your opinions?
3. Do you feel I tend to lecture and preach too much to you?
4. Do you feel I show an interest in your interests and activities?
5. Do you feel I consider your opinion in making decisions that concern you?

By Noting What Annoys You in Another

Often the thing that bothers us in another is the very thing we are guilty of ourselves. The Bible says we are to examine ourselves and take the plank out of our own eye first (see Matthew 7:3–5).

Be Spirit Controlled

Having talked about the need to be sensitive to the prodding of the Holy Spirit as He points out our blind spots, we now consider another major role He has in our lives. He enables us to reach out to others as nourishers and people helpers.

The Scripture gives these instructions to all of us potential people helpers:

> Brethren, if any person is overtaken in misconduct or sin of any sort, you who are spiritual—who are responsive to and controlled by the Spirit—should set him right and restore and reinstate him, without any sense of superiority and with all gentleness, keeping an attentive eye on yourself, lest you should be tempted also. (Galatians 6:1, AMP)

When the Bible says "you who are spiritual," it does not mean that I have to be perfect, but that I need to be willing to be used by and want to be controlled by the Holy Spirit. It means counting on His presence and His help. It means being Holy Spirit controlled and letting Him produce His fruit in my life (see Ephesians 5:18–21; Galatians 5:22–23).

The person who nourishes others is not to have a spirit of superiority or self-sufficiency but must depend on the Holy Spirit to give the grace, gentleness, longsuffering, wisdom, and love to help the one in need. He is not to be self-centered or a troublemaker or impressed with his own importance.

Develop a Deep Desire to Help

"Carry each other's burdens" (Galatians 6:2). Not with a desire to have a possessive relationship, "I'm the only one who can help you." Not with a goal to make the other person your captive audience or a follower (disciple) of your own ideas. Not to build up your reputation as one who has wise counsel. But with a genuine desire to serve the other person and see that he is helped, whether that help comes through you or through someone else.

Learn Sustained Listening

We talked about developing a listening heart. We need to exercise that art of active listening for sustained periods of time. Listening conveys your interest, your concern, and your understanding. Listening encourages others to share with you, as one mother discovered.

"Now I know," she lamented, "that I did not take enough time to listen to my children. I fit their requests and desires in when and if my other activities allowed it. It always seemed as though I was rushing myself and them. Later, as they grew into their teen years, they communicated less and less. I found out via the grapevine that many of their actions and reactions in outside situations were unacceptable. Long talks with them separately brought out the same complaint: 'You don't have time to listen.'

"Suddenly I realized that in doing many good things, I had missed the best thing: always being available to my children. My kids felt I was unapproachable and not even interested in them. They had food, clothes, and proper sleep, but they didn't have me. I've adjusted my priorities and have learned to quietly listen when they are ready to talk. Now they know they can come to me at any time with anything—and they do!

"Lots of my other activities have been shelved until the years when the children are gone. Result? A more relaxed, secure family that is sensing the needs of others and trying to reach out. The children no longer complain that I'm too busy. They even 'volunteer' me to help their friends too! Life is lots more fun for all of us."

Think for a moment. In ordinary conversation with someone, what percentage of the time do you listen and how much do you talk? When someone comes to you to talk over a problem, what percentage of the time do you listen? How much do you talk? Do you need to make some adjustments in your listening habits?

Be a Humble Learner

With a humble spirit, learn from the person you are helping. When either of you makes a mistake, learn from it. Think of yourself as a learner—one who could also stumble, fail, be tempted. Notice the emphasis in Galatians 6:1 (AMP): "without any sense of superiority and with all gentleness, keeping an attentive eye on yourself, lest you should be tempted also."

We are to be realistic and honest about our own potential waywardness. We are to face the possibilities of sin in our own hearts, and we each need to be willing to confess our faults to one another (see James 5:16).

Having the attitude of a humble learner will help us to be patient with the slow progress and repeated struggles of those we are trying to help, and our own as well.

Be Nonpharisaical

When we communicate the truth of Jesus, we also need to communicate the heart of Jesus. His heart is loving, understanding, caring, forgiving. He is not accusing, censoring, shaming, or condemning. He does not "pile up backbreaking burdens for men to bear" (Luke 11:46, Phillips).

Remember the Pharisee and the tax collector? The Pharisee began his prayer, "God, I thank you that I am not like other men. . . ." What blatant pride! In Matthew 23, Jesus describes the Pharisees: They do not practice what they preach. They strain out a gnat but swallow a camel. On the outside they appear to be righteous, but on the inside they are full of hypocrisy and wickedness. Everything they do is done for men to see. They love the place of honor and to be greeted with titles.

In brief, the Pharisees tied up heavy loads and put them on men's shoulders, but they themselves were not willing to lift a finger to help them with their burden. The Pharisees were masters at shooting their wounded. They shot and shot again.

Recently I read the book *Why Do Christians Shoot Their Wounded?* by Dr. Dwight L. Carlson, a very thought-provoking work. It touched me because I have heard so much from so many wounded ones around the country, people wounded even by Christians. How do we shoot the already wounded? By piling on burdens too heavy to bear as the Pharisees did. Sometimes it is through thoughtless words; sometimes through an imbalance of truth; sometimes because of more legalism than grace, more the letter of the law than the spirit. Or perhaps we wound through not allowing for emotional weaknesses and struggles.

A lady who was confused, bruised, and wounded through a hurtful divorce and her wayward, rebellious children realized she needed help. Reluctantly and fearfully, she decided to try going to a church. In the women's Bible study she mustered courage and poured out her whole story. One woman quickly spoke up and said, "You need to straighten out your life. Then things will be different with your children." The wounded lady made up her mind to never again go back to church.

Shelia, my friend in Ohio, was considering separation. After years of struggling with her husband's addiction to pornography, she planned to seek help from the church elders. But her husband got there first and told them only a part of the story. When she went to them, they told her, in effect, "Go home and submit to your husband, and your problems will be solved." This already wounded one was shot again. Ultimately, she felt she had to go to another church for some love, understanding, support, and emotional healing.

Be a Trustworthy Confidante

You must be a *safe* person. People need to know that you won't tell others what they confide in you, unless you have their permission. They must be sure they can trust you with their most vulnerable thoughts, feelings, or personal secrets. "He who goes about as a talebearer reveals secrets, but he who is trustworthy and faithful in spirit keeps the matter hidden" (Proverbs 11:13, AMP).

Become a Woman of Prayer

Pray much for the one you are helping. And pray for yourself, for grace, wisdom, understanding, compassion, and discernment to handle the nourishing of this person in the biblical way.

Gain Some Understanding of People

We need some basic understanding of ourselves and others. We have discussed in detail the typical lies we tell ourselves and the resultant twisted thinking. Understanding this helps us understand ourselves.

It is also helpful to be aware of the *differences* between people: differences evident in personality types, spiritual gifts, natural gifts and abilities, and the differences between men and women. To be a good people helper, a nourisher, we need to understand and accept the God-given uniqueness that people have. It is because of these differences that we each have different needs. We need to walk in forbearing love, "bearing with one another and making allowances because you love one another," as Ephesians 4:2 (AMP) says.

1 Peter 3:7 (NASB) gives this advice to husbands, but it should be heeded by all of us in all relationships: "Live with your wives in an understanding way."

One Bible teacher and mentor didn't understand the unique differences between people. Instead, she would say of her weaker, struggling sister, "She has the same resources I have," implying: "She has no excuse for her weaknesses or struggles; she is not living in victory as I am."

As we consider these prerequisites for people-helping, we realize we need the power of the Holy Spirit to implement them in our lives. The good news is that we *have* the Holy Spirit, but we need to draw upon His power. As we do so, we will become more the kind of people helpers who honor Jesus and make people thirsty for Him. We want them to say or think, "I want what she or he has."

There is hope and healing, even for the wounded. The flip side of all this is that God never wastes anything. He's never baffled as to how He's going to cause this wound, this hurt, this problem to work together for good. He's gifted at giving "beauty for ashes, the oil of joy for mourning, the garment of praise for the spirit of heaviness" (and Isaiah 61:3, KJV). And He will do it for those who will put their woundedness in His hands, trust Him, and see what He will do (see Romans 8:28).

THOUGHTS TO REMEMBER

One of the most vital ways you can be a people helper is to develop a listening heart. Listening conveys your interest, your concern, your understanding, and it encourages others to share with you.

"Therefore encourage one another and build each other up, just as in fact you are doing" (1 Thessalonians 5:11).

PRACTICING AND JOURNALING

As you review the subhead "Be Willing to See and Admit Your Faults" ask the Lord to reveal to you one of your blind spots. Is this blind spot giving an impression of a know-it-all attitude?

Write an example of the way you displayed one of these negative attitudes this week. Tell how you became aware of it and what you did about it.

12

Guides for People-Helping

Before we get into a discussion of the Guides for People-Helping, come with me back in time to visit a man whose very name has become synonymous with suffering. After all those tragedies struck Job, some friends came to visit him, friends Job later called "miserable comforters."

JOB'S MISERABLE COMFORTERS

In preparation for teaching my first Linx class, I read the Book of Job again, asking myself, "What did these men do wrong?" Later in this chapter we will be taking a good look at that, but first, as you read Job 2:11–13, see if you can discover three things they did right.

> When Job's three friends, Eliphaz the Temanite, Bildad the Shuhite and Zophar the Naamathite, heard about all the troubles that had come upon him, they set out from their homes and met together by agreement to go and sympathize with him and comfort him. When they saw him from a distance, they could hardly recognize him; they began to weep aloud, and they tore their robes and sprinkled dust on their heads. Then they sat on the ground with him for seven days and seven nights. No one said a word to him, because they saw how great his suffering was.

These men had a threefold ministry to Job: (1) The ministry of their *presence*. They came from a distance and sat with him. That's compassion! (2) The ministry of *silence*. For seven days they didn't say a word. They didn't use empty words to fill the silent spaces. (3) The ministry of *tears*. They wept aloud and identified with Job in his grief, poverty, and calamity.

Their Slide Downhill

They started out so well! But from day eight on, things went only downhill. What they did from then on earned them their well-known title: miserable comforters (see Job 16:2). Eugene Peterson, in the introduction to his paraphrase of the Book of Job describes well what they (and all who follow in their train) are like.

> The moment we find ourselves in trouble of any kind—sick in the hospital, bereaved by a friend's death, dismissed from a job or relationship, depressed or bewildered—people start showing up telling us exactly what is wrong with us and what we must do to get better. Sufferers attract fixers the way road-kills attract vultures. At first we are impressed that they bother with us and amazed at their facility with answers. They know so much! How did they get to be such experts in living?
>
> More often than not, these people use the Word of God frequently and loosely. They are full of spiritual diagnosis and prescription. . . .
>
> The Book of Job is . . . our primary biblical protest against religion that has been reduced to explanations or "answers.". . . They are answers without personal relationship, intellect without intimacy. The answers are slapped onto Job's ravaged life like labels on a specimen bottle. Job rages against this secularized wisdom that has lost touch with the living realities of God. . . .
>
> On behalf of all of us who have been misled by the platitudes of the nice people who show up to tell us everything is going to be just all right if we simply think such-and-such and do such-and-such, Job issues an anguished rejoinder. He rejects the kind of advice and teaching that has God all figured out, that provides glib explanations for every circumstance.

Peterson goes on to say,

When we rush in to fix suffering, we need to keep in mind several things.

First, no matter how insightful we may be, we don't *really* understand the full nature of our friends' problems. Second, our friends may not *want* our advice. Third, the ironic fact of the matter is that more often than not, people do not suffer *less* when they are committed to following God, but *more*. When these people go through suffering, their lives are often transformed, deepened, marked with beauty and holiness, in remarkable ways that could never have been anticipated before the suffering.[1]

They Wanted to Fix Job

Job's comforters understood neither the ways of God with Job nor the mysteries of suffering nor the unseen battle going on. Because they were knowledgeable and well versed in the ways of God—or so they thought—they could not stand to not have answers for Job. They *must* fix him. So they used their human intellectual approach and gave him wrong, hurtful, noncomforting answers. In this case, even Job knew these weren't correct answers; but his friends would not hear him even when he stated this clearly. He felt the pain of his own confusion and of their misunderstanding, a situation that increased his misery.

Our Propensity for Error

We are prone to becoming miserable comforters also, whenever we try to comfort or fix people with our own wrong thinking, or when we give them untimely biblical truths or half-truths (truth out of balance). By our own effort, we will not only fail to comfort but we will also confuse and accuse, leaving the suffering, struggling ones feeling guilty, hopeless, or with a sense of shame or failure.

Like Job's friends, we can be so set in our creeds (our understanding of biblical truth, what is right and wrong) that we leave no room for being at a loss, being baffled into silence concerning God and His ways, having no explanations or advice to offer. We leave no room for God to come and work His way. We refuse to be inadequate. We feel we must have answers.

The friends believed that they had to defend and explain God and fix Job who, to their way of thinking, desperately needed to be shamed, rebuked, and corrected. So they tried hard to convince Job that his suffering was his own fault, a result of his sin.

What God Says About Their Answers

To make a very long, painful story short, look at what God said about all the clean-cut answers Job's friends produced, in keeping with their religious philosophy, creeds, and beliefs. One paraphrase puts it this way:

> After God had finished addressing Job, He turned to Eliphaz the Temanite and said, "I've had it with you and your two friends. I'm fed up! You haven't been honest either with me or about me—not the way my friend Job has. So here's what you must do. Take seven bulls and seven rams, and go to my friend Job. Sacrifice a burnt offering on your own behalf. My friend Job will pray for you, and I will accept his prayer. . . . They did it. . . . And God accepted Job's prayer. (Job 42:7–9, The Message)

We could add a fourth point to the things they did right—their obedience They humbled themselves and did as God said.

WE CAN NEITHER EXPLAIN GOD NOR FIX PEOPLE

We need to become aware that we cannot explain God and His ways, neither can we fix people. We can go to them, weep with them, sit in silence with them, and pray for them. We can humble ourselves and admit when we are wrong and when we have given wrong advice. Too often we try to fix others with a good Scripture verse. When we do this we number ourselves with the miserable comforters. Once again, we've shot our wounded.

WHAT LINX IS ALL ABOUT

This story expresses my burden, my passion, so well. In my experience of traveling around the country, listening to people,

I've seen *so many* people who have been deeply hurt by well-meaning friends.

Linx: Women Connecting with Women is all about helping us avoid being miserable comforters, becoming instead, "God with skin on," real encouragers, real comforters.

From the very first chapter we have said that as redeemed children of God, our purpose here on this earth is to represent God, to show what Jesus is really like. As His representative, His agent, I am to be:

- An *advocate:* Like Jesus, defending people against the untruth of their own twisted thinking and from what others wrongly say or imply
- A *refuge,* a *safe place:* Like God the Father, to Whom we can pour out all our maddening thoughts and pain. We are to be secure confidantes
- A *paraclete:* Like the Holy Spirit; that is, one who comes alongside to comfort, encourage, help, and support. We are to be people who will help the hurting to understand and guide them into the truth about themselves, God, others, and how the Christian life really works

"When He, the Spirit of truth, has come, He will guide you into all truth" (John 16:13, NKJ). We cannot and should not try to take the place of the Holy Spirit, but we can help guide people into truth against false assumptions about the Christian life and how to live it. We can help them see the lies we tell ourselves about self, others, and God. We can make them aware when truth is out of balance and show them other kinds of twisted thinking

God Was a Refuge for Job

Job had only one place to turn for refuge. God was that safe place—so safe, in fact, that throughout the book Job trusts God with his angry thoughts and feelings. Notice this example:

> Surely, O God, you have worn me out; you have devastated my entire household. You have bound me—and it has become a

witness; my gauntness rises up and testifies against me. God assails me and tears me in his anger and gnashes his teeth at me; my opponent fastens on me his piercing eyes. Men open their mouths to jeer at me; they strike my cheek in scorn and unite together against me. God has turned me over to evil men and thrown me into the clutches of the wicked. All was well with me, but he shattered me; . . . (Job 16:7–11)

After such honest words as these that express anguish, pain, and helpless rejection, now listen to Job's words of trust in this very same God.

Even now my witness is in heaven; my advocate is on high. My intercessor is my friend as my eyes pour out tears to God; on behalf of a man he pleads with God as a man pleads for his friend. (vv. 19–21)

What They Did Wrong

THEY JUDGED JOB

These three men judged Job and accused him of all kinds of wrongdoing and sin. Oswald Chambers in *Baffled to Fight Better* cautions us:

It is a good thing to be careful of our judgment of other men. A man may utter apparently blasphemous things against God and we say, "How appalling"; but if we look further we find that the man is in pain, he is maddened and hurt by something. The mood he is talking in is a passing one and out of his suffering will come a totally different relationship to things. [2]

THEY DIDN'T TRY TO UNDERSTAND

They didn't listen or take any cues from Job. They did not understand what was behind his talk, nor did they try to get in touch with his pain. They couldn't stand to hear Job speak to God with such honesty. Oswald Chambers summarizes it. They didn't realize that "God and Satan had made a battleground of [Job's] soul."

To the rescue came the three misguided, well-meaning friends to comfort and encourage. One friend concludes that Job has sinned against God; another torments him with endless questions; and the third friend accuses Job of faulty doctrine. In short, they weren't "God with skin on" for Job.

No wonder Job called them miserable comforters.

> I have heard many things like these; miserable comforters are you all! Will your long-winded speeches never end? What ails you that you keep on arguing? I also could speak like you, if you were in my place; I could make fine speeches against you and shake my head at you. But my mouth would encourage you; comfort from my lips would bring you relief. (Job 16:2–5)

THEY DIDN'T LISTEN

If his friends had listened to Job and considered what he said, they could have been corrected in their wrong thinking. Instead, they simply continued to judge, accuse, preach, and try to correct him. They built their case on a wrong assumption that good things happen to good people and bad things happen to bad people. And obviously, since bad things were happening to Job, he was a bad person—Job had sinned and was the cause of his own suffering.

THEY DIDN'T PRAY FOR HIM

Oswald Chambers goes on to say:

> The biggest benediction one man can find in another is not in his words, but what he implies: "I do not know the answer to your problem, all I can say is that God alone must know; let us go to Him." It would have been much more to the point if the friends had begun to intercede for Job; if they had said, "This is a matter for God, not for us; our creed cannot begin to touch it"; but all they did was to take to "chattermagging" and telling Job that he was wrong. . . . The biggest thing you can do for those who are suffering is not to talk platitudes, not to ask questions, but to get into contact with God, and the "greater works" will be done by prayer (John 14:12–13). Job's friends never once

prayed for him; all they did was try to prove a point to enrich their own creed out of his sufferings. [3]

How I wish I could say that all Christians really do know how to comfort, love, and give grace as Jesus did. But I've heard so many stories that contradict that hope. These are stories, in some cases, of Christians who have spent years studying the Word, who have grown up surrounded by the preaching of the Word, and who usually have a ready verse to quote for those "in need." In the process, however, they bring more hurt than comfort.

After Joan got some shocking, tragic news, her friend—intending to help—said, "You know 'All things work together for good to them that love God.'" Joan knew that verse and had lived in the comfort of it for quite a long time, but because it was given so glibly now, when she was in the depths despair, she had a strong reaction against it. She said she came to "hate" the verse. It was two years before she was able to again take comfort from that precious verse. It had been unwisely given to a deeply hurting person at the wrong time and in the wrong way.

So many others have shared similar stories of hurt and pain when people have tried to fix them with a good but untimely verse, a quickly spoken cliché or a pat answer that conveyed no compassionate understanding. Hurting people then feel more preached at than cared for.

GUIDES FOR PEOPLE-HELPING

In contrast to this description about the miserable comforters, we're going to turn a sharp corner and think through some simple guidelines we can follow as we seek to help people and be encouragers.

Many times we know the Word and we have a heart desire to help others, but we don't understand people—their struggles and their real needs. We have already stressed the importance of active listening. Here we are going to consider it in detail.

When you listen and give another person the opportunity to express herself, you will be amazed at what you learn and communicate by simply *listening,* and also what she learns about herself and her own situation. Sometimes she even comes up with her own solutions.

The following three verses speak volumes of advice for the people helper:

> Be quick to hear, slow to speak and slow to anger. . . . (James 1:19, NASB)

> He who answers a matter before he hears it, it is folly and shame to him. (Proverbs 18:13, NKJV)

> But the wisdom that is from above is first pure, then peaceable, gentle, willing to yield, full of mercy and good fruits, without partiality and without hypocrisy. (James 3:17, NKJV)

As we study the guidelines for helping people, you may be surprised how often you'll hear the word *listen.* Listening conveys your interest, your concern, your understanding. Listening encourages others to share with you, and it communicates your desire to help bear their burden. One of the best ways to convey your interest and concern is to develop the art of active listening.

In one of my favorite devotional books, *Joy and Strength,* Frederick William Faber gives these pointed thoughts about listening:

> There is a grace of kind listening, as well as a grace of kind speaking. Some men listen with an abstracted air, which shows that their thoughts are elsewhere. Or they seem to listen, but by wide answers and irrelevant questions show that they have been occupied with their own thoughts, as being more interesting, at least in their own estimation, than what you have been saying. Some interrupt, and will not hear you to the end. Some hear you to the end, and then forthwith begin to talk to you about a similar experience which has befallen themselves, making your case only an illustration of their own. Some, meaning to be kind, listen with such a determined, lively, violent attention, that you are at once made uncomfortable, and the charm of conversation

is at an end. Many persons, whose manners will stand the test of speaking, break down under the trial of listening.

—Frederick Wm Faber (1815–1863)[4]

As you study the following guidelines for listening, ask yourself, How will doing this help me to understand this person? and What will my listening communicate to the person regarding my heart and desires for her?

Listen Without Distraction

Not looking out the window, not looking at your watch, not looking at others, but giving undivided attention to the person, *listen*. Make sure you look at the person directly and with interest. Listening in this way is an expression of love. Someone has said that when you listen lovingly, you invite that person into your life.

Listen—Hear What People Say

Periodically repeat or rephrase their words to let them know you are listening and to give them opportunity to clarify their thoughts if your understanding seems inaccurate to them. It is important that you don't just assume you know what they are saying or how they are feeling.

One person shared, "I am learning not to assume that I know what another person is saying or how he is feeling. After eighteen years, our marriage broke down. During the difficult months of counseling, I discovered that instead of really listening to what my family was saying, I had unconsciously adopted this *assuming* attitude. This was true in the case of our wife-husband relationship, but it also flowed over into my attitudes toward our two daughters. I often assumed how they felt or what their desires would be, and most often I decided that it was exactly how I felt or what I thought about the subject. In other words, I didn't really hear what they had to say.

"Now as I have learned to listen to what they think, feel, and desire, I have not only had the privilege of seeing the Lord mend our marriage, but I have also been blessed with a very treasured relationship with my daughters."

The following three verses from Proverbs 18 give us significant principles for people-helping:

> He who answers before listening—that is his folly and his shame. (v. 13)

> The heart of the discerning acquires knowledge; the ears of the wise seek it out. (v. 15)

> The first to present his case seems right, till another comes forward and questions him. (v. 17)

The *Life Application Bible* comments:

> In these concise statements, there are three basic principles for making sound decisions: (1) get the facts before answering; (2) be open to new ideas; (3) make sure you hear both sides of the story before judging. All three principles center around seeking additional information. This is difficult work, but the only alternative is prejudice—judging before getting the facts.[5]

And the only way to get the facts and hear both sides of the story is to *hear* what people say—*listen*. That's what Job's miserable comforters failed to do.

Listen for the Meaning Behind Their Words

At significant times, to confirm or correct your understanding, you might say, "You said . . . What did you mean?" or, "Did you mean to imply . . . ?"

One mother was tuned into the meaning behind her teenager's words. "Often when the children are ready for bed I go into their bedroom, turn the light out, and rub their back—providing they were in bed at the proper time. Even our sixteen-year-old boy, who has been quite rebellious, still calls out, 'Mom!' as he goes into his bedroom. I know this means, 'Come rub my back, I have something I want to talk about.' This gives a private, peaceful, special and individual time with the children when they want to share problems, concerns, and worries without interruptions. And they don't even have to look me in the eye if they don't want to! Of course, there are ages and times when they do not seem to want this, and I try to honor that too."

Listen with Understanding

As much as you can, seek to identify with the person's thoughts and feelings. People go through deep trials. Even though you may never have experienced anything like someone's trial and can in no way comprehend it, you can still communicate love and care.

Consider some of the difficulties they may be struggling to overcome. Perhaps their temperament or background, their responses learned in childhood, or their weak reactions to life make it more difficult for them to face the trial. Realize they may need extra doses of reassurance, encouragement, and patience. It is important for the person to see you react to his problem with genuine understanding, longsuffering, and hope.

At times, verbally communicate your understanding by brief comments such as: "That makes good sense," or, "Tell me more about . . ." or, "I see what you mean," or, "I can see why that would make you feel the way you do."

Listen and Build Confidence by Being Quiet

These verses from Proverbs clearly indicate that we can build confidence by being quiet:

> He who has knowledge spares his words, and a man of understanding is of a calm spirit. Even a fool is counted wise when he holds his peace; when he shuts his lips, he is considered perceptive. (Proverbs 17:27–28, NKJV)

One mother discovered the value of being quiet and listening to her teenage son. "My seventeen-year-old son had repeatedly told me, 'Mom, you never listen!' I couldn't see what he was talking about, so I passed it off as 'just his age.' I *always* listened to him! He gradually talked to me less and less, and then no longer confided in me at all. This bothered me, but I couldn't figure out why.

"In a sharing time one day, my sister told me I needed to learn to *actually* listen. She told a story she had read about 'active listening.' It made sense! So I decided to try it. Gradually, I began to see that I had not been listening to my son—or to anyone else. I had been listening with one ear, but I was thinking of all the advice the person needed, or why they shouldn't think and feel the way they do, or how I understood because I had gone through it before myself!

"As I began to see this, I realized I needed to first listen quietly—keeping my mouth shut, in other words—then acknowledge their feelings and thoughts and not jump in with advice. Well, since I've learned to be quiet, my son has been talking to me more. Things are not perfect yet, but it is encouraging to see even a little progress, knowing more will come. What a reward for learning to be quiet!"

Listen for Three Basic Needs

Three common attitudes characterize people who have been hurt. Listen for them because one or more may be present when someone shares her thoughts, hurts, and problems with you.

BITTERNESS

Bitterness is often a major problem. It might be expressed toward *people* for the wrongs they have done, toward *God* for the way He has ordered their lives, or toward *circumstances* that are not according to their choosing.

In helping them to be free from the bitterness you need to help them identify it, become aware of it, acknowledge it. Then gently and lovingly take them through these steps:

1. Asking God's forgiveness for the resentment and bitterness they have had toward Him for what happened

2. Thanking God for that trial, remembering that thanking God is a way of letting go of the bitterness and resentment
3. Telling the Lord that their deep desire and purpose of heart is to cooperate with Him in whatever He wants to do in their life; that they purpose to trust His love, goodness, and power on their behalf

GUILT

Guilt is the second problem to look for. It may be invalid guilt; that is, guilt feelings over something they are not responsible for or had no control over.

It may be guilt over past sin that has already been forgiven. If this is the case, they need to be pointed again and again to the forgiving love of Christ and be led to rest in His sure forgiveness (see Psalm 86:5 and 103:12).

It may be valid guilt over sin that they are unwilling to face or forsake. In such a case, the sin needs to be gently and lovingly addressed with a view to helping them face it, be cleansed of it, and be free from the guilt. "If we confess our sins, he is faithful and just to forgive us our sins, and to cleanse us from all unrighteousness" (1 John 1:9, KJV).

A LOW SELF-CONCEPT

A low self-concept is the third area. Are they downgrading themselves and their attitudes? Do they need reassurance that they are very special? A low sense of worth is a very common area of need. Often negative thought patterns regarding self-worth are well established. The need is to build new, positive patterns of thinking about their worth, especially from God's viewpoint, and to help them really come to believe in God's love for them and acceptance of them. There are many resources you can guide them to for help in changing their attitude toward themselves. You might suggest they read my book *You Are Very Special* and work through the projects given.

Other Problems to Listen For

In addition to listening for the three basic needs, also be alert for the things we discussed earlier:

- *Twisted Thinking*—the all-or-nothing stance. Look for black-and-white statements the person is making
- *Distorted Views* of self, God, others, and how the Christian life works
- *Negative Self-Talk* that can grow out of the above distorted views or twisted thinking
- *False Assumptions* as to how the Christian life works, such as, "It's selfish to think of my needs," or, "If I have God, I don't need people."
- *Truth Out of Balance*—Is the person looking at only one side of a truth?

No Murmuring and Complaining

Jamie was struggling with accepting a difficult situation. She said, "I realize that basically I'm angry with God. I even told Him exactly how I feel about Him. I know I shouldn't feel this way. I know the Bible says 'no murmuring and complaining.' But is it all right to tell God how I feel? I guess this is wrong, isn't it?"

We talked about what *murmuring* and *complaining* means in that context, and then how the writer of Psalms continually poured out his feelings to God. Job did this too. Notice how Job graphically expressed to God just how he felt in the following passages:

Job spoke, and cursed the day of his birth. . . . Why is a man allowed to be born if God is only going to give him a hopeless life of uselessness and frustration? I cannot eat for sighing; my groans pour out like water. (Job 3:1, 23–24, TLB)

My heart is broken. Depression haunts my days. My weary nights are filled with pain. . . . All night long I toss and turn. . . . I cry to you, O God, but you don't answer me. (Job 30:16–18, 20; TLB)

I encouraged Jamie to remember that in spite of Job's honest expression of his anger and depression, both toward God and to his friends, the Bible says, "In all this, Job did not sin" (Job 1:22). And in the very last chapter, God vindicates Job and says his friends were wrong (see Job 42:7).

Jamie had gotten truth out of balance. While I shared these thoughts with her, she was able to think, bring truth into balance, and was freed from the feelings of guilt she experienced when she expressed her anger to God.

Listen without Condemnation

It is important not to appear shocked by what people share. Our shock can so easily communicate to them that we are rejecting them as people or have a judgmental attitude about their actions. They must sense that we accept them but do not condone their sinful behavior.

One dear lady shared, "Verna, adopting this practice of listening to our children without condemnation became a life-and-death matter for my husband and me.

"About twelve years ago I came to the workshop and realized that God wanted us to become more and more like Him and to treat others more and more as He treats us. Both my husband and I have endeavored by God's grace to have this attitude toward our children. And we have had a beautiful family relationship.

"So it was a shocking surprise when my daughter came to me and said, 'Mom, I really need your help!' She shared that she was trapped in drugs. I listened with inward shock. I had no idea she was even involved. I had heard of many other families facing drug problems, but I thought that was one problem we wouldn't experience with our children.

"Even though we were shocked and devastated, both my husband and I were able to respond with unconditional love, acceptance, and a genuine desire to help her in her time of desperate need.

"One day during counseling, she shared that she could have justified continuing on drugs if only we had not loved her and been so good to her. The guilt was so great that she had to turn from drugs.

"Sometime later she shared that she had seriously considered suicide. I really believe that if we had not responded in love and acceptance and a desire to help, we would not have her today. That's why I say that adopting and following this practice of listening without condemnation was a life-and-death matter for us."

We are never to condemn others. Appearing shocked can feel like condemnation to someone with a heavy burden.

THOUGHTS TO REMEMBER

We need to be aware that we cannot explain God and His ways, nor can we fix people. We can go to them, weep with them, sit in silence with them, listen to them, pray for them, and humble ourselves and admit when we are wrong.

"My dear brothers, take note of this: Everyone should be quick to listen, slow to speak and slow to become angry" (James 1:19).

PRACTICING AND JOURNALING

1. Pray this Scripture-based prayer each day this week: "Father, help me to listen well. Guide me in my thoughts and speech so that no unwholesome words come out of my mouth but only words that are good, words that edify others according to the need of the moment. May my words give grace to those who hear. Help me to say only what is good and helpful to those I am talking to. Let my words give them a blessing." (See Ephesians 4:29, NASB and TLB.)

2. Work at really listening to each of your family members and close friends this week. How did they respond to your listening style? How did that make you feel?

3. Write an illustration of how you showed genuine interest in a friend by listening to her and asking her questions about her activities and interests.

13

More Guides for People-Helping

In chapter 12 we emphasized the importance of developing the grace and art of active listening. Listening conveys our interest, our concern, and our understanding. We continue the guides for people-helping.

More Guides for People-Helping

Listen for the Real Problem

The real problem a person is facing may not be evident in the first comment stated or the first question asked. One mother told what happened when she did not discern the real problem.

"After someone speaks, I immediately jump to conclusions and do not really listen to what the child is communicating. My daughter, a high-school student, asked if she could drop her Spanish class. My immediate reaction was, 'No, why should you drop a class?' And there was no more discussion! She honored my wish and completed the quarter. After that, she never took another Spanish course. I found out later that two-thirds of the class had dropped Spanish because of the teacher's attitude.

"If I could do it over, I would calmly question her to find out why she wanted to do what she asked for. Hindsight is slowly teaching me not to jump to conclusions."

At one of our workshops a lady came up to me and asked, "How do you know God's will in a matter? He doesn't speak in words. He doesn't write in the sky!" Her tone of voice and obvious, sarcastic exaggeration were significant. Though I detected this negative, accusing, blaming attitude, I didn't mention it. I did wonder if the stated question was the real problem; but, to answer her verbal question, I briefly shared with her four significant criteria in determining God's will: (1) What God's Word says, (2) circumstances, (3) the witness of people, and (4) inner peace—"Let the peace of God rule . . ." (Colossians 3:15, KJV).

Then I asked, "Do you have a specific situation in mind?"

In answering she made a significant statement, which led to the real problem: "I want another child and my husband doesn't. He thinks our time in life is against us and that we shouldn't for financial reasons. He just doesn't seem to have the desire. I guess, really . . . he doesn't want that responsibility at our age."

So it was a big issue of contention, a point of argument between them. Then I realized her actual question was, "How do I get my way when my husband doesn't want what I want?" From that point on we talked about the real issue and the solution for it.

Listen for Their Own Conclusions

Listen for or encourage them to share the answers they have already concluded for themselves. Many times they know the right answer and simply need reassurance and reinforcement that they are going the right way.

A single woman said she finds it very difficult to be with couples who are happily married. "That makes me more and more dissatisfied with my single life, and it greatly increases my desire for marriage. I find it very difficult to handle. Now it is true that I have been neglecting my time alone with the Lord. I haven't had a time in the Word for a long, long time. Guess I really need to start there and get back to spending time in the Word with the Lord."

After sharing, she drew her own conclusions as to what her first step should be. I simply affirmed and underscored the importance of her stated conclusion. She was trying to fill her God-shaped vacuum with other things.

Listen for Clues

Look for clues people might give you. Use their words to get your point across.

A lady wanted me to help her solve her problem with immoral thoughts, which she said turned into immoral actions. She said these thoughts were stimulated by a certain kind of music she listened to over the radio. As she listened, her thoughts fed her imagination, and then she would commit the act.

After she had shared the basics of her concern, I simply made a few comments and asked a couple of questions based on what she had said or implied. "Did I hear you say it begins in your thoughts, especially when you listen to a certain kind of music, and then it moves out into actions? What do you think you should do when that offensive kind of music comes over the radio?"

Would you believe she had the right answer? But it was much better for her to draw that conclusion and state it than for me to tell her what she ought to do. She gave the clue to her need, and I underscored it.

Listen Through Periods of Silence

Be comfortable during what may seem like long periods of silence. Be patient while they struggle to verbalize their need. Do not feel you have to fill the silence with words. During silences, they may be working through a deep soul struggle, attempting to decide whether or not to face the situation realistically, make the right decision, and take the necessary follow-through steps.

You may recall how I listened to Hannah for over two hours with long periods of silence and what that meant to her (chapter 1).

Listen to Ask Profitable Questions

Carefully worded questions can help the person clarify her own problem. But we must listen in order to know how to ask profitable questions.

"You stated. . . . What do you think you ought to do about this?" This approach will help you better understand how far along the person is in her own mind toward a solution.

If she asks, "What do you do if? . . ."

You might ask, "Are you thinking of a specific situation?"

Listen to Determine Their Conscience

What is conscience? It is that internal *voice* in the soul that dictates what a person should or should not allow. In one of his messages, my pastor, Ben Cross, defined it, "Our conscience is that structure in our soul that gives us the ability to feel whether something is right or wrong."

How is conscience developed? Pastor Ben explained it this way:

> Conscience is influenced, shaped, and developed throughout our life by significant relationships (parents and peers), by our culture and our experiences. However, you know that our parents and peers, our culture and our experiences were not always truthful. Therefore, we have the capacity in our conscience to feel that something is very right when, in fact, it is very wrong, or that something is very wrong when in fact it is okay.
>
> When we get saved our conscience isn't suddenly erased or transformed so that we read and interpret life completely accurately according to the Word of God. We carry old baggage on into our new life. Over a whole lifetime God transforms our conscience, but it is a slow process.[1]

THE WEAK CONSCIENCE

Not all issues of right and wrong are clear and definite in Scripture. There are some gray areas of Christian behavior that are not actually forbidden by Scripture. In these gray areas Christians may have different views of what is right or wrong. To some, these become a conscience issue—"Christians shouldn't do that." The basic scriptural teaching that applies is found in 1 Corinthians 8:9–12:

> Be careful, however, that the exercise of your freedom does not become a stumbling block to the weak. For if anyone with a

weak conscience sees you who have this knowledge eating in an idol's temple, won't he be emboldened to eat what has been sacrificed to idols? So this weak brother, for whom Christ died, is destroyed by your knowledge.

The apostle Paul admonishes us to honor the person with the weak conscience. We are not to flaunt our liberty or expect or pressure others to live according to our conscience. We may have greater liberty of conscience because of our knowledge.

"Therefore," Pastor Ben explained, "some things become sin for some because they are wrong according to their personal theology (their conscience), but they are not sin for another because they are not wrong according to God's theology. If by the practice of your liberty, you embolden another to do something that violates his conscience, you cause him to sin, and his conscience could become seared and his ability to hear the voice of God diminished. Hence, you have caused him to stumble, and that would not only be sin against him, but also sin against Christ."

WEAK OR LEGALISTIC?

"Let me clarify the difference between a *weak* conscience and a *legalistic* conscience," Pastor Ben continued:

> When Paul talks about the brother or sister with the weak conscience, he's not talking about the legalist. He's talking about a believer whose conscience tells him the behavior is wrong, but after watching you he will be tempted to go ahead and do it and thus violate his conscience and sin against God. That's not a legalist. That's a person with a weak conscience who might stumble.
>
> A legalist could have a strong opinion on an issue but would not be tempted to do something he thinks is wrong. So, in exercising your liberty, you may have offended his opinion, but you have not caused him to stumble because he would not follow your example.
>
> It's very important that you understand the difference between a legalist and someone with a weak conscience. You should

not allow people with a more conservative or simplistic view of morality to dictate what you can and cannot do in your liberty in Jesus Christ. In 1 Corinthians, Paul is talking about restricting your liberty for the sake of protecting the brother or sister with a *weak* conscience who would follow you in your activity and destroy himself in the process. There's a huge difference.[1]

Pastor Ben illustrates this out of his own life. A couple years into his first pastorate he decided to start growing a beard. Some of the church people didn't like it, but since there was nothing in the Bible that said you couldn't grow a beard, he knew he was just offending their opinions and he would not cause any of them to stumble. So he kept his beard even though it irritated some.

Later he learned that a former hippie who had recently come to the Lord under his ministry had stopped coming to church because he was genuinely offended by Ben's beard. It represented everything he had lived for in the hippie lifestyle—dope, sex, and rebellion. To him, a beard was a sign of that rebellion. Now the fellow was confused and about ready to give up his faith because of Ben's beard.

When Ben learned of this, he immediately shaved off his beard, and in the weeks to come that fellow was restored to a walk of obedience and became a glowing Christian gentleman with a lovely Christian family. Ben said, "I was glad to shave my beard for the sake of a man's soul, but not to satisfy somebody's opinion. There's the difference."

SUE'S CONSCIENCE RIGHTLY CONDEMNED HER

Jay Adams in his book, *Competent to Counsel,* gives another very helpful illustration of this conscience issue. This is an old book and the illustration is of an issue you may never have had a problem with, but the conscience principle is the same. He speaks of Sue, a woman who feels guilty about wearing lipstick.

> How could Sue be guilty of wearing lipstick? She could if [she] had come from a home where she had been taught that wearing lipstick was a sin. Now, if in college she has begun to

wear lipstick in order not to look peculiar, but is doing so against her standards, she will be guilty of sin, and her guilt will be real. Even if wearing lipstick is not sinful in itself, Sue's act is sinful because it did not proceed from faith (see Romans 14:21–23).

When Sue used lipstick, she thought her act was (or might have been) a sin against God, and yet she did it anyway. It is this rebellion against God for which she is guilty and about which her conscience rightly condemns her. Sue must confess her sin to find forgiveness and relief, and must not be told that her guilt is false. Later, if it is important to do so, the matter of whether Sue's standard is biblical may be discussed; but these are two distinct questions. Yet they have been confused consistently.[2]

Don't let the legalists who are bound by some nonbiblical rules and regulations control you. On the other hand, keep your eyes and ears out for the weak brother or sister who might stumble because they don't acknowledge your liberty.

Let each be fully convinced in his own mind. . . . But he who doubts is condemned if he eats, because he does not eat from faith; for whatever is not from faith is sin. (Romans 14:5, 23: NKJV)

BE SENSITIVE TO THE OTHER PERSON'S CONSCIENCE

I continually meet women who are struggling with the gray areas of Christian conduct. There are two basic ways you can help a woman acknowledge the importance of her conscience and its role in her behavior: (1) Discover where her conscience stands, and (2) Don't impose your conscience on her.

Does she have a well-taught, maturing conscience, or is it weak or legalistic? To help clarify her understanding of her conscience, you might ask thoughtful questions such as: "What do you think you should do about this? What does the Bible say about this? Do you have any idea what the right thing is for you to do?" Once she understands where her conscience stands, encourage her to not violate it in her actions.

We are not to impose our conscience on another person; that is, to expect or encourage him or her to live by *our* conscience.

"For several months, I was trying to be my husband's conscience, pressuring him to be more spiritual. I felt that I was growing in the Lord, and he was losing interest. I would ask him if he had been having quiet times and prayer, instead of letting him alone and letting the Lord take care of the situation. I handed this to the Lord, and in less than two weeks my husband asked me to pray with him. He prayed specifically to be forgiven for not being my spiritual leader. This is exactly what I had been trying to *make* him be. Isn't it good! The Lord really knows His business and how best to accomplish it!"

Listen, but Don't Repeat to Others What You Have Heard

Keep the confidence of the one who has shared the deep things of her heart with you. Proverbs says:

> A talebearer reveals secrets, but he who is of a faithful spirit conceals a matter. (Proverbs 11:13, NKJV)

> The words of a talebearer are like tasty trifles, and they go down into the inmost body. (Proverbs 18:8, NKJV)

> A gossip betrays a confidence; so avoid a man who talks too much. (Proverbs 20:19, NIV)

Speak—but Not Too Soon

While listening to a person, you may think of several biblical principles that would apply to her situation. Usually she will not be ready to receive these if you share them too abruptly or too soon. She will want to be sure you really understand. She may just need to talk the whole situation out. This was true of Rita, a college freshman.

From the time she was twelve until she was sixteen, Rita attended the camp where I was a counselor. Each summer we would plan for some special time together when she could ask questions and share her thoughts. It was a thrill to share with this young, deeply committed Christian who had such a tender heart and intelligent, inquiring mind.

Now she was a college freshman, and she invited me to visit for a weekend. She and some other top students loved to get together and discuss philosophical and biblical ideas. From the time that I arrived, she shared some of the questions they had been discussing but had not yet found answers to.

Immediately, I recognized that the answers to some of the questions were very simply stated in the Word of God. Since she was asking me the questions, and since she had invited me with the intention of hearing my point of view, I caught my breath to begin to answer one of the questions. When she heard me about to answer, she quickly said, "Don't answer it yet. Really think about it for a while. We've been talking about this for quite some time."

This cue was clear. How could I have an answer so quickly when they had been discussing it so long? I didn't answer, but just continued to listen; in fact, I listened for most of the rest of weekend. When our last day together came, I felt that I now should have the privilege of talking just a bit. So I gave her the same simple answer that I would have given two days before.

First, I cautioned her about not "worshiping at the shrine of intellectual curiosity." Then I suggested that we read Colossians, using Phillips' paraphrase. As we read the whole book aloud, she realized that it was speaking very clearly to her need. Now we could talk a little more, and she was ready to listen.

She had not wanted me to have an answer right away—not even a simple, clear answer from the Word. She had wanted me to think philosophically and intellectually, as she and her friends had done. She wanted me to speak, but not too soon.

On the other hand, in a confident relationship, it is certainly appropriate to share your comforting words, verses of Scripture, poems, and devotional thoughts.

Speak—Asking Careful Questions at Proper Times

Earlier, we stressed the importance of listening so we would be able to ask helpful questions. Now we look at how careful questions can help the person see for herself whether she needs to change her attitude or actions.

Notice Jesus' example when He appeared to two men walking from Jerusalem to Emmaus after the resurrection. He began with two questions that led them to tell Him of their sorrow, bewilderment, and dashed hopes.

> He asked them, "What are you discussing together as you walk along?"
>
> They stood still, their faces downcast. One of them, named Cleopas, asked him, "Are you only a visitor to Jerusalem and do not know the things that have happened there in these days?"
>
> "What things?" he asked.
>
> "About Jesus of Nazareth," they replied. "He was a prophet, powerful in word and deed before God and all the people. The chief priests and our rulers handed him over to be sentenced to death, and they crucified him; but we had hoped that he was the one who was going to redeem Israel. And what is more, it is the third day since all this took place. In addition, some of our women amazed us. They went to the tomb early this morning but didn't find his body. They came and told us that they had seen a vision of angels, who said he was alive. Then some of our companions went to the tomb and found it just as the women had said, but him they did not see." (Luke 24:17–24)

Two little questions brought out their feelings and gave them courage to share their deep confusion with this kind stranger who listened compassionately. Some questions you might use as you're listening to someone share a problem:

- Can you give me an example of that situation?
- How does this make the children (husband, friend) feel?
- How do you feel about . . . ?
- Is this your situation?
- What advice did your pastor/counselor give to you?
- Have you had other counseling on this?
- What have you already tried?
- What do you think you ought to do?
- What do you think God's Word teaches about this?

Speak to Clarify Their Response

After you have heard the person out and have communicated love and understanding, you may need to correct or clarify her own response to hear her evaluation of the situation or need.

A friend was receiving strong teaching on the subject of having large families. One day she shared that she was thinking of having her tubes untied. I asked her why she was considering this.

"Well, the children really want me to have another baby."

I sensed this comment might be stemming from the teaching she had been hearing, so I asked, "Totally apart from the children, how do you feel about having a baby at this time in your life?"

"Well, kinda excited; but then another part of me isn't."

"Does your husband want a baby?"

"No! He really doesn't. He says we can't afford it, and besides he really doesn't want another child. He's really against it."

She needed someone to help her sort out her thinking.

Speak—Suggesting a Project

As a mentor, it is often wise to assign or suggest a project that will help the person follow through on a solution to her problem. This could be something as simple as memorizing a Bible verse and repeating it morning and evening, or it might be to prepare her husband's favorite dinners two times this week or have the house picked up by 5 P.M. for the next three days. Plan short, realistic goals that can be met.

PROJECT: WORK TOGETHER

You might work together to help another person with a need. One lady became burdened for a friend who had both weight and marital problems. She thought of a project that they could do together. The friend lost fifty pounds, and her self-esteem and marriage greatly improved.

PROJECT: KNOW GOD LOVES YOU

One lady would not allow herself to really believe or verbally admit that God loved her. I gave her a four-week project about confessing God's love on a regular basis, along with specific ways of doing it.

PROJECT: FOR SOMEONE WITH A POOR FATHER IMAGE

One woman found it difficult to have positive thoughts about God, so I gave her a project to help her to come to believe in our Heavenly Father's loving character.

PROJECT: CREATE YOUR OWN

We can encourage others to create a project of their own. A friend shared how she had recently heard a message on the importance of joy in the Christian life. The speaker taught that joy comes as a result of resting in four great fundamental truths:

1. I am accepted and loved by God
2. My circumstances are under God's blessed control
3. I have someone worth having—Christ
4. I have someone worth sharing—Christ

Her heart responded, "I want my life to be filled with that kind of joy!" She decided to review these thoughts each morning in her quiet time, asking God to make them true in her experience that day.

PROJECT: USING SONGS AND HYMNS

One friend said, "A project I have enjoyed this year is selecting a 'Hymn of the Month.' This turns my attention and trust toward the Lord."

Another help is to change a few words in a chorus or hymn you know. Or make up and sing your own words to a comfortable tune. When my housemate was traveling alone by car, she took the song "God Is So Good" and sang through a number of the attributes of God: He loves me so, He changes not, He is my peace, He's merciful, He's faithful too, etc.

Projects! What a simple yet sure means of growth. It is good to plan projects for ourselves as well as to help others design projects that will more deeply imbed the life-changing truth of the Word of God into our hearts and minds.

Also, assigning projects with accountability can help you determine whether the person you are trying to help is serious about wanting help and is willing to work toward a change.

Speak—Words of Encouragement

Encourage! Encourage! Encourage! That's what people-helping is all about. A people helper is to be an encourager.

Encouragement is actually the ministry of all three persons of the Triune God. The following verses bring this out:

> [GOD THE FATHER]
> Praise be to the God and Father of our Lord Jesus Christ, the Father of compassion and the God of all comfort [encouragement]. . . . (2 Corinthians 1:3)

> [GOD THE SON]
> "May our Lord Jesus Christ himself . . . encourage your hearts and strengthen you in every good deed and word." (2 Thessalonians 2:16–17)

> [GOD THE HOLY SPIRIT]
> And I will ask the Father, and He will give you another Comforter (Counselor, Helper, Intercessor, Advocate, Strengthener and Standby) that He may remain with you forever. (John 14:16, AMP)

That's encouragement! We should look for ways to encourage others in our daily encounters. Encourage people at church. Encourage those who have ministered to you. Write that note; make that phone call; take time to speak those kind, thoughtful words. One person wrote:

> Dear Verna,
> About ten years ago I purchased a complete set of audio cassettes on your Enriched Living Workshops. I am interested

in beginning this study again with my future daughter-in-law. Is it still possible to purchase the study guides? I first attended your workshop twenty years ago. The principles I learned then have been invaluable to me as I have raised five children and sought to be the kind of person that only God could make me. When my first daughter-in-law approached me about doing a study together, I immediately thought of your course. I'm looking forward to sharing with her what has been so valuable to me."

This note came in an order for five cassettes:

Please send me five more *Input for a Rejoicing Heart* tapes. I can't tell you how many women (including myself) have been blessed by these tapes. Sharing these is one of my ways of encouraging others.

At my dad's funeral, we all were taking pictures of the families. Being single, I didn't have a family for a picture. Immediately Suzannah, my niece, became aware of and sensitive to that and said, "Verna, come be a part of our family." That simple, sensitive, thoughtful word comforted me deep down in my soul for a long time. It was so meaningful that I cried over the very specialness of it.

A simple, well-timed word of encouragement can have a very positive influence on a person. Before you know it, she will touch another, and that one will touch another. Your little word of encouragement could have tremendous implications for eternity and bring great joy to your own heart.

Eighty-four-year-old Bernice wrote what a blessing she receives when she reaches out and ministers to others by sharing a principle the Lord made real to her in the workshop.

Dear Miss Birkey,
"Drop a stone into the water—in a moment it is gone, but there are a hundred ripples circling on and on and on. Say a word of cheer—in a moment it is gone, but there are a hundred ripples circling on and on and on."

You really dropped a stone at your last workshop here when you told about the girl whose boyfriend jilted her, owed her money, and hadn't paid her back. The principles you gave were:

1. confessing her wrong attitude of resentment
2. thanking God for her situation—that he jilted her, owed her money, and hadn't yet paid it back; and
3. cooperating with God in the situation

Let me tell you the joy I've had in passing on these three principles.

A friend asked me to write to a mutual friend in California who was depressed. Her husband had left for India to continue their work there, and now she discovered she was pregnant. She is not well, has three children, and felt this was more than she could stand. She was terribly frustrated and discouraged. I wrote to her and took her through these three steps. This set her free.

A converted Jewess visited my California friend and was so impressed with these principles that she wanted a copy. Later this Jewess wrote to me thanking me for passing them on. They were helping her and (she wrote in large capital letters) OTHERS.

Then I shared these steps with a friend whose son was on drugs. She asked for a copy.

Some friends in Seattle with whom I shared put these principles to work as they waited for a word from the hospital concerning their daughter.

Would you believe it? I am eighty-four and still teach a class of women! Some are young mothers, and I have shared all this with them. Thanks for dropping the stone.

That's what I hope and pray will happen as you apply the principles given in this book, that you will reach out to others and cause the ripples to expand. We will each have our personal methods—some structured and some nonstructured. But God's principles will work through anyone who puts them into action.

A pastor's wife in New York called to order three copies of my book, *If God Is in Control, Why Is My World Falling Apart?* She told me her remarkable "ripple" story.

About three years prior to our conversation, she had studied the book thoroughly—looking up all the verses and answering all the questions. When the ladies in her church asked her to suggest material for a spring Bible study, she mentioned how this book had helped her so much.

The ladies asked her to lead them through the study. They really worked hard at the lessons, and the pastor's wife reported seeing a tremendous difference in each of their lives. Then several of them began leading the study with even more ladies. The ripples were going out.

"Also," she added, "My husband has led a young man to the Lord and now wants to take him through this book because he saw what a difference it has made in my life. Our women are now encouraging the pastor to take all the men through the book."

It just keeps snowballing and the encouragement keeps flowing.

Speak—Pray for or with That One

If someone shares a burden with you personally or by phone, ask if she would like you to pray right then—if you sense that it is the appropriate time—or assure her that you will be praying for her.

POWER FOR THE PEOPLE HELPER

There are several key areas that are fundamental to our appropriating God's power for people-helping.

Claim God's Promises

Over and over in His Word, God promises His help and power to those who are doing His work. It is our responsibility to read, study, and claim His promises. Depend on God to arrange your thoughts in an orderly and meaningful way and to help you give the right answer for the need of the moment. As you deliberately trust Him for answers, God will give wisdom (see James 1:5). Additional verses that are promises of His wisdom and help as we trust Him:

The plans of the mind and orderly thinking belong to man, but from the Lord comes the [wise] answer of the tongue. (Proverbs 16:1, AMP)

The Lord God has given Me the tongue of the learned, that I should know how to speak a word in season to him who is weary. He awakens Me morning by morning, He awakens my ear to hear as the learned. (Isaiah 50:4, NKJV)

I am full of power by the Spirit of the Lord. . . . (Micah 3:8, NKJV) [You can personally apply this to yourself by saying, "I am full of power by the Spirit of the Lord to do all the will of God for me."]

I can do all things through Christ who strengthens me. (Philippians 4:13, NKJV)

For God has not given us a spirit of fear, but of power and of love and of a sound mind. (2 Timothy 1:7, NKJV)

So we can lift our hearts to God and say, "Create in me now orderly thinking, the tongue of the learned, the right words which will refresh and help this one, and give me the wisdom and power to do Your will in this situation."

Be Sure of God's Will

The assurance that we are walking in the way of God's purpose for us at this particular time of our lives gives us strength. If we are confident of His call, we can also be confident that He will enable, giving power to carry out His assignment. If I am walking in His will, then I must not look at my own resources and judge my adequacy by my own limitations. Instead, I must keep focused on His call, His plan, and His promises. One of my college professors put it this way, "God's callings are His enablings!"

When I first sensed that God was calling me into a ministry to women, a friend asked, "Do you really think you can do that?"

My answer at that time was, "If it's God's will, I can. If not, I can't."

Many times since then, I have seen that when I am walking in His way, obedient to His will, His power is fully available to me for that assignment. The most recent illustration of this is developing the *Linx* course and writing this book. Sometimes I wonder, "What am I doing? I'm so inadequate for this." When I have those thoughts, I go back to the basics and check to see if the indicators of God's guidance are still in order. What are those indicators? (1) The Word, (2) prayer, (3) the inner witness of the Spirit, (4) circumstances, (5) the church.

The Lord clearly affirmed these indicators again when I was in New York and Pennsylvania on a speaking trip. During those days, I had quite a bit of time alone on the plane and in the motel, so I decided to work through the *Experiencing God* workbook. Many, many times I underscored and highlighted thoughts and then wrote in the margin: *"Linx."* Without question, the Lord was confirming again and again that this was His assignment for me at this time.

The Lord used all five of the indicators of His guidance, but the last two seemed especially evident to me. Two years prior to this, during a casual conversation, our director of Women's Ministry, had asked me to start a mentoring program. I realized during this trip that her request was the Holy Spirit confirming His will through the church. This was and is further encouragement to me that *Linx* is not only God's idea, but it came in God's timing. And wonder of wonders, it is His appointment for me at this time. I'm awed, but greatly comforted and encouraged that it is His doing, His assignment, not simply my idea.

Therefore, no more "I can't." Instead it is, "I can with Jesus!" Obviously this calls for dependence on Him. I like the way the Amplified Bible puts Philippians 4:13: "I have strength for all things in Christ Who empowers me—I am ready for anything and equal to anything through Him Who infuses inner strength into me; that is, I am self-sufficient in Christ's sufficiency."

That's the power the Triune God gives us to carry out His assignments as we live in obedience to Him.

Being sure of God's will has increased my passion to both motivate women to love God with all their hearts and to equip them to reach out in love, understanding, and compassion to others. Connecting with other women on a one-on-one or small-group basis and giving friendship and encouragement to them is what servant-mentoring is all about.

Will You Join God in What He Is Doing?

Are you willing to step out in faith, relying on His power, to see what He will do? You may feel very inadequate or too small for such a big job. Jeremiah did. Look at his response to the Lord when God called him:

> The word of the Lord came to me, saying, "Before I formed you in the womb I knew you, before you were born I set you apart; I appointed you as a prophet to the nations."
>
> "Ah, Sovereign Lord," I said, "I do not know how to speak; I am only a child."
>
> But the Lord said to me, "Do not say, 'I am only a child.' You must go to everyone I send you to and say whatever I command you. Do not be afraid of them, for I am with you and will rescue you," declares the Lord.
>
> Then the Lord reached out his hand and touched my mouth and said to me, "Now, I have put my words in your mouth." (Jeremiah 1:4–9)

Although Jeremiah started out by making excuses, "I'm far too inadequate. I don't know what to say, and I'm far too inexperienced," God simply answered, "Don't say that. Trust Me. I'll do it through you, and you will do a great work under My appointment and My enablement." Jeremiah did it, together with God.

Whatever God is calling you to do, will you step out and trust Him? Or will you argue with Him, "Lord, You really don't know what You are doing. Surely, You haven't considered all the facts—my inabilities, my inexperience, my limitations."

Are you available to let Him take you beyond your comfort zone, beyond your experiences thus far? Are you ready to hear from Him regarding His calling, His assignment to you, without giving excuses. Will you step out in faith and become involved in the lives of other women?

Remember *Linx: Women Connecting with Women* has a twofold purpose. One is to equip women, helping us to identify our needs and make life changes so that we can become more effective dispensers of God's grace to others. We learn to truly listen to and become sensitive to the particular hurts of others. And we learn how to come alongside with support and encouragement. God will do the work in hearts, but He gives us the privilege of cooperating with Him as He works!

The second purpose is to develop meaningful, significant connections with a few other women. These links can help women to be knit together in love in supportive friendships, refreshing others, and being refreshed by them.

Will you join God in the work that He wants to accomplish through you in a *Linx* friendship ministry? A *Linx* friendship can be tailored to meet your needs or the needs of someone you want to help. It might be one on one or a small group of two to four, women who connect for friendship, mentoring, general support, or encouragement.

The groups can be a combination of study, social times, and spiritual support: doing a Bible study, sharing day-to-day events together, having coffee or lunch, going shopping or walking, learning a new skill, praying together—whatever your *Linx* friendship connection decides.

Or, you might want to lead a group through this book. We've designed it so that it's easy to use in small or large groups. I'd love to see many little home study groups spring up using the *Textbook* and companion *Study Guide* (see page 333 for how to order). God is using this course in amazing ways to help even mature Christians become more comfortable comforters, encouragers, mentors, and people helpers. Here's a few of their comments:

The emphasis in *Linx* is on becoming prepared to help others, but in doing that, I found that I was examining my own life. That revealed some problem areas, and now I've experienced freedom in those areas. I've been a part of many other Bible studies but this was the most helpful, practical, life-related Bible study I've ever taken! —*Active in Bible Studies for 25 Years*

Women Connecting with Women showed me areas of twisted thinking in my own life. For a lot of years I believed that being a good Christian meant doing anything anyone asked of me. Every session of Linx has been positive and hope-giving. The course is a lot like going to a group counseling session but without the high cost. —*Head Nurse, Bible Study Leader, Wife, and Mother*

Linx has provided in an organized and concise curriculum the principles I want to pass on to the women of my church. Verna has brought it all together in a format that provides building blocks for personal growth and for developing practical skills in all relationships. —*A Director of Women's Ministries*

THOUGHTS TO REMEMBER

Listen, but don't repeat to others what you heard. "A talebearer reveals secrets, but he who is of a faithful spirit conceals a matter" (Proverbs 11:13, NKJV).

Power for people-helping comes from the Holy Spirit. "The plans of the mind and orderly thinking belong to man, but from the Lord comes the [wise] answer of the tongue" (Proverbs 16:1, AMP).

PRACTICING AND JOURNALING

1. Review the points under the importance of listening. Which ones do you feel you need to work on the most?
2. Speak some words of encouragement to each family member this week. Jot down what you said, along with their response.

3. Write a note or call a friend to encourage her. Ask her to go out for a cup of coffee or for a walk. Learn to take risks, initiate, and go beyond your comfort zone.

14

Helping People in Crisis

Mrs. Cardinal is in the hospital. The book *Birdlife in Wington* describes two of her visitors:

Mrs. Cardinal is in the hospital as a result of an airplane accident, and has had a relapse. She was doing quite well until Friday when Mrs. Owl and Mrs. Pelican made a call. That night she took a sudden turn for the worse, and now the doctor is quite concerned. He has put on a special nurse and issued a strict order, "Absolutely no visitors." Mrs. Owl and Mrs. Pelican cannot understand it, because they know their visit cheered her up to no end!

They arrived at the hospital just after lunch when the patients were supposed to be resting. It was best to go early, they had agreed, so their visit would not be rushed. Upon their arrival, they did not inquire at the desk, but started down the hall, peering into every room. Naturally, this was embarrassing to a number of patients, but Mrs. Owl and Mrs. Pelican didn't mind.

Finally, they came to a door marked, "No visitors, please!" "This must be it," said Mrs. Owl as she pushed open the door.

"Yes, here is Mrs. Cardinal, but I do believe she is asleep. Do you think we should waken her?"

"Yes, of course," replied Mrs. Pelican. "She wouldn't want to miss our visit. Besides, she has nothing to do all day but sleep."

By this time they had shed their coats and pitched them on the bed. "Just us," said Mrs. Pelican, "we dropped in to cheer you up. My! but you have a lot of flowers; your room reminds me of a funeral parlor."

"You're a lucky bird," said Mrs. Owl, as she settled down in a chair with her arm resting on the side of the bed, with the result that she shook it every time she moved, "to be lying up there in a nice soft bed where you can get a good rest. That's where I ought to be. No one knows how I've suffered lately. But I just can't take time to go to bed. Some birds can, but I can't."

"You couldn't possibly feel as bad as I do," Mrs. Pelican broke in. "I'm so nervous, and I've completely lost my appetite. Last night we had fish for supper. Mr. Pelican seemed to enjoy it, but all I could possibly eat was a shrimp cocktail, a bowl of oyster stew, four or five perch, three crab cakes—then I just forced myself to eat a piece of pie for dessert. The little I did eat gave me indigestion. I really don't have the appetite of a Sparrow."

"More like the appetite of an Ostrich!" thought Mrs. Owl, but she didn't say it.

"But let us talk about your aches and pains rather than ours," continued Mrs. Pelican. "Was it only one wing you broke when you collided with that airplane?"

"Do let us see the wound," said Mrs. Owl before Mrs. Cardinal could answer, pulling back the cover as she talked. "My! it does look bad. Do you suppose gangrene has set in?"

"I don't like the way it is bandaged," said Mrs. Pelican. "Who is your physician anyway?"

"Dr. Snowbird," replied Mrs. Cardinal weakly.

"I thought so," said Mrs. Pelican. "You remember poor old Mrs. Grosbeak was a patient of his!"

"Her death was such a shock," said Mrs. Owl. "Mrs. Pelican and I called on her two days before she passed away, and we had no idea the end was near. She looked no worse than you do, my dear."

"Yes, and she had failed to make her will," added Mrs. Pelican. "I am sure you have attended to that, Mrs. Cardinal. Just think how unhappy you would be in the next world if Mr. Cardinal's second wife should get all your property!"

At this point the two callers were interrupted by the arrival of the nurse with Mrs. Cardinal's supper tray.

"Don't tell me it is supper time," said Mrs. Owl. "How time does fly. Who would have thought we have been here three hours! Well, we just must go. Don't be disappointed if you don't feel like eating all of your supper. Hospital food is terrible."

At the door Mrs. Pelican turned back. "You are very wise to have this 'No Visitors' sign on the door," she said. "It should keep out a lot of undesirables. Some birds can be so thoughtless."

"It really makes one feel good to do a 'bird scout' deed each day, doesn't it?" said Mrs. Owl, as they walked down the hall.

"It certainly does," replied Mrs. Pelican. "Next week perhaps we can do another by attending a funeral together."

Strange, isn't it, that Mrs. Owl and Mrs. Pelican are the only two birds in Wington that do not understand why Mrs. Cardinal had a relapse.[1]

Times of crisis come to all of us. Some forms of crisis are:

- The sudden death of a loved one
- A broken engagement
- Breakdown in marriage, divorce
- Personal injury
- Sudden loss of job or retirement
- Loss of health
- Trouble with children
- Trouble in child's marriage
- Work upsets or new job

What we need at these times is not a Mrs. Owl or a Mrs. Pelican, but someone who will stand with us to understand, listen, comfort, and encourage.

At times we may feel that we don't have a lot to say to someone who is going through a difficult experience. We feel we have no wise words of advice. Wise words are not always necessary. Through our presence we communicate our concern and love. We are there to listen and to let the person express her varied emotions. To empathize, not condemn. To support, not sermonize. God wants each of us to be a comfortable comforter as 2 Corinthians 1:2–4 encourages us:

> Grace and peace to you from God our Father and the Lord Jesus Christ. Praise be to the God and Father of our Lord Jesus Christ, the Father of compassion and the God of all comfort, who comforts us in all our troubles, so that we can comfort those in any trouble with the comfort we ourselves have received from God.

Many times as the person openly expresses how she feels, she is better able to identify her true feelings. In more acute crises she may experience anxiety, confusion, anger, depression, and guilt. Sometimes there is anger over the situation—toward herself, toward others, or toward the Lord. As she senses your calmness, concern, and acceptance of her (including her varied emotions), she is more prepared to accept herself and the situation.

UNDERSTANDING THE CRISIS CYCLE

If we understand the crisis cycle, we can better anticipate reactions and can better understand both ourselves and the other person. The following diagram of the stages in a crisis experience will help us visualize this process.

These are stages that a person typically goes through when experiencing a crisis in life, as well as the crisis of a death.

Denial
"No, not me! It cannot be true." A stunned state of shock and disbelief that may be accompanied by uncontrolled emotions.

Guilt
A feeling of having failed in some way, or a sense of regret and self-accusation.

Anger
"Why me? Why couldn't it have been ————?" A response of irritability, resentment, and questioning.

Bargaining

Especially with God, endeavoring to determine some way to postpone or avert the inevitable happening.

Depression

"What's the use?" Mournfully thinking of the impending loss of everything and everybody the person loves. A sense of unreality and inability to cope.

Isolation

A sense of acute loneliness and seemingly unbearable anguish.

Acceptance

Not in despair, but with peace. Readjusting the lifestyle to accept both the loss and the struggle that accompanies new patterns of living.

APPLYING THE CRISIS CYCLE

These stages are not absolute, but the description does provide a general pattern. The way they play out varies as much as individuals do, and the various emotions may recur from time to time.

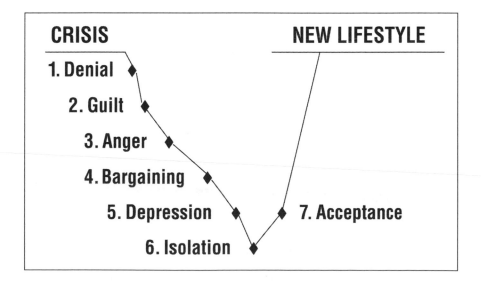

As you are able to share this description of the "normal" journey, when appropriate, with those who are going through it, you can be a source of hope and encouragement to them. The hurting ones can begin to understand and take comfort in the fact that their questions and reactions are normal. They can begin to see that there is hope in acceptance.

Each Stage Takes Time

Hurting people need to realize that each one of these stages may take time, especially the ultimate acceptance of the situation. We can assure them that each tiny step they take in dealing with the problem will move them toward inner healing and toward developing a new lifestyle. They will gradually learn new ways to cope with the difficulties and trials related to the situation and new ways of appropriating the resources of the Lord by faith.

God Has a Purpose for Good

God uses crises in our lives to help us grow as Christians, to lead us to a richer life in Him and a deeper dependence upon Him. Many times we learn better habits and attitudes and grow into a whole new lifestyle.

Oswald Chambers makes these comments in reference to Revelation 1:7 (NKJV), "Behold, He is coming with clouds":

> In the Bible clouds are always associated with God. Clouds are those sorrows, sufferings, or providential circumstances, within or without our personal lives, which actually seem to contradict the sovereignty of God. Yet it is through these very clouds that the Spirit of God is teaching us how to walk by faith. If there were never any clouds in our lives, we would have no faith. "The clouds are the dust of [our Father's] feet" (Nahum 1:3). They are a sign that God is there. What a revelation it is to know that sorrow, bereavement, and suffering are actually the clouds that come along with God! God cannot come near us without clouds—He does not come in clear-shining brightness.
>
> It is not true to say that God wants to teach us something in our trials. Through every cloud He brings our way, He wants us to unlearn something. His purpose in using the cloud is to sim-

plify our beliefs until our relationship to Him is exactly like that of a child.[2]

GENERAL GUIDELINES FOR HELPING PEOPLE IN CRISIS

Help Them . . .
Face the Problem

Help them face the fact that there is a problem and assist them toward a more thorough understanding of the situation.

Acknowledge Negative Feelings

Encourage them to acknowledge their negative feelings and to realize they are normal. Help them to gain freedom from the feelings of guilt, anxiety, and resentment.

Explore Ways of Coping

Explore with them practical ways of coping with the situation. Encourage them to assume the responsibility to change the things that can be changed and accept the things that cannot be changed. Help them to sift through these things and act on what they know they ought to do.

Draw Close to People

Encourage them to make an effort to draw close to people—a support group, family, friends, and pastor. If suitable, you might plan periodic phone calls or regular get-togethers for sharing, prayer, or Bible study.

Reinforce Time with the Lord

Encourage them to reinforce their own personal time alone with the Lord and to memorize appropriate Scriptures and meaningful hymns and choruses.

And . . .
Assist Them in Practical Ways

Do what you can in practical ways to assist them in their daily tasks or in mobilizing prayer support for them.

HELPING PEOPLE IN A SPECIFIC CRISIS

By offering the following suggestions for providing support to people who may find themselves in four different situations that devastate, I am not implying that the process is easy or that these are the only possibilities for helping. These are suggestions for you to consider when you find yourself with someone who is going through one of these situations.

The person you are helping will continue to need your patience, understanding, and support all along the way.

Help for One Left Alone

In giving helps for the widow, divorcee, or persons left alone, Virginia Watts, in her book, *The Single Parent,* gives the following suggestions:

> Acknowledge your true feelings of loneliness, anger, guilt, grief, depression, others.
>
> Recognize aloneness as the first feeling most newly single [people and other alone persons] experience.
>
> Realize that it takes time to heal. [It doesn't happen overnight.]
>
> Be prepared for special days which may be difficult to face. [Plan ahead to keep from being alone—anniversary, anniversary of death, etc.]
>
> Begin to develop your own unique personality—this is God's will for you. Study Psalm 139; Isaiah 43:1–4, 7; Philippians 2:1–18. [After her husband died, one friend said, "I don't really know who I am now. I've always been Al's wife."]
>
> Learn more about God and how He helps people through crisis experiences. Study 2 Chronicles 20:1–12; Acts 7:1–50.
>
> Believe that the Bible is true. Memorize the following passages to help you through your personal crisis: Psalm 23; Joshua 1:9; and Hebrews 13:5.
>
> Read to gain understanding of yourself, your problems, and God.[3]

To Mrs. Watts' list I would add: Find a support person or group that understands your kind of situation and the pain it brings. Those who have gone through a similar experience and understand something of your thoughts, feelings, and questions can help you realize how typical they are. This can be a real help to you in your readjustment time.

Helping Children of Divorce

Many times the question comes, "How and what do we share with the children when my husband has said he plans to divorce me?" We are not, of course, in any way encouraging easy divorce. But when it happens, it is so important to give the children some of the facts at the appropriate time, and to communicate as much sense of security and love as possible. Here are a few guidelines. These also apply to separation.

TELL THEM ONLY WHEN IT IS DEFINITE

When a definite decision to separate has been made, share this with the children. Do not share when you are simply discussing a possibility; but when the decision to separate or divorce is irrevocable, tell the children at once. Give them the honor of hearing it directly from their parents, not through hearsay.

BE TRUTHFUL

The child already knows there is a problem. Avoid making up such stories as, "Daddy is away on a long business trip." When he discovers that you have been deceiving him, this could cause confusion and distrust. Let him know that you know this decision is painful for him and difficult to understand.

LET YOUR CHILD HEAR IT FROM BOTH PARENTS

In some situations it may be an advantage for the child to hear it from both parents.

EMPHASIZE HE IS NOT TO BLAME

Emphasize and reemphasize that in no way is your child to blame for this problem between his parents—they are not breaking up because of him or anything he has done. It is very common for children to figure out some reason why they must be to blame and then assume guilt for the separation. They need reassurances that they are not the cause, but rather that they have brought joy into the home. One child thought that because he accepted Christ as his Savior he was the cause of his parents' divorce.

Assure the Child of Your Love

Give him the assurance, and continued reassurance, that you both still love him dearly. And even though you will no longer be husband and wife, you are still his parents and will always love him.

Strengthen Your Relationship to God

Do what you can to strengthen your own personal relationship to God, and give the child a positive example from which he can form his concept of God. Your attitude toward the Lord will be significant to his adjustment.

Helping During Times of Loss and Grief

Another very important time of ministering very sensitively and compassionately to the needs of others is when they have just lost a loved one.

These helps for the grieving person are drawn (with their permission) from the experience of Earl and Rose McQuay in their book, *Beyond Eagles*[4]. The book springs from their experiences after the accidental death of their twenty-three-year old son. The following suggestions for comforting one another in such a critical time of intense loss are adapted from the final chapter.

Be Aware of the Grief Process

It is important to be aware of and understand the "Crisis Cycle" which we discussed earlier.

Act Promptly in Providing Physical Aid

The initial reaction to tragic news may be physical—a tightness in the throat, choking, shortness of breath, or an uncontrollable emotional outburst. If you are present at that time, the best help you can give is to respond with calm, confident assistance.

DO SOMETHING RATHER THAN JUST OFFER HELP

Perhaps it's best not to say, "Please let me know if there is anything I can do to help." How often has a grieving person said, "Could you bring something over for dinner tonight?" Instead, you can initiate a suggestion of how you might help. Remember soup is soothing to one who is hurting.

Rose's friends would call, "Rose, I'm coming to get you at noon today. I want you to be ready to go with me for lunch." Or, "I'm coming to do one of three things for you today: vacuum the house, prepare a meal, take you shopping for groceries." In other words, call and offer several possibilities.

SHOW THAT YOU CARE

Showing that we care may not be so much what we say, but our willingness to be there in the moment of pain and hear the hurt in the life. It may mean simply being there, listening to the bereaved, and showing genuine sympathy. Speak quietly and reassuringly. Let your tone of voice be soothing, not jarring. Your presence, your voice, your eyes, the touch of your hand speak volumes. "We pray for you." "You are constantly in our thoughts." "We love you." "You are dear to us." "We admire your courage."

AVOID VAGUE QUESTIONS AND EMPTY WORDS

Vague or pious questions such as, "Well, how are you doing?" "What has the Lord been teaching you through this?" do not comfort. Rather, ask questions that encourage discussion if he chooses: "Have you been able to sleep all right at night?" "Have you been tired by a lot of visits?"

Empty statements such as, "I know how you feel," will not make the person feel better. We cannot really know how he feels. Or, "God will use this for good." "Jesus never fails." Though these are true, this may not be the appropriate time to remind them.

ENCOURAGE HIM TO WORK THROUGH HIS GRIEF

Assure him grief is normal and that expressing his emotions furthers the healing process. It may be helpful to encourage him to talk about his loss and his feelings rather than to flee into some form of escapism.

EXPRESS YOUR SYMPATHY

Don't be afraid to talk about the deceased person. Perhaps one of the most hurtful things that you could do to is to say nothing about the person's loss. Recall something special you remember about the deceased—some little thing he said or did that was meaningful to you.

It is not a time for you to talk about your own troubles, your tales of woe. And don't think you have to have all the answers. None of us has all the answers. Avoid pat answers like, "It's God's will." It is best that we do not try to give a bereaved person a reason for his loss.

Be positive in your sympathy. Tell the person that you share his sorrow, that you love him, and that you are praying for him. A simple expression of your feelings, "I'm very sorry" is often enough.

BE BIBLICAL IN YOUR RESPONSE

I do not necessarily mean that you should quote Scripture verses. That may have its place, but do not overdo it. But offer counsel in keeping with the truths of Scripture. If a person is filled with guilt regarding his relation to the deceased, guide him toward the grace, forgiveness, and love of Christ. Let the Holy Spirit bring him to conviction and confession. He will do that; you will not need to.

SHARE READING MATERIAL ON GRIEF

In the first year of their grief the McQuays read over 50 books on the subjects of death, grief and suffering, heaven, and personal accounts of people's loss through death. The book of Job was especially meaningful to them.

REMEMBER, THE HURT GOES ON

Don't forget that the hurt goes on weeks, months, sometimes years after the person's loss. During that time you may comfort by again expressing your sympathy in some small way. McQuay said that some had written notes to them at the anniversary of their son's death and these kind gestures were greatly treasured.

Sometimes during times of sickness and loss it's the children who suffer the most. They are often left with babysitters during long trips to specialists or hospitals. Children go through crises, too. They experience many of these same emotions. They experience loss of security both in parent and now, apparently, in God. Their teachers should be informed of the prolonged illness or death of the children's parent so they can better understand what the child is going through.

Dr. David Jeremiah warns,

> We need to be careful that we don't assume we know what other people are feeling. Every experience of suffering is totally unique to the person who is experiencing it. It is unique in the sense that it is this suffering for this person at this particular time in this particular context, and there is no way we can know how they feel. We can tell them we care for them and we know they are hurting. But not, 'I know exactly how you feel,' or 'I know what you're going through.' And this is not the time to preach the verse, 'All things work together for good to those who love God.'[5]

Joseph Bayly, who laid three of his sons in the grave and knew what grief was all about, says in one of his books, "I was sitting, torn by grief. Someone came and talked to me of God's dealings and why it happened, of hope beyond the grave. He talked constantly. He said things I knew were true. I was unmoved except to wish he'd go away. He finally did. Another came and sat beside me. He just sat beside me for an hour and more, listened when I said something, answered briefly, prayed simply, and left. I was moved. I was encouraged. I hated to see him go."[6]

The Painful Experience of a Wayward Adult Child

When you discover that your adult child is going contrary to what he has been taught in your home, there are two possible approaches. The wrong approach is to banish your child from the family, have nothing to do with him, and forbid him to ever visit you. The right approach is to let him know that while you do not approve of his lifestyle or choices, your love for him will never change or fade.

Some suggestions for facing this painful time:

Don't Expect Immediate Answers

Only the Lord knows the real and full explanation as to why things have happened this way, and only He has the answer to all our problems and questions. Don't expect immediate answers, but do keep up your prayers and confidence in the Lord's power to break through and bring beauty out of ashes and make all things beautiful in His time. (See Isaiah 61:1–3 and Ecclesiastes 3:11.)

Forgive the Adult Child

Forgive the adult child who has caused this pain. Remember, ignoring, minimizing, denying, or excusing is not the same as forgiving. Admit the pain, admit the wrong done to you, but then try to see the person who hurt you as a weak and needy person. Try to understand their pain, their frustration, confusion, and weakness, and choose forgiveness.

Love Unconditionally

Choose to love him or her unconditionally. Purpose to learn what that means for each person involved. Balance tender love and tough love.

Winston Churchill said he always tried to think things through ahead of time so that he could give the best answer when the time came. If you have children, I would suggest that you do the same in regard to some of these difficult things that are happening even in Christian families today.

It is wise to ask yourself, What do I want my response to be should I discover that:

- my son is a homosexual or my daughter is a lesbian?
- my unwed daughter is pregnant?
- my daughter is planning or has gotten an abortion?
- my child is bent on marrying one I don't approve of?
- my child is living with his girlfriend?

A friend's sixteen-year-old daughter finally admitted to her mother that she was pregnant. The mother had no idea that her daughter had been living a promiscuous lifestyle for the previous year and a half. "But," she said, "the Lord gave me the grace not to tell her off, as would be my usual way, but to calmly show her love and support and assure her that I will stick by her as she makes the decision about keeping the baby or putting her up for adoption. I need to keep the relationship open with this girl. She needs my support."

Relinquish Your Hold

Realize that you cannot *fix* your child. You cannot change him. Learn to put him in God's loving hands. In short, learn how to "let go and let God." The adult child is responsible for his own choices. You cannot control him and his choices—nor should you. As has been said, "Where there is no control there is no responsibility." And you cannot take responsibility to fix him. As Joy, my counselee, said, "I don't want you to fix me. . . . I know it is up to God and me to fix me."

Realize You Can Change Yourself

Realize that you can change your own attitude, even though you cannot change your child. You can adjust to the difficult situation and learn to accept the people in your life who are engaged in unacceptable behavior. Trust God for supernatural grace to accept the person. Press close to the Lord for your own learning, healing, and growing. Do what you must to take care of yourself and get on with your life.

DEAL WITH GUILT

Deal with guilt, both valid and invalid. Just because your child has chosen a wrong lifestyle does not mean that you are to blame, that it is your fault, that you did not raise him right. There are many pressures and opportunities out there to do wrong, but he is responsible for his choices. And don't let the enemy harass you with the guilt or regrets of the *if onlys:* "If only I had . . ." or "If only I hadn't . . ." You must be content with the realization that you did what you thought was best at the time.

On the other hand, where you know you did do some things wrong, it is important to face these, confess them to the Lord, and believe in and accept His forgiveness and cleansing. God says, "If we confess our sins, he is faithful and just and will forgive us our sins and purify us from all unrighteousness" (1 John 1:9). Then confess them to the child, asking for his forgiveness.

Oswald Chambers says:

> Our yesterdays hold broken and irreversible things to us. It is true that we have lost opportunities that will never return, but God can transform this destructive anxiety into a constructive thoughtfulness for the future. Let the past rest, but let it rest in the sweet embrace of Christ. Leave the broken, irreversible past in His hands, and step out into the invincible future with Him.[7]

"Let the past rest in the sweet embrace of Christ," and move on. That is, get on with your life, and in the right sense, do as Paul admonishes, "Forgetting what is behind and straining toward what is ahead, I press on . . . " (Philippians 3:13–14).

REACH OUT TO OTHERS

Reach out to others in the Body to help you with the adjusting and healing process. Pray for and endeavor to find one friend to whom you can pour out your heart with all its anger and confusion, without being judged or condemned. You need *a* paraclete to stand with you; to weep with you; to pray for, support, help, and encourage you. But also, if you see someone else going through this painful experience, reach out to support and encourage her in her healing and growing process. Proverbs 11:25 says, "He who refreshes others will himself be refreshed."

LEARN TO LAUGH AGAIN

There will be tears, deep grief, heart anguish, and painful memories. Allow for the grieving process and know that healing takes time. But also remember the bright side of life—the goodness of the Lord and of His people. "A cheerful heart is good medicine . . ." (Proverbs 17:22).

REMEMBER GOD IS STILL ON THE THRONE

Above all things remember that God is still in control. He loves you more than anyone can, and He has promised to work all things together for good as you trust Him. He will redeem this circumstance and make it work for your growth and His glory. 1 Timothy 6:15 (Phillips): "God . . . is the blessed controller of all things."

DRAW NEAR TO GOD

Above all things, seek to know more of God and His heart. Hold on to God and His character, and walk with Him in obedience, giving up your way for His way. Declare each morning, "God *is* love; only God is good; God cares for me; God is for me; God is working. You, O Lord are strong and You, O Lord, are loving."

Don't demand an answer to your questions. Remember only God knows the whys and hows. Focus on your need to know Him more fully, love Him more dearly, and walk with Him more closely.

The Importance of Prayer

Intercessory prayer for others in crisis times is the encourager's primary responsibility. Be available to the Lord for this kind of prayer. One night in the middle of the night I awakened and remembered two dear friends, whom I knew were in the midst of working through their grief after losing their mother. I took that as a call to pray for them.

SIX SIMPLE SUGGESTIONS FOR PEOPLE-HELPING

I do not intend to imply that the suggestions given in this book provide a formula that everyone should follow in every situation. God deals with individuals where they are, in His unique, creative way. We must let God be God in each individual's life. God is a God of great variety. We cannot predetermine how He will work in someone's life. Though I have presented some possible plans and steps, God may or may not choose to follow that procedure in the case you are facing.

Let me end with six simple suggestions that usually are a part of every people-helping situation, whether it be friend with friend, mother with child, or family members with each other.

Empathize with Understanding

Endeavor to enter into the other person's feelings. Try to see the problem from her perspective, yet remain objective: "If this were my mother or sister, how would she feel and what advice would I give her?"

Communicate Concern

"I do care about you." The good relationship you build through your genuine concern for her will strengthen her confidence in you and the advice you give her.

Communicate Hope

Give her hope as you begin your time together. "No temptation has seized you except what is common to man. And God is faithful; he will not let you be tempted beyond what you can bear. But when you are tempted, he will also provide a way out so that you can stand up under it" (1 Corinthians 10:13).

Then as she reports to you periodically, point out specific areas of improvement that you see. This will give her added hope. Hope is a powerful motivating force that can encourage her to pay the price for change.

Clarify the Problem

You may need to gently and lovingly, yet firmly, guide her to see and confront the real issues regarding her problem.

Help Her Take Action

Lead her to take the steps of action that she clearly knows she must take. If appropriate, provide the opportunity or support for her to act.

Design Projects

Design projects that will help her to move toward healing, such as those we talked about in chapter 13.

Remember, the last chapter in anyone's story hasn't yet been written. God is in the business of redeeming bad situations and bringing good out of them. He promises to transform, restore, rebuild, and renew. We can be sure that Jeremiah 29:11 applies to each of us, "'For I know the plans I have for you,' declares the Lord, 'plans to prosper you and not to harm you, plans to give you hope and a future.'"

Let us be comforted and comfort others with such words of hope from God as these:

I will restore to you the years that the swarming locust has eaten. (Joel 2:25, NKJV)

For I am with you. . . . I will strengthen you and help you; I will uphold you with my righteous right hand. (Isaiah 41:10)

The desert shall rejoice and blossom as the rose. It shall blossom abundantly, and rejoice even with joy and singing. (Isaiah 35:1–2, NKJV)

. . . to give them beauty for ashes, the oil of joy for mourning, the garment of praise for the spirit of heaviness; . . . that He may be glorified. (Isaiah 61:3, NKJV)

For your encouragement let me briefly outline the events that took place during about five years in one mother's life. After many, many years of enduring her husband's sexual addictive behavior, Karen went through the horrendous pain of divorce. During this time three of her children turned against her. Her daughter was raped, and she herself was mugged near their home in Chicago's inner city. Her oldest son was living an ungodly, rebellious lifestyle. Then her teenager got pregnant. Her oldest daughter, who had been her very best friend, distanced herself from her mother. Friends at church didn't support her during these crises. The story goes on and on, hurt upon hurt.

Yet Karen's greatest desire was to live a godly life, to be the kind of daughter, wife, mother, and churchwoman who would honor the Lord. We might ask, "Why did God allow all this?" or, "What is the solution to all these problems?" Karen didn't have any answers, only painful questions.

That was several years ago. Here's the sequel—things are different now. The oldest daughter married a fine Christian man, and they both have a close, warm relationship to Karen. The oldest son is walking with the Lord and is a strong witness for Him. He's concerned about being a good example and influence on his younger brother. The younger daughter, though she still vacillates in her spiritual walk, is a good mother to her child.

Recently, Karen has had the long-dreamed privilege of serving the Lord in Africa. She plans now to spend six months each year in Africa and six months in the States, working in the mission's office. God has made "the desert rejoice and blossom as the rose."

Don't expect immediate answers, but keep praying with confidence in the Lord's power to break through and bring beauty out of ashes and make all things beautiful in His time (see Isaiah 61:3 and Ecclesiastes 3:11).

> May the God of hope fill you with all joy and peace as you trust in him, so that you may overflow with hope by the power of the Holy Spirit. (Romans 15:13)

> "I, even I, am He who comforts you." (Isaiah 51:12, NKJV)

"Comfort, yes, comfort My people!" (Isaiah 40:1, NKJV)

THOUGHTS TO REMEMBER

God uses crises in our lives to help us to grow as Christians, to lead us to a richer life in Him and a deeper dependence upon Him. Oswald Chambers says, "The clouds are the dust of our Father's feet."

> Praise be to the God and Father of our Lord Jesus Christ, the Father of compassion and the God of all comfort, who comforts us in all our troubles, so that we can comfort those in any trouble with the comfort we ourselves have received from God. (2 Corinthians 1:3–4)

PRACTICING AND JOURNALING

Do something to support and encourage someone this week. Perhaps it will be to approach someone you didn't know before. Write what you did.

Sources

PART ONE—THE TRUTH WILL SET YOU FREE

Chapter 1: Needed: Safe People, Safe Places

[1]Henry Blackaby and Claude V. King, *Experiencing God.* (Nashville, TN: Broadman and Holman, 1994), p. 32

Chapter 2: Free to Nourish Others

[1]Ronald Enroth, *Churches that Abuse.* (Grand Rapids, MI: Zondervan, 1992), pp. 216–217
[2]Ronald Enroth, *Churches that Abuse.* (Grand Rapids, MI: Zondervan, 1992), pp. 223–224

Chapter 3: Free to Be Nourished

[1]Rich Buhler, *New Choices, New Boundaries.* (Nashville, TN: Thomas Nelson, 1991), p. 41
[2]George F. Root, hymn, "Why Do You Wait?" Public Domain
[3]Jo Coudert, "The Pig Who Loved People," in *Reader's Digest,* April 1992

PART TWO—FREEDOM FROM MALNOURISHMENT

Chapter 5: Hurtful, Twisted Thinking

[1]Dr. Albert Ellis, on ABC approach, adapted from Chris Thurman, *The Lies We Believe.* (Nashville, TN: Thomas Nelson, 1989), p. 55

Chapter 6: Dealing with Negative Self-Talk

[1]Verna Birkey, *If God Is in Control, Why Is My World Falling Apart?* (Portland, OR: Multnomah, 1990) p. 88

[2]Verna Birkey, *Less Stress, More Peace.* (Grand Rapids, MI: Fleming H. Revell, 1995), pp. 87–96

[3]Jan Frank, *A Door of Hope.* (San Bernardino, CA: Here's Life, 1987), pp. 119–120

PART THREE—FREE TO NOURISH OTHERS WITH BOLD LOVE

Chapter 7: Boundaries

[1]David Augsburger/John Faul, *Beyond Assertiveness.* (Waco, TX: Word Books, 1980), pp. 156–157

Chapter 9: Conflict Resolution

[1]David Augsburger/John Faul, *Beyond Assertiveness.* (Waco, TX: Word Books, 1980), story of Pauline adapted from pp. 24–25

Chapter 10: Confrontation

[1]David Augsburger, *Caring Enough to Confront.* (Glendale, CA: Regal Books, 1973), pp. 2–3, and Preface

[2]David Augsburger, *When Caring Is Not Enough.* (Ventura, CA: Regal Books, 1983), pp. 27–28

PART FOUR—NOURISHING OTHERS THROUGH PEOPLE-HELPING

Chapter 11: Be a People Helper

[1]James Freeman Clarke, quoted in *Joy and Strength,* compiled by Mary Wilder Tileston. (Minneapolis, MN: World Wide, copyright 1929), p. 95

[2]*Life Application Bible*, New International Version. (Wheaton, Ill.: Tyndale House and Grand Rapids, MI: Zondervan, 1995), p. 1277

Chapter 12: Guides for People-Helping

[1]Eugene H. Peterson, *The Message, the Wisdom Books.* (Colorado Springs, CO: NavPress, 1996), pp. 11–13

[2]Oswald Chambers, *Baffled to Fight Better.* (Grand Rapids, MI: Discovery House, 1990), p. 32

[3]Oswald Chambers, *Baffled to Fight Better.* (Grand Rapids, MI: Discovery House, 1990), pp. 47–48

[4]Frederick Wm. Faber, quoted in *Joy and Strength,* compiled by Mary Wilder Tileston. (Minneapolis, MN: World Wide, copyright 1929), p. 295

[5]*Life Application Bible*, New International Version. (Wheaton, IL: Tyndale House, and Grand Rapids, MI: Zondervan, 1995), p. 1315

Chapter 13: More Guides for People-Helping

[1]Material on "Conscience" quoted from a message by Pastor Ben Cross, by permission

[2]Jay E. Adams, *Competent to Counsel. (Grand Rapids, MI: Zondervan, 1970)*

Chapter 14: Helping People in Crisis

[1]John Calvin Reid, *Bird Life in Wington.* (Grand Rapids, MI: Wm. B. Erdmans Publishing Co., 1948), pp. 62–66

[2]Oswald Chambers, *My Utmost for His Highest, An Updated Edition in Today's Language*. (Grand Rapids, MI: Discovery House, 1992), July 29

[3]Virginia Watts, *The Single Parent*. (Old Tappan, NJ: Fleming H. Revell, 1976), pp. 22 and 114

[4]Earl McQuay, *Beyond Eagles*. (Columbus, GA: Quill Publications, 1987). Material on "Helping During Times of Loss and Grief" is adapted from chapter 13.

[5]David Jeremiah, *The Power of Encouragement*. (Atlanta, GA: Walk Thru the Bible Ministries, 1994), pp. 108, 114

[6]Joseph Bayly quote taken from David Jeremiah, *The Power of Encouragement*. (Atlanta, GA: Walk Thru the Bible Ministries, 1994), page 107

[7]Oswald Chambers, *My Utmost for His Highest, An Updated Edition in Today's Language*. (Grand Rapids, MI: Discovery House, 1992), December 31

Suggested Resources

Allender, Dan B. *The Wounded Heart*. Colorado Spring, CO: NavPress, 1990.

Arthur, Kay. *Lord, Heal My Hurts*. Sisters, OR: Multnomah, 1989.

Augsburger, David. *Caring Enough to Confront*. Glendale, CA: Regal Books, 1973.

Bacus, William and Chapian, Marie. *Telling Yourself the Truth*. Minneapolis, MN: Bethany House, 1980.

Birkey, Verna. *God's Promises of Peace*. Kent, WA: Enriched Living.

———. *If God Is in Control, Why Is My World Falling Apart?* Portland, OR: Multnomah, 1990.

———. *Input for a Rejoicing Heart* (Cassette and Booklet). Kent, WA: Enriched Living.

———. *Less Stress, More Peace*. Grand Rapids, MI: Fleming H. Revell, 1995.

———. *Linx: Study Guide*. Mukilteo, WA: WinePress, 1997

———. *You Are Very Special*. Grand Rapids, MI: Fleming H. Revell, 1977.

Blackaby, Henry, and King, Claude V. *Experiencing God*. Nashville, TN: Broadman and Holman, 1994.

Brestin, Dee. *The Friendships of Women*. Wheaton, IL: Victor Books, 1988.

Buhler, Rich. *New Choices, New Boundaries*. Nashville, TN: Thomas Nelson, 1991.

Carlson, Dwight L. *Why Do Christians Shoot Their Wounded?* Downers Grove, IL: InterVarsity, 1994.

Chambers, Oswald. *Baffled to Fight Better.* Grand Rapids, MI: Discovery House, 1990.

———. *My Utmost for His Highest: An Updated Edition in Today's Language.* Grand Rapids, MI: Discovery House, 1992.

Cloud, Henry and Townsend, John. *Boundaries.* Grand Rapids, MI: Zondervan, 1992.

———. *12 "Christian Beliefs That Can Drive You Crazy.* Grand Rapids, MI: Zondervan, 1995.

Crabb, Larry. *Connecting.* Nashville, TN: Word, 1997

Crab, Larry and Allender, Dan. *Hope When You're Hurting.* Grand Rapids, MI: Zondervan, 1996.

Dobson, James. *Love Must Be Tough.* Waco, TX: Word Books, 1983.

Enroth, Ronald. *Churches that Abuse.* Grand Rapids, MI: Zondervan, 1992.

Frank, Jan. *A Door of Hope.* San Bernardino, CA: Here's Life, 1987.

Jeremiah, David. *The Power of Encouragement.* Atlanta, GA: Walk Thru the Bible Ministries, 1994.

Johnson, Barbara. *Stick a Geranium in Your Hat and Be Happy.* Dallas, TX: Word, 1990.

Mayhall, Carole. *Help Lord My Whole Life Hurts.* Cororado Springs, CO: NavPress, 1988.

McQuay, Earl. *Beyond Eagles.* Columbus, GA: Quill Publications, 1987.

Otto, Donna. *Between Women of God.* Eugene, OR: Harvest House, 1995.

Reeve, Pamela. *Relationships, What It Takes to Be a Friend.* Sisters, OR: Multnomah, 1997.

Senter, Ruth. *Longing for Love.* Colorado Springs, CO: NavPress, 1991.

Sloat, Donald E. *The Dangers of Growing Up in a Christian Home.* Nashville, TN: Thomas Nelson, 1986.

Stoop, David. *Self-Talk: Key to Personal Growth.* Grand Rapids, MI: Fleming H. Revell, 1982.

Swindoll, Charles. *Grace Awakening.* Dallas, TX: Word, 1990.

Tileston, Mary Wilder. Compiler, *Joy and Strength*. Minneapolis, MN: World Wide, 1986.

Thurman, Chris. *The Lies We Believe, The #1 Cause of Our Unhappiness*. Nashville, TN: Thomas Nelson, 1989.

Van Vonderen, Jeff. *When God's People Let You Down*. Minneapolis, MN: Bethany House, 1995.

Virkler, Henry. *Speaking the Truth in Love*. Kearney, NE: Morris Publishing, 1991.

Wilson, Sandra D. *Released from Shame*. Downers Grove, IL: InterVarsity, 1990.

Wright, H. Norman. *Recovering from the Losses of Life*. Grand Rapids, MI: Fleming H. Revell, 1991.

To order additional copies of:

Linx:
Women Connecting with Women

or for *Linx: Study Guides*, call

1-800-917-BOOK

or write to:

Enriched Living
PO Box 3039
Kent, WA 98032

DATE DUE

MAY 1 4 2021			